THE LEISURE OF AN EG

Lord Edward Cecil, known as 'Nigs' lived ..om 1867 to 1918 and belonged to the distinguished family of English statesmen. The fourth child of the third Marquis of Salisbury, who became Conservative prime minister in 1885, Lord Edward enjoyed the reputation of being the wittiest man in England and Ireland. According to his wife, he could be said to be the real inspiration behind the Boy Scout movement which was born in Mafeking during the Boer War, where Lord Edward served as a senior officer under Baden-Powell. In his younger days he was certainly a mainstay of the Garrick Club, where his company was sought out by those who admired his entertaining humour, a humour with an appeal that has not diminished over the years as this book clearly illustrates.

The Leisure of an Egyptian Official is drawn from the eighteen years the author spent attached to the Civil Service in Egypt before and after the First World War. Lord Edward was based in Cairo and gives us a sketch of his daily routine there which conveys, in the most diverting way, a picture of life in Egyptian society as it used to be in the days of the English Civil Servants.

THE LEISURE OF AN EGYPTIAN OFFICIAL

LORD EDWARD CECIL

CENTURY PUBLISHING
LONDON

HIPPOCRENE BOOKS INC.
NEW YORK

LESTER & ORPEN DENNYS DENEAU
MARKETING SERVICES LTD TORONTO

Introduction copyright © Lord Hardinge of Penshurst 1984

First published in Great Britain in 1921 by Hodder & Stoughton

This edition published in 1984 by Century Publishing Co. Ltd,
Portland House, 12–13 Greek Street, London W1V 5LE

Published in the United States of America by
Hippocrene Books Inc.
171 Madison Avenue
New York, NY 10016

Published in Canada by
Lester & Orpen Dennys Deneau Marketing Services Ltd
78 Sullivan Street, Ontario, Canada

ISBN 0 7126 0444 8

*The cover painting is from the collection at the
Mathaf Gallery, 24 Motcomb Street, London SW1*

Reprinted in Great Britain by
Richard Clay (The Chaucer Press) Ltd, Bungay, Suffolk

INTRODUCTION

My Cecil grandfather died in 1918, three years before I
was born. He was ill in Switzerland and possibly fell
victim to the killer flu that was about to multiply the
appalling ravages of the first world war. Evidently his
death was a sad blow to those who knew him as not just
a brave and honourable man but a man of deep feelings, melancholy and humorous.

From the frontispiece of the first edition of this book
his photograph stares out at us in a magnificent military
uniform, Egyptian style, fez and all. And, indeed, he
served in the Egyptian army from 1901 until he trans-
ferred to government service in Egypt where the jobs he
held successively were Under Secretary for War (1904),
Under Secretary for Finance (1905) and Financial
Adviser (1912). It would seem that he himself was by
no means unaware of some irony in such financial
responsibility falling on one whose handling of his
personal finances had never been especially earnest,
cautious or perspicacious.

Although it was his way to meet life bravely and with
humour, his experiences were not the stuff of which
happiness is made. It has scarcely been a secret since
1906 that his marriage to my grandmother (whom I
knew well and adored) was not a success. They had met

in Dublin in 1894 when 'Nigs' (as Lord Edward was known to his family and friends) was serving as A.D.C. to Viscount Wolseley. The marriage produced two children, my mother and my uncle George: George Gascoyne-Cecil was killed in France in September 1914 at the age of nineteen.

During the Boer War Lord Edward was a senior officer among the British troops trapped in Mafeking under Baden-Powell. The Boy Scout movement is supposed to have been invented in Mafeking during the siege, and Baden-Powell of course went on later to turn it into a worldwide organisation. In her later years my grandmother used to claim that it was really Lord Edward who had invented the Boy Scouts – but no doubt there could be much debate about that. She used to tell me how – as a young man, before Mafeking – he was sought after in the Garrick Club where he was regarded as a great wit, the best of company: and this we can all believe.

'Hatfield is the capital of Philistia', was a quotation also passed on to me from my grandmother from the early days of her marriage and visits to Hatfield House. This was a joke the young Cecils made against themselves, and referred to the freedom of wide-ranging conversation, humorous iconoclasm, provocation and argument which were evidently the staple of meal-time exchanges, even encouraged by their father, the Prime Minister. There is much to be learned of this brilliant generation, part of the late and second flowering of this extraordinary family, from Kenneth Rose's book, *The Later Cecils*.

Old family rumours have it that by publishing, after his death, what were supposedly private letters written by her first husband, my grandmother had acted imprudently and caused offence in some quarters. But she was not given to doing things without careful judgment, and was very well aware of the power of mischief of the written word. She was the least mercenary person I have ever known. I'm quite sure it was a considered decision that the world should not be deprived of the wit and good cheer to be gained by reading these papers. She would also have taken the advice of Lord Milner, her second husband, a man not known for stupidity or greed.

Making jokes, making fun and making mockery are all close cousins: at the time of publication some people may have thought that so far as fun had been made of people, places and customs, the first publication was too close in time to the author's experiences. That cannot be said today even though a re-reading shows that the irony and wit have not faded at all over the years. My grandfather's humorous writings have worn extraordinarily well, a great achievement considering that humour is often so ephemeral.

Criticisms can of course be made of this book – so they can of any book, it's not just a hazard of publication, it's a certainty. But it seems to me that the many reprints over the years – the vast delight it has given so many people, the sheer laughter – is something for which my grandfather is and will be gratefully remembered.

For myself I'm especially happy to see it reissued now, and predict that it may again have a huge success.

At Xmas 1957, only ten months before she died, my grandmother inscribed a copy of the book (from the fifth edition dated 1931) as follows:

INTRODUCTION

'It was written by the wittiest Englishman I have ever known.'

We did not know him, but we can easily take her word for it. As an introduction to this charmingly humorous and sometimes uproarious book it can scarcely be improved upon.

LORD HARDINGE OF PENSHURST

PREFACE TO THE FIRST EDITION

THESE sketches were written by Lord Edward Cecil at various times during the eighteen years of his service in Egypt. " My Daily Life " and most of the other papers, including the unfinished " Going on Leave," belong to a period long anterior to the War. Only two of them, " Lord Kitchener " and " An Official Correspondence," are of comparatively recent date.

Though they were only written for the amusement of his family, it is thought that these pictures of the lighter side of Egyptian life may be of interest to a wider public. The characters introduced are, of course, not drawn from any individuals.

July, 1921.

CONTENTS

MY DAILY LIFE

CONTENTS

GOING ON LEAVE

MY DAILY LIFE

"Here lies a fool who tried to hustle the East."
RUDYARD KIPLING.

CHAPTER I   GETTING UP AND BREAKFASTING

MY first sensation in the morning is usually a confused impression of noise. It is often combined or half combined with my dreams. There is an earthquake, and the house is falling. There is a battle, and they are shelling the house. As my consciousness returns, I become aware that it is my servant.

He is four foot odd high, and weighs about as much as a big retriever dog, but he makes more row than a giant. He has never yet come into my room of a morning without falling foul of something. Sometimes it is the table, sometimes a chair, or sometimes he does his great feat, which is to catch his foot, fall against the table, upset my tea, and bang the door, all in one movement. After years of careful practice, he has discovered how to drop a woollen garment on a thick carpet and make it sound like a plank falling on a pavement.

He is a quaint personality belonging to a curious people, people literally without a history. Older than the old Egyptians, they have lived on from the dawn of history as hewers of wood and drawers of water, producing countless servants, watchmen, grooms, and cooks, and no single man of eminence, or even partial eminence. They are intelligent and, when not spoilt, faithful and not devoid of some virtues, but without that something which enables some negroes even to rise to eminence among their fellow-men.

I say they are, up to a point, virtuous when they are not spoilt, but it must be remembered that they are all more or less spoilt. They vary in morals from the Pasha's old servant, who, beyond the ordinary Eastern vices and petty dishonesty, is quite respectable, to the outrage on humanity who is taken on by the American tourists for the winter. One of the most pleasing sights we sojourners in the land see, is American young women chaffing men whom one would not willingly speak to oneself, unless it was to tell them to go away.

My retainer stands fairly high up the list, unlike the servants of most of my friends. How men who have been as long in the country as Jones, Smith, and Robinson can employ the ruffians they do, is a mystery to me. I think it is because so few of us are really good judges of character, or understand these people, or the Egyptians, for that matter. I actually overheard Jones alluding to my servant the other day in very deprecatory language. I know he is not perfect in any sense, but compared with Jones's Ahmed, my Suleiman is an angel of light.

Having banged his way through tidying up my room, the angel retires with a final crash, and I resign myself to the inevitable getting up! I proceed to get out of bed, and stroll out on to the balcony according to my custom. It is curious, if one lives alone, how one follows unconsciously the same routine day after day. I believe it is only the interference of others that ever makes one change one's habits.

I feel sure that the view from my balcony in the early morning is a subject of legitimate pride, though why, it is hard to say; probably because seeing anything in the early morning, or even being awake then, is universally admitted to be a matter for self-congratulation, and possibly because it would have been clever of me to find a lodging with such a view if I had noticed it at the time I took it, which I did not. When I first look there is, however, nothing to be seen but masses of white mist lazily moving in the light morning air. In a minute or two, as the sun strikes over the hills behind me and the mist turns a delicate pink, in the far distance the bright blue hills of the western desert begin to show, and the horizon line is cut by the pyramids, starting out of the sea of blushing cloud. Incredibly quickly change follows change. The cloud now turns to liquid translucent gold, and through it dimly appear the feathery palms and the graceful sails of the passing boats. In a moment more the rising breeze has swept away the cloud, and the houses round show again their familiar but not beautiful forms. The morning pageant is over, and though I have seen it more times than I care to be reminded of, it never finishes without causing me a slight pang of regret that anything so beautiful should cease to be.

From below in the street a familiar noise strikes on the ear. It is the early tram. I live over a tram line, and in front of my abode the line makes a curve which was obviously designed by an optimist.

Unless the driver slows down to the pace of an ordinary beetle, the car goes off the line. As no Egyptian ever profits by experience, and as when it is cold he cannot think at all, the early tram runs off the line five days in seven. I watch it as it approaches, and, sure enough, it goes off the line and pulls up. The driver carefully gets on the brake, and, spreading his hands before him in the national gesture of expostulation and complaint, calls Heaven to witness that he is an unlucky man, and that the company treats him like a dog. The conductor, who has dismounted, joins in, and they continue to bewail their lot until the conductor hints that the driver was in fault. The driver replies hotly that he was not, adding that the conductor's relations are not respectable. The passengers, who have also dismounted, form a circle round the two, and after listening to a short biographical sketch of the driver by the conductor, take sides, and the row becomes general. As the voices become shriller and shriller in the fury of the quarrel, which has all the appearance of being about to lead to bloodshed, and which, in reality, would never lead to the lightest blow, a sleepy policeman approaches the group. Every one appeals to him, and he, with great impartiality, abuses every one. He, however, has the sense to suggest that the tram ought to go on. The driver and the conductor, still raging, admit this, and with the assistance of the crowd shove the car back on to the lines in that hopelessly unmethodical and eminently successful manner pursued by Egyptians when dealing with heavy weights. The driver and conductor take their places, the passengers scramble back to their seats, and the car jolts away into the distance.

Seeing that it is getting late, and that I particularly want to be early at the office to-day, in order to get the memorandum on the sale of public lands on the instalment principle written for the Adviser, and to look up the case of Hassan Pasha Yghen's pension, which the Agency have been asking about, I commence to wash and dress.

The water of my bath is cold, and I bellow for Suleiman; he at once denies that it is cold, but on my marching into the kitchen and pointing out that the boiler itself is barely warm, he says it is a very bad boiler, for there has been a roaring fire for the last two hours, and that the amount of coal I use is a shame. There I agree, but that is because I supply not only himself, but also his family and friends, who, apparently, from my little bills, run a small blast furnace somewhere. I open the fire door and point to the half-consumed kindling wood which has not had time to burn yet. Suleiman is horrified, and says it is the other servant, who . . . and here follows, or would follow, the many iniquities of that youth. I, however, cut matters short with a denunciation of Suleiman and all his works, and resign myself to a tepid bath.

When I have finished dressing I send for a cab to go to the club, as I have given up breakfasting in. Suleiman "fancies" himself as a cook, but he is wrong. Whatever his natural talents are in that direction, they have been obscured by his desire to retire on a competency at an early age. No cooking will reconcile me with meat and eggs which belong to the fifth dynasty, even if I pay restaurant prices for them. He is aggrieved because he did not get my water warm, and accompanies me to the cab in a state of silent protest, and puts me into a prehistoric vehicle which has apparently been up all night. The driver, who has his head muffled up in a shawl to protect him against the cold, without waiting for orders, starts his horses off at a slow amble in the wrong direction. When my voice has penetrated the shawl, he slowly hauls them round, beating them for not knowing the way, and we proceed towards the club.

As usual, I appear to have got the worst cab obtainable. That is because I told Suleiman to get me one, and he charges too high a fee or commission. This custom of giving tips or commission runs through every class and every transaction in this country, from the superior irrigation engineer, who expects his " present " from the landholder for giving him the water he has a right to, to the office-keeper, who expects a farthing tip from the poor petitioner who wishes his complaint laid upon the great man's table. Suleiman, who follows the custom of the country most religiously, takes a commission on everything he buys for me, and even from the cabman he calls at my request. But, as I have indicated before, he is a lover of wealth, and consequently his terms are so high that only cabs which can get no other custom come when he calls. One of the cabmen told me that the fee was $2\frac{1}{2}d.$, which makes a big hole in an eight-penny fare.

Without discussing the merits of this system as a whole, the particular result is that I am now in

a cab of which the horses are living skeletons, the
driver filthier and more crassly stupid than most of
his fellows, the harness composed of relics of leather
tied together with rags and string, the covering of
the seats in holes, the springs half on one side, and
the wheels with a spoke or two missing from each.
We jolt along until, meeting another carriage, the
. driver pulls up, upon which the harness breaks in
one or two places, and he gets down to mend it
with a piece of chain, some thin string, and what
looks like an old necktie. This done, we rock on
again until suddenly the weak spring finally " goes "
with a crash; we again pull up, and I get out.
Luckily, I am only a hundred yards from the club,
so I walk there, while my driver begins to repair
the spring with a boot-lace.

I was really " well out of it," as these cabs may
break down anywhere, and it is lucky if it occurs
in a by-street and not in the way of effendi-driven
motors. No accident is impossible in these cabs.
On one occasion the driver pulled up his horses
with a vigour, and, both reins breaking simul-
taneously (as the string they were tied up with was
worn and probably of inferior quality), the driver
performed a sort of back somersault, and arrived
in a sitting posture on me. On another occasion a
similar recklessness on the part of the Jehu led to
the whole of the harness falling off the horses, who
trotted away, leaving us gravely seated in a horseless
carriage.

As I pass the clock in the club hall, I see it is
already eight o'clock, at which hour I meant to
begin work, so I rush into the dining-room and ask

17

them to hurry up my breakfast. The form used is "Breakfast quick," because, as all the waiters are Greeks or Berberines, with an imperfect knowledge of English, a complicated order leads to most unexpected results. An aged and respected member asked the other day for "eggs or anything that's handy," and got a nauseous-looking fluid in a glass, which proved to be eggs beaten up in brandy. I have always the same breakfast—cold meat, omelette, and coffee, and this, after ten years' experience, they know, so I usually have no difficulty in getting what I want.

Our club dining-room is rather a curiosity in its way. It is more like a foreign railway station restaurant than anything else I know. People are always rushing in and demanding food. The waiters go about at a trot, bang down the wrong dish in front of you, and rush away before you can object. The noise and clatter are terrific, but it is the only place where one can get decent food at a price less than that paid at a Monte Carlo restaurant.

In addition to a pot-house, our club is a place of business (unluckily), and for a senior official consequently a place of torment. You are caught and button-holed at every step. The more civil of your oppressors begin with "Excuse a word of shop," or "You won't mind my saying a word about business." Others brutally begin the subject as if they knew they had got you at a disadvantage and rejoiced over it. I have been attacked at meals and after meals, whilst reading the papers, and even while playing bridge, to the great pecuniary discomfiture of myself and partner; and one deter-

mined old concession-hunter followed me into the
washing place and caught me with my head under
the tap. At breakfast-time, however, it is nearly
deserted, and one is fairly safe, as most people
breakfast at home.

When I enter the dining-room I find, as I expected,
only half a dozen grumpy-looking members munching at their separate tables, who look up and give
vent to the usual surly " good morning," with an
obvious implication that you are not to use this
concession to good manners as an excuse for entering into conversation. As I sit down I see, to my
horror, that I am being followed into the room by
Dr. Smart. He is our Scottish conversationalist,
and I believe never stops that flow of talk which
has made so many of us feel more sympathy with
suicide than is right. Mercifully he sits down at
Colonel Brown's table, which suits him, as it is
central, and enables him to operate on a more
extended scale than if he sat in one of the corners.
I cower behind a paper the waiter has brought
me, as I hear Brown's indignant snort. " May I
have the pleasure of wishing you good morning,
Colonel? " The Colonel gives a sort of snorting
groan. " Now, I often wonder what the origin of
that custom is." " Humph," from the Colonel.
" In Scotland we say it more cordially, I think,
than you do in England." " Humph." " But then
our manners are more precise. You doubtless
remember Macwheesky says the Scottish precision
is as marked a characteristic of the race as the
Irishman's humour or the Englishman's stolidity."
" Humph." " But the custom is universal—even

the lowest races say something to one another when they meet in the morning." "Humph, worse luck," from the Colonel. "The morn, the beautiful morn, what splendid thoughts and poems have been produced in its honour! I feel very often quite poetical myself when I look out of my window in the morning and watch the beautiful landscapes, and feel the soft wind blowing on my face. Oh dear me, yes, it is wonderful, especially in this land of light and colour." "Humph." "Now, do you wake early, Colonel?" "Got to." "And, like an old campaigner, spring from your pallet couch and rush into your cold bath." "I don't take a cold bath. Liver." "You surprise me. I thought all you men of blood and iron did." I dare not look up, as the Colonel must be on the verge of apoplexy. I wish he would hit Smart, or pour boiling tea on him, or something. "Blood and iron —a terrible mixture. What a magnificent sight a great charge must be! Now, were you ever in a charge, Colonel?"

This I am sure will end badly, when Flasher, a member of the Prisons Department, creates a diversion by entering the room in his usual state of suppressed fury. He is far advanced in the national disease of irritability. "Am I," he thunders, "going to have breakfast or not, waiter? If you don't bring me kidneys in two seconds I'll . . ." The waiter, who is green with terror, murmurs, "Cook not got no kidney—only fish eggs." "D—n it all, what a rotten club. . . ." There, now he is started, and good-bye to any chance of peace and quiet. However, my frugal meal is over. I wonder

20

why all eggs in Egypt taste musty, as if, as our Irish doctor said, they had been laid by a mummy. As I pass the cashier's desk, I find that, as usual, I am short of cash, and shall have to change a sovereign. This means getting what I call the club token money. Members who become possessed of some of the many artistic imitations of our coinage produced by the artless Greek and simple-hearted Egyptians pass it at the club, where they never seem to mind what they take. This is given out to members again, and as they cannot get rid of it except in charity or to the club, it returns again and again, and becomes, in fact, a token currency in the club.

Now, at all events, I shall get a decent cab, which I want, as it is now 8.25, and I am already nearly half an hour behind my time. I recognise the cab-driver as an old friend who usually drives me in the morning. His cab is comparatively clean and his horses are decently fed. He cracks his whip and beats his horses unnecessarily, as they all do, but, generally speaking, he is less of a brute to them than most of his fellows.

His driving is peculiar. We start off at a gallop before I am well in the cab, and I sit down suddenly. This is painful, but I am used to it. We whirl round the first corner, and miss an old man who is strolling down the road, apparently with the intention of committing suicide, by a fraction of an inch. The driver yells out the whole time various remarks to the other occupants of the street who are getting, or who he thinks may get, in his way. "O my father, mind thy feet. Thy feet, my brother. To thy right, beloved. O son of all that is vile, and father of unmentionable things, where are you going?" Then a torrent of abuse which is absolutely unreproducible. The language of the barrack-room in old days was pure and mild compared with ordinary chaff of the streets here.

All this time we are galloping and missing people and vehicles by the narrowest of margins. It looks like a series of the most unparalleled flukes, but it is really due to the cleverness of the horses, who are as quick on their feet as cats, and just manage to avoid each thing in turn. It is lucky that they are so gifted, because no one keeps the rule of the road; all pedestrians walk in the roadway, usually on the wrong side, and are either engaged in conversation or are so blind as not to be able to see the carriage until it is close upon them. The shouts of the driver have less effect than one might expect from their loudness and substance, because all the other drivers are shouting at the same time. As the cabman drives with the reins loose on the horses' backs, and held in one hand, he can do very little steering. Where it is necessary to change direction, he pulls in one rein till it tightens up. This takes time, and he is usually late, so that you swing round the corners in a way that would turn the carriage over if it could be turned over, and that would certainly in any case throw down any horses but these. Beyond cannoning with another arabiyeh, we get through safely, and come through the Ministry gates as if we were riding a finish in a race.

OUR Ministry is neither a strictly beautiful building nor a convenient one. It was originally the property of a Pasha in Ismail's days, and, shall we say, reverted to the Crown when its owner died somewhat suddenly. The part we occupy was the harem of the palace, and I dare say, though I am no judge of such matters, did very well for that, but as a public office it leaves much to be desired. It is, inside, an aggregation of innumerable small and for the most part ill-lighted rooms, connected by a labyrinth of dark passages. Like so many buildings of that date, it is constructed principally of lath and plaster, and is always threatening to fall down; but we go on patching it up, hoping that we shall be rich enough to build a new Ministry some day. Its interior decoration is not artistic. The leading features are painted ceilings, with adhesive goddesses sitting on them; gilt, red plush, and inferior looking-glasses, all very faded and fly-blown.

I mount the stairs under the protection of two orderlies and a policeman—the orderlies to shove unoffending people, who are not in it, out of the way, and the policeman to walk as close behind me as possible without treading on my heels. Whether this is to prevent an assassin getting at one unbeknownst from behind, or to see that I don't steal anything on the way up, I have never found out.

I enter my room just thirty minutes later than I meant to, and, dropping into my chair, begin looking at my post as a preliminary to starting the day's work.

Though, of course, like all sane men, I dislike work, and, consequently, the beginning of work, there is a grain of optimism in my constitution, which makes opening my letters a certain pleasure to me. One knows the odds are enormously against their being interesting, and that some must be annoying, possibly even painful, but one still hopes that one day one will get a letter which will really please one. An easy enough matter when one was young—an invitation one wanted or a few words of praise from a superior, and the world went rose-coloured in a moment. Now it would require definite assurances from an unimpeachable source of a gift of health, wealth, and happiness for a period of ten years at least to produce that glow of hope and contentment which used to come so easily.

Now this train of thought indicates liver, and nothing else. I wish to goodness I had had the strength of mind not to play that last rubber of bridge, which has cost me so much from both a pecuniary and a hygienic point of view. Let me see what my letters are. Not an encouraging-looking lot.

No. I.—DEAR CECIL,—What on earth does the Finance mean by their recent order with regard to cash payments? I can only tell you if this policy of pin-pricks is to continue I and many others will have to reconsider their positions, etc.

(Signed) A. WORRY.

There now, I wonder what that is? Some Accounts Circular which they don't like. I will send for it and see. I wish there was one week in

the year in which Worry did not resign, or, better
still, that he would really go altogether.

No. 2 (in French).—Cher Lord,—I recommend to your un-
failing kindness a young man called, I think, Ahmed Kairy,
who, *I am told*, is an excellent fellow of high principles and
extraordinary attainments. The sources from which I obtain
my information are the very best.

(Signed)   MOHAMMED SULEIMAN,

Under-Secretary, Towns and
Buildings Dept.

The very best!—I should think they were. He's
his nephew, if I remember rightly; and I last heard
of the young paragon as having raised a subscription for erecting a monument to the martyrs of
Sersenna, and having retired to Paris to spend the
proceeds.

No. 3.—DEAR SIR,—I am fifty years of age, and have never
had a profession. It was suggested to me by a friend who
lives near me, and whom I see almost every day, that the
only cure for the weak health from which I have been suffering for some years would be to go abroad for a long period.
He suggested some hot climate would suit me best. I thought
of Egypt. Could you give me a post under Government with
light duties and a moderate salary? I write a good hand
and am a great admirer of Mr. Balfour, whose governess's
second cousin married a connection of my wife's. Awaiting
a favourable reply,—Believe me, Yours.

P.S.—I should add that I am slightly deaf.

No wonder his friend gave him that disinterested
advice.

No. 4.—SIR,—Knowing the deep interest you take in the
welfare of this ancient country, with which the names of so
many of our famous men have been associated, I venture to
bring to your notice a scheme which, if it were carried into
effect, would, I am sure, be of the greatest benefit to Egypt
generally, and more especially to that most interesting class,

the peasantry. I enclose the written proposal, which I understand it is usual to send in on such occasions, and beg to assure you that I remain, etc., etc.

A. TUBBS.

The scheme consists apparently in making a new fertiliser out of old bricks, which the Government is to supply gratis. Thank you.

No. 5.—DEAR LORD EDWARD,—I am sure you will not mind my writing to you about a personal matter. Dear Charlie is so depressed because he did not get any recognition this year. Of course, he does not care for such things in themselves, but he feels it hard that so many others who have done so much less than he has should receive them, and he be left out. He tells me even the messengers in the office salute him with less respect than they used to, which shows what the natives think about it. Could you do anything in the matter, do you think?—Believe me, etc.

ANNIE BROOK.

Mean beast, to make his poor wife write! She is worth exactly a dozen of him, and I'd give her any decoration she liked, for I suppose that's what he is after. Luckily I can write back to say it is not in my power to do anything. If it were, he would not get one, but that don't matter.

No. 6.—DEAR LORD EDWARD.—I felt after our conversation the other day that perhaps I had not explained my position quite clearly enough. It is, as you are aware, very complicated, and in fairness to myself I think I must claim to put the whole of the matter before you. At the risk, therefore, of trespassing unduly on your very valuable time, I must request you to grant me another interview.

Trusting that you will forgive my importunity, etc., etc.

J. MAUNDERS PROSY.

Now, upon my word, this is the pinnacle! He stayed in my office for two hours the first time, and left me with a bad headache and a portfolio of documents which he asked me—ironically, I con-

clude—to read at my leisure. I did so with the
assistance of two trained experts and a magnifying
glass. They proved to be his household accounts
for the years 1880 to 1887, and were mostly wrongly
added up. He came back to explain he had given
me the wrong documents, which had dawned on
me in the interval, as his case is a shadowy claim to
compensation for having done nothing and not got
killed in the Alexandrian riots of 1882. If I could
get at the rioters I would have them punished very
severely for their remissness in not braining him or
burning him alive or something. The second time
he came he told me all his early life, which made
one wonder why he had not committed suicide, as
it was so dull. He only got to the year seventy-
nine, however, when a merciful message from the
Minister that he wished to see me stopped the flow
of his conversation, which I had enjoyed for an
hour and a half. The third time we had a cheery
little talk for three hours on men he remembered
in old days, whose chief consolation in leaving this
world must have been that they escaped his chatter.

The fourth time we went minutely over his so-
called case several times, besides those of a lot of
poisonous friends of his, and now he wants to begin
again. Well, I know it is no good putting him
off. He is perfectly persistent and entirely equable.

There, it seems I was wrong, as usual, to expect
an interesting mail. To my joy, however, I see I
have overlooked three letters with English stamps
which have concealed themselves under the torn
envelopes of those I have read. This is grand!
Let us see what is in them. I open the first. It is

the notice of a flower show held a month ago at a place I used to live in five years since. This is not encouraging. The second looks better—let us see.

DEAR LORD EDWARD,—I have been meaning to write to you for a long time, but, I don't know how it is, something always seems to stop me. I am longing for news of all our old friends, and to hear what they are doing and where they all are. Is the Savoy as full as ever, and do you still play golf every day? Do write and tell me all about it. I had hoped that we should come out to Egypt this year, as Charles is in need of a rest, but the doctors have sent us to the Riviera, which I *hate*. Is it not unlucky? I met an old friend of yours the other day, Colonel Blogger, and he asked most affectionately after you. He is trying to get his son into some profession. The poor boy broke down at college and had to be taken away, and has now nothing to do. He is very intelligent, nice and steady, etc., etc., etc.

Now that is what I call (ironically) gratitude! I looked after Mrs. Lever for a whole season. I lent her my boat, got her reserved compartments, and ran about on her errands for three solid months. She has never written a line to me, after her formal letter of thanks, for two years, and now she is trying to engineer young Blogger into the service. Young Blogger of all people! His father was Principal Medical Officer of the Army of Occupation in 1902, and was nicknamed " the Pestilence that walketh in the noonday," as he always lured unsuspecting acquaintances into accompanying him on long and tiresome walks, during which he explained his own merits and the organised conspiracy which existed in the War Office to delay his well-earned right to something very abstruse. I will send a civil answer, and that is more than she deserves.

On opening the third and last letter, I am rewarded for patient submission to unmerited adversity. It is from my much-beloved and re-spected niece Emma, and is doubtless full of family news, etc.

DEAR UNCLE N.,—We have just left . . . [can't read this] for London, where we are now. We thought the sooner we moved the better [why?], and I am sure you will agree with our point of view. It is all very tiresome. [Very!]

Turning to a more pleasant topic, we are all delighted about . . . [can't read—it's an initial X, I think] success. [Wonder what he or she has done.] Of course we expected it would be all right, but one cannot ever be quite sure [I expect it's her brother's examination; I know he was in for one—bravo, Charlie!], and the doctor was doubtful. [That don't sound right. Perhaps the poor beggar was seedy.] It was very painful, and —— was almost delirious [Charlie does not seem to like exams.—I sympathise], but as soon as they cut it open it was all right. [This can't be an examina-tion. It is too drastic—let us look again. Of course not—it's " abscess," not " success." She does write indistinctly.] She was wonderfully brave. [Not Charlie, obviously some one else.] Mamma told me to tell you that the [looks like Broughton] family are coming to Cairo in December or January, and she thinks they are going to stay in a hotel somewhere near where you live, but she cannot remember the name. Will you be an angel and look after them? [Cheer-ful prospect. I wonder who they are.] One of the daughters is nice-looking, I am told. [How many are there, I wonder?] Mamma thinks they will amuse you. [Anne was always an optimist.]

I have lots more to tell you, only the post is going. Was it not sad about Bart? Your affec. niece,

EMMA.

There you are. That is the kind of maddening letter one gets. First the family left some place for reasons unknown, but as Emma thinks I should approve of them, I presume not discreditable. Secondly, some woman underwent a successful operation. Thirdly, a family of the possible name of Broughton are coming some time during the winter to an unknown locality, where I have to find them on the chance of being amused. Fourthly, Bart, who is my second cousin, has died, or got convicted, or something.

I shall worry my head all day about these problems. No, the mail has been a failure to-day.

Now for work. I will just polish off the submitted questions, and then see the people who have appointments, and put in an hour between one and two at the memorandum and the pension case.

I ring for Mr. Tomkins.

Mr. Tomkins is my shorthand clerk—at least he was so, but he has gradually edged himself into the title of secretary. He comes from my native village —London, to wit—and is my great stand-by. He is obviously cross this morning, because he bangs the slate, on which the names of the people I have to see are written down, on the table with an aggressive and aggrieved air. It is curious that all people of a certain social grade sniff when they are out of temper. I wonder if there is any medical reason for this.

Let us see the list: two heads of Departments at 9.30, 9.45, respectively. At 10 a.m. the Under-Secretary of the Ministry of Justice. At 10.15, Freiherr von Gompnitz. Good lord, the German Chargé d'Affaires! He is perfectly awful. At 10.30, M. de Signorini. Signorini is a kind of land broker, and is both a joy and a terror—a joy because of the amount of amusement he affords, a terror on account of the amount out of which he annually swindles the Government. 11.0, Ahmed Bey Kalaam —he is a crank about Arabic literature, and is under high protection. 11.15, Mr. Simson. Who is Mr. Simson? Mr. Tomkins thinks he is connected with one of the companies, and he has left a letter for me. The letter, on examination, shows that Mr. Simson and two other gentlemen are representatives of the Borneo and West Australian Fibre and Silk Growing Association, and that they will call on me to lay certain matters before me. Concession-hunters.

Nothing more? No, Mr. Tomkins admits, grudgingly, there is nothing more at present, though some gentlemen are sure to come without appointments. He adds, with a gleam of satisfaction, that there is a committee at six this afternoon. This pleases him, because he knows I hate committees. I wonder what he is cross about.

Mr. Tomkins, when he has banged down on my table the first pile of dossiers, as we call them, leaves the room, and I proceed to deal with the papers.

My written routine work can readily be divided into two classes: covering other people's responsibility and answering riddles. We call these in the office signatures and decisions, because it sounds nicer. Each question comes up with all the papers concerning it from its earliest infancy, and the last document is a letter or a note. If it is a signature that is required, it is a letter; if a decision, a note.

I have to sign letters because in theory the heads of other Ministries consider it below their dignity to receive letters signed by subordinates. This is the theory, but the fact is that subordinates prefer to be covered by one's authority. This is, of course, especially true of the Syrians, Moslems, and Copts. They have often a playful way of getting you to

sign innocent-looking documents, and then producing them later on as a justification for some
iniquity or other. This at one time became so
common as to be dangerous, and we had to put an
end to it by calmly reversing the ruling or decision
contained in the original letter as one given in error.
This was regarded as mean, but stopped the practice,
which we made still further unpopular by declaring
that the drafter of a letter was responsible for its
contents.

Decisions, on the contrary, are given on a set of
facts (save the mark!) set forward in a note by the
head of the Department concerned. They always
remind me of the hard cases in *Truth*, as they
usually end in a question of the nature of " What
should A do? " Of course, beyond this one has
one's own notes to write for the Council or Minister,
or the Adviser or the Agency, as the case may be,
but they are a different class of thing, and deal with
questions of policy and legislation, and not with
matters of routine.

My first batch of dossiers this morning are seventeen in number, and all look simple except two.

Let me see. For signature, letter informing
P. W. D. that a credit of £10,000 has been placed
at their disposal for making a new road in Cairo.
Letter to Public Instruction, informing them that
their proposal to start a new school for girls in
Tanta cannot be considered before the preparation
of the next Budget. Letter to the War Department, asking why they have exceeded a credit of
£30,000 by £1 5s., and so on, and so on.

The decisions are for the most part quite simple

too, as one has decided heaps of similar cases before. There are two difficult ones, however, which are rather typical of the kind of thing one has to decide.

The first is a pension case.

One Mohammed el Tawari wishes to have his case treated under the pension law of Said Pasha rather than under the present law. Only people who joined the service before the year 1875 can claim this privilege, which is a very substantial one, as the old law was far more generous than the present one. Mohammed Bey founds his claim on the following considerations:—

His entry into the regular service (Ministry of Justice) was in 1877, but he claims to have been a corporal, and subsequently a sergeant, in the Government schools from 1874 to 1877. In old days the Government schools were military in their organisation; and though service as an ordinary scholar or private did not count as Government service, the time passed as a non-commissioned officer did. So if we, in a moment of enthusiasm, believed what he said, his service began in 1874, and his pension must be granted according to the provisions of the older and more generous law.

What makes the real difficulty of these cases is, that all the records of these schools were burnt in the 1882 rebellion. So we have no document to prove whether a man was or was not a non-commissioned officer on any particular date.

Some genius in the Ministry some years back got the Government to decide that if any one claiming to count service as a non-commissioned officer in the schools could produce the written testimony of four senior Government officials to the effect that he had served as an N.C.O., it would be accepted as sufficient proof.

Mohammed Bey has produced written statements from seven of these worthies to the effect that he was a corporal in the Saidieh School in the year 1874. The statements are most circumstantial, and the witnesses are two judges of the High Court, three generals of brigade, a controller in the Public Works Ministry, and an ex-Under-Secretary of State.

So far it appears simple. According to our rules, Mohammed ought to be allowed to reckon his service from 1874, and have his pension calculated according to the Said Pasha law.

Unluckily for him, he fell out with a cousin of his, called Ibrahim Pasha Murad, over a question of inheritance and outmanœuvred him. Ibrahim Pasha, smarting under his defeat and its concomitant pecuniary loss, came to see me. We discussed the weather and the crops rather more fully than was natural, and he then mentioned incidentally his cousin in the most laudatory terms. He praised him particularly for his charming manners, which he casually mentioned had been acquired in Paris, when he was at school there in 1876, and he in the course of his innocent family reminiscences mentioned the name of the school.

I naturally wrote to Paris on the strength of this information, and have received a most clear and authentic extract from the records of that institution that Mohammed el Tawari, the son of Shefik Pasha Raschid, the then Minister of Public Works in Egypt, was accorded a prize by, I conclude,

34

some swindle which was not found out, in November 1876. The record also stated that at this time Mohammed was a scholar of the third year. When I as gently as possible brought this to the notice of Mohammed Bey, he was horrified, and explained that it was all a mistake. The individual alluded to in the records was his brother, who had died young. On examination this proved to be only partially accurate, as the brother in question had died in infancy at Constantinople in 1867.

What is A (that is, I) to do?

Of course the French record is the true one, and the written statements are benevolent or properly rewarded fictions. Still, it is a little hard to tell all these perjurers the truth about themselves. On the whole, I shall refuse the request civilly without giving my reasons. The fear of exposure will probably make them eventually " take it lying down," even if they do try to " bluff " a bit at first.

The second case is a land case.

Some dozen years ago a man called Aziz Effendi Neguib took five hundred acres of Government land in exchange for some land of his own that the Government wanted for something or other in another part of the country. Here in the dossier are all the deeds of the transaction perfectly in order. The paper work of the Land Department was always very good, but they were much less careful about measuring the land up than they are now, and for a slight payment I have no doubt you could vary the measurements within reasonable limits.

The Government now wants to repurchase this same land for the new Agricultural School hard by.

When we came to measuring up the land, we found that there are only four hundred acres instead of five hundred, and the present owner, the son of Aziz Effendi, now wants the Government to make good the amount out of which he alleges we swindled his father.

At first there seems some justice in this demand, as we delivered a hundred acres less than we mention in the deeds of transfer, but on examination there are one or two points which make one alter one's opinion. First, the price at which we valued the nominal five hundred acres twelve years ago seems curiously low, but you find that if you take the land at its real area, the price works out at the price of such land in those days. It is only when you call the four hundred acres five, that the price seems low.

Now supposing that this was a fraud, what was his object? Simple enough. Aziz Effendi got his four hundred acres at a fair price. It is true he had to pay land-tax on five hundred, but what of that compared with the power of mortgaging the land as five hundred acres instead of four, which he duly did?

Whether this son can attack us in the Courts now is another matter, but in any case I mark the papers, " That the Law Officers be instructed to resist this claim."

CHAPTER III   OFFICE—PART II

AT this point Mr. Tomkins comes in and wants to know if I will see Mr. Driller, head of the Department of Unappropriated Revenue. Certainly, and in bangs Mr. Driller. He is a valuable public servant, but works always under a head of steam that is positively dangerous. He rushes into the question he wants to discuss at the point where he has met the difficulty, not at the beginning, explains his reasons in a torrent of words, touches on the beginning of the matter in an incomprehensible way, says he is sure the right action is to refuse, but as perhaps I would like to consider it he will come round to-morrow, but hopes the Government will back him up, and disappears in a sort of whirlwind.

I get my breath back and ask Mr. Tomkins to get the papers about the case, so that I may form some dim idea of what it is all about.

Driller is succeeded by Langworthy, Director-General of State Properties. He is an excellent contrast to the other. He enters the room wearily, and says he has nothing of any interest to discuss except the Marini case. Would I like to go into it? "Yes, certainly." Langworthy, after mentioning he is far from well, and would I mind the window being closed, begins at Count Marini, who flourished forty years ago, and had obscure claims to some Government land, works slowly down with a wealth of detail that obscures the slender thread of the story, and wearily arrives at the present day. It is the usual long tissue of cheating and muddling. I suggest declining to have anything to do with Marini, and leaving him to sue us in the courts, if he wishes to.

" I thought you would say that," says Langworthy, in a sepulchral tone, and totters out, presumably to see about his funeral. He has never been ill in his life, but believes he has a mortal disease—a different one every month. It's consumption this month, so he coughs; last month it was paralysis, so he dragged his leg. He is a queer fellow, but an excellent official.

Mr. Tomkins now brings in a letter from the Agency asking me to see Mr. Adalbert Langton, an English gentleman of position, the bearer of the highest recommendations, etc., who wishes to purchase land in Egypt.

I see him for ten minutes, discover that he does not know why, where, or how he wants to buy land, and send him on to Langworthy, who is used to dealing with these followers of Nebuchadnezzar who want to know both the dream and the interpretation thereof.

My next visitor is the Under-Secretary of the Ministry of Justice, a dapper little Egyptian. He goes by the name of " Oliver Twist," as he is never satisfied. He sits down and chats amiably about the weather and the crops, mentioning in a non-committal way several matters in dispute between our departments, and then most artistically works the conversation round to his house. He is or has been building a new house, which apparently he thinks ought to be constructed by the aid of departmental subscription. Thus he got the stone half-price from the Public Works, transported it by the State railways at quarter-rate, and had its erection supervised by a wise Egyptian architect of the Public Works at no rate at all.

Now he wants me to ask the Water Company to lay on water free of charge. To this I naturally demur, as we don't like asking favours of the companies—they cost too much in the long run. He smiles and apparently acquiesces, but he will get it eventually. He will worry and bore every one about his beastly water until the Khedive or the Prime Minister or the Agency will ask us to get it done for him in the interests of the peace and quietness of all concerned.

I have tried everything with him—brutality, fencing, delay, counter-pressure—but it is no good. His ancestress must have been the Widow who dealt with the Unjust Judge. Our business over, he tells me a little malicious gossip about one of our colleagues—a pretty little story, accusing him of every form of vile rascality, a story one would not dare to tell under one's breath at home; but here such things are regarded as amiable eccentricities, and we part with expressions of mutual esteem.

My next visitor is an abnormally tall man, whose body and limbs appear to be made of wood. They don't seem to move naturally, and it would cause one no surprise if he creaked when he walked. His face is large and round, with a set half-smile on it. His hair is short and carefully brushed à la militaire, and the fixity and vacuity of his gaze indicate that he suffers from extreme short-sightedness.

The moment he has entered my room he bends suddenly in the middle, as if he were seized by a sudden abdominal spasm which he is too self-controlled to show in any other way.

He has another spasm on my offering him a chair, and he sits down as if it were a part of his military drill, and a separate word of command were required for each movement.

39

I inquire politely after his health, which gives him another spasm.

He then sits looking at me as if I were a curious anatomical specimen in a bottle, but without attempting to break the silence.

Seeing that, according to Prussian rules, it is obviously my turn to lead, I ask him to what I am indebted for the honour of his visit. He has a modified spasm, draws off his gloves very deliberately "by numbers," and opening his enormous mouth gives vent in deeply guttural tones to the following :—

"You are very amiable. I haf a gomblaint."

Taken literally, this is what I should have expected. He ought by his appearance to be suffering from *rigor pokeritis* or some such disease, but I know better from bitter experience. So I say that I am extremely sorry to hear it, and ask him to be kind enough to tell me what is the matter.

In the tones of a man to whom expectoration is on the whole more usual than conversation, he replied, " Ve vant to gif you blacks."

This is a little difficult to translate. I am sure he does not want to give us anything we should like to get, so I think " gif " must be translated " sell." What " blacks " or " placks " are is a matter which will be cleared up as we go on. I ask him what sort of placks he alludes to, slurring the " p " so that it will do for " p " or " b," as the case may be.

" Gobber," is the reply.

Copper blacks is impossible; it must be . . . and then with a flash I get it. It is " plaques." Now the only " plaques " I can remember purchasing are the brass ones some of our messengers wear on their arms, but they are undoubtedly of brass, and we don't buy twenty a year. He cannot be bothering about those. With a view of clearing matters up, I suggest, " Don't you mean brass? "

" I am instrugded gobber," is the uncompromising reply.

" Could you tell me what the copper plaques are for? " I ask.

" They was as changes," replies the Freiherr.

No! I am out of it. I guess, from previous experience, that this is probably a complaint from the German merchants that they have not been treated on an equality with others in connection with a Government order for copper plaques or something of the sort.

I have another try at elucidating the mystery. " Do you remember what Department of the Government required these plaques? " I ask. He ruminates for a moment, and then rasps out:

" I haf no zertain knowledge, but I tink you."

Now what on earth could the Finance want with copper plaques? " Please," I say in despair, " tell me the whole story, as I cannot remember any case such as you mention."

" Yaas," he grunts, " is besser. You haf a note inzerted in the *Journal* that you vant fife hundert tousand gobber blacks, but it is so late that Shermans cannot abbly."

" But why should it be worse for them than any one else, even if the time allowed for tendering was short? " I ask.

" It is for us longer."

" But why? "

" Ve must alzo write to Shermany and have answers, and so."

" But that is the same for all nations, Freiherr. How does Germany (I very nearly say Shermany) suffer more than the others? And we have had no complaints from them."

He ruminates, and seems to me to be going to ruminate for some time, so I say as helpfully as a strong desire to tell him and his Government to go to—South Sahara will allow me:

" I will note your complaint, Freiherr, and see if there is anything in it, and I will let you know the result."

" I tank you," he grates out. " I vill call some more."

He gets up after this threat, has three spasms of a peculiarly painful nature, and goes. I ring the bell, and on Mr. Tomkins appearing, ask him what copper plaques we have been ordering lately, and for what purpose we wanted them. He indignantly denies any knowledge of an order for copper plaques, but he says we have been asking for tenders for five hundred thousand copper coins.

Of course! What an ass I am! The idiot did not know the word for " coins," and called them plaques. And our respected friends the Shermans are at their old tricks. The dodge is a simple one. They don't tender, but wait to see what the lowest offer is. They then try to get the adjudication annulled on the ground that they had not time to tender or some nonsense of that sort, and when the order is put up to adjudication again, they compete with the

42

advantage of knowing the lowest tender. If they cannot carry out this swindle, then they make a grievance of the question, and demand that they shall be compensated by being given some particularly lucrative piece of business by the Egyptian Government. Oh, they are a sweet, straightforward, honest lot, the Meinherrs! I will write presently and tell the Freiherr I see no foundation for his " gomblaint."

As Mr. Tomkins shows in Signorini, I see a gleam of pleasure in his eye. He knows that these interviews result badly for the Government as a rule. Signorini is a middle-aged gentleman, faultlessly dressed in the newest fashion. His grey hair gives him an appearance of respectability, and his open and candid expression inspires confidence from the first moment you see him; and it is on that candid expression that he has lived in luxury ever since he attained the dignity of manhood. His mind is well cultivated, and his knowledge of history and literature extensive. He speaks five languages with fluency and accuracy, and is an amateur of no small merit in music and painting. His collection of Ptolemaic antiquities is one of the finest in Egypt, and he has published a very readable treatise on the subject. In conversation he is quick and witty, and he has a pleasant geniality of expression.

And he would swindle the coat off the back of a blind beggar.

After a few desultory remarks on the heat of the weather and the prospects of the cotton crop, he opens his business.

He is a master of his art. He does not nauseate

43

one with platitudes about progress or try to persuade one that he is a philanthropist. He begins
by telling me that he, or rather those he represents,
wish to buy a large area of Government land on
the outskirts of Cairo. They would then level it,
lay it out in streets, build houses on it, and sell them
off to the public.

It is true he wants the land at a low price, but
unless it is sold for some such scheme, what can the
Government do with it? The expense of levelling
and laying out streets, putting in water and gas
mains, etc., will be heavy, and can only be done by
people who are prepared to spend a lot of money,
so the Government cannot sell the area piecemeal
to small buyers, and produce the same results.
Again, at present, as waste land, it brings in no
revenue, but if it was built over we should get our
house-tax, always worth something.

If I were another sort of man, he says, he might
point out the advantages to the public and to the
country which would be gained by the carrying out
of such a scheme, but he knows that I can appreciate
these things without his telling me, and frankly he
does not care a button for the public. He, or
rather his syndicate, are prepared to carry out
whatever bargain they make fairly and loyally, but
what they want is the profit, and they don't conceal
the fact. Of course it is a big gamble. They may
all lose their money over it. He thinks not, or he
would not have gone in for it—of that he can assure
me. The Government can be assured the work will
be well done, because if it is not so the syndicate
will not be able to sell the houses, so the scheme has

the best of all guarantees, viz. that the interests of the syndicate and Government are identical. The Government, he agrees, make no great profit, but they sell land which is otherwise unsaleable, and they get their house-tax, besides the indirect advantages to this famous public we hear so much about, and they take no risks at all. He mentions the price he is prepared to give, which, though low, is not unreasonably so, considering the levelling, etc.

Of course, like all his proposals, it sounds admirable. I wonder where the flaw is.

He continues that he does not want to make a complicated agreement. Where interests are identical this is not necessary. He simply wants to buy the land and agree to level it. The rest is a matter for the syndicate. He proposes, therefore, that they should be given possession of the land at once and allowed two years in which to level it, with an option of purchase on each hundred square metres levelled. Will I consider it and let him know, and will I be so kind as to keep the matter a profound secret—at all events as to the actual place? because otherwise all the small proprietors, of whom there are twenty or thirty on land adjoining the plot in question, and whom it will be necessary to buy out quietly, will get wind of the scheme and put their prices up to fantastic figures.

That is all, he says airily, and it was most kind of me to have seen him.

He must now return to Alexandria, where he lives, and see after the unhappy Duclos, whose house he is living in. Have I not heard? Oh, but it is the best story in the world. This miserable Duclos, who is

45

sixty and shaped like a tun, must play the gay
Lothario. It is too comic for words, and then follows
a story which I was just going to write down, but on
reflection think I had better not. When S. tells
them they sound so light and amusing one does not
realise that they are unfit for publication.

I admit that this one makes me laugh, and S.
swaggers off to his carriage.

Mr. Tomkins brings in a note from Carter, the
general manager of the State railways.

DEAR C.—We have found a site for the new goods station.
I cannot at present tell you the exact locality, but the syndicate
who own it have offered to level and deliver in two years at a
fairly reasonable price. Much less than we should have to
pay if we expropriated and levelled it, for you know what
the Courts make us pay in such cases.

The matter, at the request of the syndicate, is to be kept a
dead secret, as they have certain negotiations on with regard
to outlying small proprietors which they wish to terminate
before the scheme becomes public property. I promised to
tell no one, but cannot help letting you know privately. I
believe the land was old Government land, but has been
recently sold.

Well, I am blessed! Of all the calm cheek I ever
heard of! S. has solemnly fooled the railways
(probably bribed a clerk or two) into believing that
the land is the syndicate's, and he very nearly succeeded in buying it from me. Telling Carter that it
used to belong to the Government was an artistic
touch. It would explain away any awkward description of the land on any plan Carter looked at. He
would not be surprised or frightened by its being
marked as Government land. The railways too
have a separate land department from the rest of
the Government, and S. hoped to slip through
between the two of us.

I ring up Carter on the telephone and put a few questions to him. Yes, just as I thought: the profit would have been just over 200 per cent. I feel almost sorry that so noble a scheme has failed, but I sit down and write:—

MY DEAR SIGNORINI,—I am so sorry, but I stupidly forgot that the land you want to purchase is not for sale. We want it for the new railway goods station. Please treat this as confidential.—Yours, etc.

For once I am even with him.

Ahmed Bey Kalaam, who now enters my room, is a fat little man with a round pink face and short grey hair, and a pair of small bright black eyes. He is attired in a rather *négligé* manner, as becomes a man of culture and artistic temperament, and wears the low tarbush indicating a Nationalist. He is, though an ardent patriot, a friend of mine, and often comes to me to pour out his overcharged soul and try to obtain some money for one or other of his literary or patriotic schemes.

He is obviously to-day in a highly excited condition. He sinks into the chair I offer him as if he could no longer bear the weight that is pressing on his patriotic shoulders.

After asking after his health, which he says is as good as he can hope for, I ask him what I can do for him. He replies that he feels absolutely disheartened, his spirit, though it has for a long time resisted the worries and troubles of life, is almost broken.

I express my sorrow, but suggest that if he will tell me his trouble I may be able to assist him.

He now produces his handkerchief and wipes

47

away a tear, and proceeds, in a voice broken with emotion, to tell me his sad history. He begins by informing me that from his boyhood up he has loved his country more than his life. He was born of a military family who have habitually given up their lives on the glorious field of battle, so it is, so to speak, bred in him and he cannot help it. If he, too, could have fought for his country and died for her, he would have done so with enthusiasm. He will ever mourn over the fact—I must not mind his saying this—that, owing to a severe attack of liver trouble, he was absent from the field of Tel-el-Kebir. There he could have died as his fathers had died, and by now he would have been forgotten by all except perhaps a few devoted friends.

Here the thought of his might-have-been-heroic end again overcomes his manly pride, and he weeps silently into his handkerchief.

With an effort, however, he recovers himself and continues that, as the tented field was not for him, he had thrown himself heart and soul, in spite of the repeated remonstrances of his doctor, into every scheme which was started for the benefit and advancement of his compatriots. He had sacrificed health, money (though this he despises), and even his literary ambitions in order to carry out his duty. What was the result? Was he assisted and encouraged? Was he met with approbation and help? No, a thousand times no! He was met with jealousy and ill-will, he was hindered and thwarted at every turn. He was at last disgusted. He would bear it no more. He would retire to Mecca, and pass the rest of his days in meditation and literary pursuits.

He works himself up as he goes on, and unless I do something he will have an apoplectic fit or something of the sort. I say to him, as soothingly as I can, that I am deeply grieved to hear that he has been so badly treated, but he must remember he has still friends who respect and esteem him, and he must not let the petty jealousies of unworthy men grieve him to so great an extent. Perhaps if he would confide the matter to me I might be of service to him.

He murmurs his thanks, and adds that I have always been a father to him. This is the painful story. Some time back he suggested the idea of founding a patriotic library in Egypt, exclusively for the collection and preservation of works by Egyptian authors. There was to be a reading-room attached, where true patriots could come and imbue their souls with the spirit of their country—their beloved, unhappy country—for half a piastre a time. The idea was received with favour, money was subscribed, and a large sum was given by Prince Ahmed Ibrahim, who, though undoubtedly eccentric, was by no means, as some low-minded dogs pretended, insane (one of the low-minded dogs in question, if I remember rightly, was the director of the lunatic asylum). The building was constructed and many valuable books were bought (among others, Kalaam's, I think), but, alas, it was not a success. The youth of Egypt were not yet sufficiently raised from that deep abyss of despair into which the misfortunes of their unhappy country had plunged them to appreciate the religious commentaries of the Middle Ages, which form the richest portion of Egyptian literature.

They still preferred the lighter works of modern French authors. No one came to the Library, and, as I doubtless remembered, the books were given to the Khedivial Library, and the building was devoted to carrying on a patriotic music-hall. He regrets that even this has been since closed by the orders of the tyrannical police because they pretended that the performance was not decent. How could totally inartistic people like the police know what was or was not decent? (I remember. It had the distinction of being one of the very few music-halls ever closed by the police in Egypt. We cannot be accused of undue prudery here.) But with this act of high-handed injustice he was not now concerned.

When the scheme of the Egyptian Library was abandoned there were still a few pounds of the money originally subscribed left over in his, Kalaam's, charge. He, Kalaam, thought earnestly what should be done with these. He did not merely consider the matter in a superficial way, but devoted his whole intellect to the question. It kept him awake at nights; it was never absent from his thoughts during the day.

At last one day an idea came to him, like a flash of light, an idea which he felt sure would be agreeable and applauded by all. He would send the money to the poor of Mecca. He felt so sure that this would be in accordance with the wishes of all that he did not even consult any one about it, as perhaps he might otherwise have done.

Had he known the dogs he had to deal with he would have cast the filthy money back in their dirty and ignoble faces. As it was, because he could not imagine that there could be on this globe such moral obliquity, such black turpitude, he sent it off next day to a friend in Mecca for distribution amongst the deserving poor of that holy place. Now, was it possible to believe that, instead of applauding his action, the family of the poor Prince Ahmed Ibrahim, who has been most unjustly deprived by the courts of law of the management of his affairs, claimed that the money should have been returned to them? Not content with this outrageous suggestion, they dared to say that the Prince, their own kinsman, was mad when he gave the money originally, and, plunging still deeper into the filth from which they sprang, they demanded from him, Ahmed Kalaam, an honest gentleman and patriot, a receipt to show that the money had been sent to the poor of Mecca. What degradation and what foolishness! As if one took receipts from the poor! Still, in spite of the dignified protests which he had made at this treatment, they were actually proceeding in the courts of law against him, Ahmed Kalaam, the patriot, as if he were a common trader, for the return of this sum which now, it might be hoped, was rejoicing the hearts of the aged, the widows, and the fatherless in the Sacred City.

Here, again overcome by his feelings, the patriot sobs afresh.

I do my best to comfort him by saying that ingratitude is the commonest of crimes, and that often the best motives are misunderstood. At the same time, though his action would doubtless be perfectly understood by his friends and by all the artistic and cultivated sections of the community, it might not seem so easy of explanation to the judges, who have even less artistic sense than the police, whom in this respect they much resemble. On the whole, then, as I know that money is no object to him, and rather a thing he despises, and as it is important that no breath of suspicion, however unjust, should rest on a patriot, and in view of the narrow, inartistic point of view of the judges, I should advise him to send back to his traducers a sum of money equal to that which he has sent to Mecca, thus taking that charitable deed to his own account.

At this advice the patriot is even more bitterly affected than ever; but, on my pressing him to consider it, he says he will do so, and takes leave of me mournfully, doubtless to think out carefully from what other patriotic source he can obtain the necessary sum to satisfy the grovelling, money-grubbing relatives of the eccentric and unfortunate Prince, who incidentally, I heard recently, is in considerable trouble himself, as he is convinced that he is a water-wheel, and they won't give him any oxen to turn him round.

One cannot tell if friend Ahmed has stolen the money or merely muddled it away. In any case, one's only chance of getting him to behave properly is to pretend to believe him.

The three gentlemen who next appear before me file into the room with the air of being the bearers of responsibility almost too great to be borne.

They are obviously the usual " cast," the capitalist, the lawyer, and the local expert.

The first is a portly gentleman with a large extent of waistcoat, irreproachably but a trifle over dressed, and as full of dignity as a turkey cock. His ancestry probably formed the rearguard of Moses' army when they left this country, and gave particular attention to the borrowing of the jewels.

The lawyer, of Greco-French extraction, with a smattering of Italian, Smyrniot, and Armenian blood in him, was born in Malta, and is therefore a fellow-countryman. He carries some large bundles of papers, and has a defiant you-can't-bully-me air.

The third is a very dark gentleman, whose subservient manner and semi-Semitic features betray the Syrian. He carries a huge roll of maps and an extraordinary tall hat, made apparently of black satin. He wears what he conceives to be an air of frankness and conscious virtue, and his eye continually wanders to the capitalist, whom he regards with the air of hungry worship.

Mr. Simson (late Simeon) introduces his two confederates (using my official title of " Lord Seesil ") as " Mr. Dupong, our legal adviser in this country, and Mr. Cassab, who is acting as our local representative." I beg them to be seated, and after a remark or two in a low tone to Dupong, the lawyer, Mr. Simson begins as follows :—

" Lord Seesil, I am here on behalf of a certain very influential group of capitalists to lay certain proposals before you, as the representative of the Egyptian Government. I may as well say at once that the proposal is a very important one, involving large sums of money, and one which I think it will be very much in the interest of the Egyptian people to accept. I will not, Lord Seesil, conceal from you that we did not take this matter up with any eagerness. I may say I was extremely unwilling to go into it. I will be quite frank with you, and tell you that as a business man this proposal is not worth taking up."

Here the other two nod their approval.

"There is no doubt, Lord Seesil," he proceeds, "a possibility—I cannot say, I am sorry to say, a probability—of substantial profit, but it is altogether too remote to tempt one to put money which might be much better employed elsewhere into this venture. So to start with, I may say we do not, at all events for many years, look for great, or even sufficient return for our money."

"No," from the other two, in low but convinced tones.

"Mr. Dupong will tell you that when he examined the papers, he said to me, 'Mr. Simson, sir, I hope I am not called upon to advise as to the desirability of the scheme from a financial point of view.' 'Mr. Dupong,' I replied, 'you are not, but I should be very glad to have your opinion.' He replied, as he will tell you, 'There is very little in it.'"

Here the lawyer, who had been nodding his adherence to and appreciation of the Lion's roaring, interposes, "Pardon me, Mr. Simson—I said there is nothing in it."

"I beg your pardon, Mr. Dupong, you are right. You said there is nothing in it."

"I replied to Mr. Dupong that I knew that only too well, but that other considerations came in. Now, before I lay the actual proposal before you, I should like to make my position quite clear in this matter.

"You will naturally ask, if there is little or no profit in this scheme, why do I, and the gentlemen acting with me, wish or consent to take it up? My reply is this.

"In the first place, I and my friends have always taken a deep interest in the country, both on account of its great history, its commercial importance to the civilised world, and the part which our country" (by this, by the way, Mr. Simson means England, not Judæa) "has recently taken in its reorganisation and progress, so that, if other things are equal, we consider it a very suitable place for the employment of our capital. Now, in order to employ that capital to the best advantage of ourselves (for I don't pretend to be anything but a business man) and of the country of Egypt, it is necessary for us to obtain a position in the country, to be known as reliable and respectable men of business, and, most important of all, to obtain the confidence and respect of the Egyptian Government. We want to be in the position to be able to come to you or Sir John, and say we have this or that proposal to lay before you for our mutual advantage, and for you to trust us, knowing from past experience that you can fully rely on the soundness and fairness of the business we propose. And it is to this future business, and not to our present venture, that we look for a fair return on our money. I also wish to say that I made it very clear when I joined this group that I would have nothing to do with any scheme which was not run on the most strictly honourable and business-like lines, or which did not meet with the heartiest approval and support of the Egyptian Government. Mr. Dupong here will tell you that that has been my line from the first, as it has always been in all business I have taken up."

Here Mr. Dupong murmured, "Most undoubtedly, you made that point quite clear—no possible doubt of that," and other laudatory and confirmatory remarks.

I see I am supposed to say something, but I can think of nothing but remarks like " You surprise me!" "How odd!" "Extraordinary!" and such like, which obviously would not do. So, like the great Lord Burghley, I gravely incline my head and say nothing. Mr. Simson appears satisfied, for he now turns on Dupong and says, " Perhaps you would not mind reading out to Lord Seesil that short memorandum we prepared on the subject."

Mr. Dupong immediately opens his largest bundle of papers, and proceeds to select the required document. During the process he shows or repeats the names of most of the leading firms and financiers in Europe and Egypt in the following way. " Let me see. Cassel, no, that's not it; Rothschild, no; Baring, no; Benachi, no; Delta Railways, no; ah! here it is!" and, adjusting his glasses, he begins to read it out.

After some paragraphs which bear a striking resemblance to the speech of Mr. Simson, both in style and purport, the scheme unfolds itself. I recognise, with a sort of unholy joy, an old friend in a new dress. It is a land concession.

The substance of this particular sort of swindle is always the same, though the details differ, as the cookery book says, to taste. The concessionaire asks for a large area of waste unirrigated land at a nominal price, and declares he only wants drainage water, *i.e.* water that has been already used for irrigation, and which is full of salt and other impurities, and which is therefore quite useless for ordinary crops. He explains that he is going to grow Californian hemp or Paraguayan fibre plant or mulberry trees for silk-worm raising, all of which plants, let us suppose, don't mind bad water.

When he has obtained his concession (if he gets it), he proceeds to put all sorts of pressure on the Government to get good water brought to the land, and probably eventually gets it. He then sells the land for cotton cultivation for more pounds than he paid pennies for it.

I hear all the dear old phrases I am used to in such cases—increased taxable area, large profit to the Government, new industry, remedy for the danger caused by depending only on cotton, and so on.

After the reading of this document has come to an end with an unusually nauseating paragraph about future progress and the benevolent Egyptian Government, Mr. Simson again addresses me on the merits of the proposition, with the air of one who is prepared to confer a great benefit on the community at large, and on me in particular. He has a kind of " you-don't-often-get-a-chance-like-this-my-lad-but-there-my-benevolence-is-so-great-I-cannot-help-it " air. He adds graciously that he does not wish to press me for an opinion on the proposal until I have had time to think it over, as the more it is examined, the better he will be pleased. He then directs the Syrian to show me the plans.

57

That worthy, whose admiration is obviously un-
bounded for the man who steals thousands while he
has had to content himself with an odd fiver here
and there, unfolds the plans and glibly explains
them with a half-imploring glance at his chief from
time to time, as much as to say, " Lion, when you
kill, don't forget your faithful jackal, who is lying
his throat sore for you now."

The plans are really works of art. Ground plans
showing the plantations and factory, the latter of
great extent. Elevations showing most magnificent
buildings and sheds with large chimneys pouring out
dense clouds of smoke, houses bristling with veran-
dahs, and covered with climbing roses and Bougain-
villeas, interiors and sections showing the costly
machinery and magnificent installation and furniture. The manager's house is a palace, the sub-
manager's is a mansion, and even the sub-assistant
engineer lives in a villa which would be cheap at
£300 a year. I duly admire the plans, and listen to
the strings of figures which Mr. Cassab pours forth,
showing the enormous expenditure the syndicate is
prepared to undertake.

It is always amusing to notice the accuracy of the
details in an imaginary concern like this. Cassab
explains volubly that the quality of the machinery
renders it more expensive than was intended, but
that, owing to the conditions of the country, this is
necessary. The sum estimated for the manager's
palace ends in four shillings and threepence, and so
on. When Cassab has finished this monument of
mendacity, Mr. Simson gravely commends the question to our earnest consideration, mentions that the

Government can rely on the honour of himself and his fellows, and retires with great dignity, accompanied by his satellites, while I send the papers to a noble institution called the Concessions Committee, whose business it is to put an end to such schemes by asking for adequate guarantees and legal undertakings, which friend Simson and his confederates would never think of giving, even if they could.

I am glad Simson mentioned his honour, as it completes the picture, so to speak. I have never met a real rogue who could keep that word off his lips for long.

CHAPTER IV   COUNCIL

I HAVE scarcely had time to dispose of a dozen papers after Mr. Simson's departure, when I am summoned to the presence of his Excellency the President of the Council, by his secretary, a particularly greasy individual, with a cast in the eye and a supreme lack of those principles which are so inconvenient in the transaction of business, who informs me that their Excellencies wish to consult me about their summer offices at Alexandria. From this I deduce that a sort of informal council is sitting —a practice to which their Excellencies are much given, as it enables them to weave those remarkable webs of, shall we say, arrangements in which their souls delight, without the interfering presence of a brutal and stupid foreigner. The question of their summer offices is one of the few which really stirs that august body, our council, to its depths. Up to now we have occupied temporary offices, but it has been proposed to change this and build, buy, or hire adequate permanent accommodation. As I am their Excellencies' adviser during the summer months, they doubtless consider that I should be consulted in the matter, or, to put it more formally, receive their personal instructions on the point.

On entering the President's room, I find that all the Ministers are there—that is, those in charge of the Departments of Public Instruction, Foreign Affairs, Public Works and War (combined), Justice, and my own Minister of Finance. The President, who is also Minister of the Interior, receives me with a limp " handshake," and waves me courteously to a seat. After shaking hands with the august body individually, I settle myself in the only armchair vacant, and prepare for what I know will probably be a lengthy interview. The President, with an oleaginous smile, opens the question. He wishes to know what has been done about providing the Ministers with offices for the coming summer.

Before I can answer that nothing has been done pending his instructions, Foreign Affairs, who resembles a football in figure, breaks in by asking me whether I do not think we had better revert to the old arrangement of taking rooms in the principal hotel. This is the signal for a general murmur of dissent, and the President raises his hand with a deprecatory gesture and begs Foreign Affairs to be silent. " First," he says majestically, " let us hear what has been done; afterwards we can discuss the various proposals." I hasten to explain that so far nothing has been done.

"That," says his Excellency, placing one hand inside his waistcoat in a ministerial attitude, "makes matters much easier, as it leaves us a free hand." This optimistic opinion is received with dignified approval.

"Very well," says the irrepressible Foreign Affairs, "we will take rooms in the hotel."

"What reasons do you put forward for such a step?" asks the President. "We must not act without reason." Now this puts Foreign Affairs in a hole, because he has been asked by the hotel proprietor to get this scheme adopted on the understanding that the grateful proprietor will continue to inflate his football-like figure free of charge, and this, though a good, sound reason, is not one which can be given in council.

"It is simpler; there are no formalities, and one is near one's work," says Foreign Affairs, after a slight pause. "In the summer one should always be near one's work."

"I do not like a hotel," growls Justice, whose digestion has long since practically ceased to exist, and for whom free food is a mockery. "It is not dignified to have a Ministry with a number on the door; besides this, there is a band which plays. I cannot work with a band playing."

"I prefer a band," says Foreign Affairs; "it is more gay; besides, you need not listen."

"It is so loud that one cannot hear," joins in Public Works; "how can one discuss grave matters to a polka?"

The cause is virtually lost, but Public Instruction, who is, or was twenty years ago, rather a gay "dog," but considers it necessary, since he assumed his present office, to take a high moral line, gives it the finishing blow, by saying with a puritanical air: " Undesirable people of both sexes live in hotels. It is not fitting that the seat of Government should be in such a place."

Foreign Affairs, with a look at Public Instruction which implies that he would like to enter on Lady Cardiganesque reminiscences with regard to his colleague, sinks into a sulky silence.

Justice now growls out that " the only thing to do is to hire a quiet villa near the sea, where we can live in quiet; and besides that, the sea air is excellent for the health." It would be both dignified and comfortable.

This suggestion is not received with enthusiasm. Our President, however, remarks that there is much to be said for a villa. The Romans lived in villas.

" And baths," adds Public Instruction, who feels it incumbent on him to display a little departmental learning.

" I won't work in a bath," Foreign Affairs says indignantly. " Do you call that dignified? "

This plagiarism on *Sartor Resartus* is received with pitying contempt by Public Instruction, who says, " Their baths were quite different to ours. When I was in Rome I went often . . .! " Here the President breaks in with, " There is no suggestion of baths; we are discussing villas."

Fixing his bilious eye with stern reprobation on his colleague of the Foreign Affairs, his Excellency of Justice continues his remarks. He points out that they must either construct a suitable house for their accommodation or acquire an existing building, and as they have no time to erect the necessary construction, which would take much thought and consideration even before the plans could be drawn, nothing remains but to take an existing building. Of course they could buy a house, but again this would take some time before the necessary formalities could be accomplished, and, moreover, if they were to take permanent quarters, it would be better to build. " But you have just said we have no time, *mon cher*," from Foreign Affairs. Justice, more outraged than ever, wishes to know if this is a serious discussion, and the President has again to intervene. " I think," he says, with the air of one solving a profound problem, " our colleague of the Justice has not finished his remarks. I am not sure, but I think so." Justice, who is now getting obviously sulky, continues : " If there is no time to build——"

" What sort of house would you build if you did build ? " asks Public Instruction, intervening. " If you want a cheap house built quickly, a thoroughly satisfactory house in every way, there is, I am told, an excellent contractor, a charming fellow, they tell me."

At this point his Excellency of Public Works, a stolid and fish-like individual, who has been regarding Public Instruction with stony disapproval, says, in tones as distinct as his adipose deposit will allow : " All building is a matter for the consideration of the Public Works."

" Unluckily," breaks in the irrepressible Foreign Affairs.

" How unluckily ? " says the Minister of Public

Works, turning his fish-like gaze on his other colleague. Foreign Affairs is a little dashed by the tone and look, but he tries to carry it off gaily. " *Mon cher*, it must be agreed that your Department's buildings are not of the cheapest, and they fall down."

" How fall down? " wheezes the Minister of Public Works, with awful emphasis.

" How do I know? " replies Foreign Affairs. " In the usual way, flat. Look at the Law Courts at Tanta."

" Or the school at Beni Suef," chimes in Public Instruction.

" Or the new wing of the Mixed Court at Zagazig," adds the Minister of Justice malevolently.

The Minister of Public Works looks on his colleagues with cold but contemptuous dislike. " These buildings were built," he wheezes, " before I became Minister. I could not hold them up. Besides, it is a technical matter, and——"

At this point the Prime Minister again intervenes and mildly reproves the Council, expresses his confidence in the Department of Public Works, in which he says, " Every one has seen great improvements since Ahmed Pasha became Minister; of course, there are accidents, but when one considers the difficulty of building a house, one only wonders that they do not fall down more often."

He adds that " he, however, believes the Minister of Justice is not advocating the building of a house. He may be wrong, but he understood him to say that it took too long."

His Excellency of Justice says that the Prime

Minister has rightly interpreted his views. If there is, as he said before, no time to build or buy, and it has been rightly decided to do away with the undignified custom of the Council meeting at an inn, there only remains one course, to hire a suitable villa somewhere in an agreeable situation. Of course it is not easy to hire a really good house, but in this matter perhaps he can help their Excellencies. The villa of Ahmed Bey Nessim would, he thinks, be not unsuitable—in fact, perhaps the best that could be obtained. He does not conceal from the Council that he has, in order to be prepared for such an eventuality, spoken to Ahmed Bey, who, though he was not at all willing to let, has been public-spirited enough to say he would place his house at the disposal of the Ministry for a very moderate rent, considering the inconvenience he must necessarily be put to by letting it.

This proposal is received in stony silence by the meeting. We are all aware that Ahmed Bey Nessim, pressed by gambling debts, has been moving heaven and earth to let his house, which is old-fashioned and rather ramshackle. We are also painfully aware that his Excellency of the Justice is chief creditor, and can guess what the moderate terms airily alluded to by his Excellency will probably be.

Foreign Affairs, who is still smarting under his defeat over the hotel scheme, starts the opposition in his best form. That, he says, is certainly an idea, and the situation of the house, though not, of course, first-class, is better than many; the fact that there is no road of access, the absence of garden, and the

65

proximity of some huts occupied by the poorer classes, which smell a little, would, no doubt, enable us to get the house at a very low figure, and this is, no doubt, an advantage (with a glance at me). Would the Under-Secretary of Finance give them some idea what that Ministry would probably pay for such a house—for what he might call a third-rate villa?

Here the Minister of Justice interrupts heatedly, saying that there is a road of access and a no doubt small, but very lovely garden, whilst the huts mentioned are far away, and no smell has ever been noticed coming from them.

Public Instruction starts giving us his views on the housing of the poor by making them build houses on the undrained lands outside the city at their own expense, when the Prime Minister checks him, and asks me for my opinion as to the rent. I reply diffidently that their Excellencies are much better judges than I am, but, in view of all the circumstances of the case, I think twenty pounds a month would be about right. Foreign Affairs exclaims that this is a very generous offer, but, on the other hand, Justice is so incensed that he can scarcely speak.

What he would have said will never be known, because Finance, who has been dozing peacefully, falls off his chair, or rather it gives way under him, and he has to be helped up and dusted.

The Prime Minister is sorry; he now remembers that that chair has a broken leg. Finance, who is slowly recovering from the shock, looks as if he would like, in street parlance, to give him something to be sorry for. However, a bell is rung, and a miserable

66

office-keeper and a secretary are heartily abused, which relieves every one's feelings. " It is very dangerous for a chair to break under one," remarks Public Instruction. " It happened to me last year."

Justice agrees, and informs us that his uncle fell off his chair, and was never right in his head afterwards.

"With me," says Public Instruction, " it was different. I hurt my back."

The Prime Minister and their other Excellencies having given their views on this interesting subject and shaken their heads over the dangers which surround us even in chairs, the Prime Minister asks the Minister of Justice what he thinks of the offer of the Finance. Justice haughtily says that, all things considered, he will withdraw his proposal. He could not ask Ahmed Bey even to consider such a rent. There is an awkward pause, which is at last broken by the Minister of Public Works, who has remained since the accident, with his huge eyes fixed on the ceiling, looking like a reflective cod-fish, saying that, in spite of the remarks which he is sorry to say have been made at this meeting, for him only one course is possible and wise. " We must build," he says.

" By contract," interposes Public Instruction. " I know an excellent contractor, a really charming fellow who——"

" No," sternly resumes Public Works. " We must build ourselves a house suitable for the occupation of the Ministers of Egypt, something really worthy of us, like ' Whitall ' or ' Down Street,' only smaller, naturally smaller." The last sentence is addressed to me, I think as a bait, but owing to a choking sensation I have some difficulty in looking as sympathetic as I could wish.

" But that will be more expensive than any villa," remarks Justice, " and besides, it would be unsuitable. I am not in favour of erecting copies of foreign buildings "—his Excellency has strong Nationalist leanings—" when we have a glorious architecture of our own."

" There is no reason," continues the impassible Public Works, " if it is desired, that we should not modify the style to make it more in accordance with Arabic Art."

" But why Arabic Art? " suggests Public Instruction, who wishes to give us the benefit of knowledge acquired on a recent trip up the Nile, in company with a German professor and a Baedeker. " Is not the art of the Ancient Egyptians even grander? "

Foreign Affairs interposes: " But it is impossible: I have seen these temples and monuments often, and none would be at all suitable for Ministries."

" I beg your pardon," replies Public Instruction, " Professor Fliegener showed me the King's House at Karnac, where it is probable that the councils were held. Of course nothing remains, and it is used as a kitchen garden, but one could see where it had been, and it was very interesting."

" Besides, who could build them? " continues Foreign Affairs. " Frankly "—to the Public Works —" can your Department build big public offices? Have they the experience? "

" Build public offices! " says Public Works with cold indignation. " We can build anything. We built a railway station, the Cairo Station, which is very large and very remarkable."

At this point Finance, who has been looking uneasy, mentions that he is sure he heard one of the chairs crack, he is not sure which. This produces general alarm, and every one gets up and examines his chair, sitting down again gingerly, and bumping up and down cautiously to test them. It is an impressive sight to see their Excellencies slowly bobbing up and down, with faces of solemn anxiety.

"You should have stronger chairs," remarks Public Works sternly to the Prime Minister, who smiles agreeably and says: " If the Finance would only refurnish this office I myself should be delighted, but——" with a smile at me.

Now this is getting dangerous; in a minute they will all be asking for office furniture, for which they have an insatiable desire, so I turn on Public Works and point out that his scheme, though in accordance with the high traditions of his Department, and worthy of his Excellency's reputation as a statesman, is, I fear, of too large and costly a nature to be considered for the present, though it might be brought forward again at a later date.

I then turn to Public Instruction and ask him if he has any suggestion.

His Excellency has. If his proposal to employ a really good contractor to build us a house, no matter if it is the man he knows personally, though he can personally vouch for his work, or not, is negatived, he suggests that we should employ some discreet person to get a list of the houses for sale in Ramleh and the vicinity, without saying for whom the information is required. He suggests that a very suitable broker would be Murad Effendi Fauzi of his Ministry, a most discreet person, and one who is thoroughly versed in business.

This proposal is really badly received. We may as a body civilly ignore that Foreign Affairs wishes to live free at the hotel, that Justice wants to recover his gambling debts, that Public Works would like the commissions he might receive on the buildings, but Murad Fauzi has married the daughter of Public Instruction, and is his agent at Ramleh, where his Excellency has indulged in a large building speculation by running up half a dozen enormous villas (built apparently from plans executed for pavilions in some exhibition, and very properly rejected by the Managing Committee). No, it is too bad. We feel that this proposal is inartistic and unworthy of our traditions. Public Instruction, however, unmindful of the gathering storm, continues to expatiate on the excellence of his scheme.

The Prime Minister rises to the occasion. "I fear," says he, "that, excellent as this plan is in many ways, it cannot be carried out."

"Why?" asks Public Instruction, in a disappointed tone; "it is an excellent plan. Now if I——"

"Because we," continues the President, with emphasis, "several of us, own villas in Ramleh, and a subordinate employé might, without knowing the extent of such a mistake, recommend that one of *our* houses should be bought by the Government, which would place us in an awkward position. The newspapers would say all sorts of things which, though untrue, would be very mortifying, and perhaps prejudice the Ministry in the eyes of the nation. We," says the Prime Minister, "must be above suspicion, even absurd suspicion."

We all nod a grave approval, rejoicing inwardly that in many respects we are above suspicion, or at all events, the effects thereof.

"*Tiens*, do you think," says Public Instruction in an astonished tone, "they would dare?"

"In this age," says the Prime Minister, "there is no respect for anything."

"Of course," says Public Instruction, "that, without question, finishes the matter; sooner than the breath of suspicion should touch us we would meet in a tent."

"That would be certainly economical," says Finance, whom a fancied creak from his chair has again aroused to a state of semi-consciousness, "but not comfortable. I lived in a tent once; it made me ill."

"I do not mean," Public Instruction begins to explain, when Foreign Affairs, who is looking at his watch, exclaims, "*Sapristi*, it is nearly one o'clock. I, for one, must go, my dear President, if you will excuse me—I have much to do."

"And I."—"And I," chime in the others, as they roll to their feet. Indeed their Excellencies' midday meal is no light matter.

Public Works remains alone unmoved. "Then what have we decided?"

There is a pause, and I suggest that now that we have discussed the matter in all its bearings, and I have had the honour and pleasure of hearing their

Excellencies' very lucid views on the subject, I think we should think matters carefully over, and that then I would venture to make some definite proposition which I trust would be acceptable to them.

" *Très bien, très bien.* Yes, yes, that is it," and, after taking a cordial leave of the Prime Minister, their Excellencies roll off to their waiting lunches and I return to my office.

CHAPTER V   OFFICE—PART III, AND LUNCH

WHEN I arrive back at my office I find my outer office crowded with a growling mob of officials, waiting to see me. Before I can attend to them however, there are between twenty and thirty letters to sign. You have to read through those prepared by Egyptian subordinates with some care, as, apart from their playful habit of inserting matter to suit their own ends, they are apt, through their limited knowledge of foreign languages, to make you say things which give an impression to your correspondent that you have become insane. For example, here is a letter about removing a wreck from the entrance to Alexandria Harbour, in which I am made to say to the Director-General of Ports and Lights that we approve of his employing dynamite " to puff up the bones of the dead ship," and another to the Controller of Government Lands in which I solemnly enjoin him to prevent trespassers from entering on a certain piece of Government land, " whensoever, howsoever, and whatsoever it is," which might well confuse him.

Having disposed of these, I begin to interview the waiting officials in turn. This is the hardest bit of the day's work. It consists in giving decisions or rulings on points submitted to you, and giving them, if possible, on the spot, as a delay is often very inconvenient to all concerned. As the rulings are, within limits, practically absolute, a faulty decision may give rise to a lot of trouble. One has to combine rapid decision with careful work, and to turn one's mind frequently on to a new subject, which is very tiring.

The native officials are far too fond of referring questions to superior authority, partly because they are timid, and partly because they have no sense of proportionate importance. This is due to the undeveloped state of their intelligence, and to the tradition of bad government which makes them live, like all whose tenure of position or livelihood is precarious, in the present. The immediate effect, not the ultimate result, is what they care about.

Their anxiety, too, to be on the winning or popular side is almost pathetic. I recently asked a high official of the Accounts Department for some figures connected with a certain subject. He immediately asked me what I wanted to prove: I told him, and the figures he produced were absolutely convincing and quite fallacious.

They also waste one's time by their love of high-sounding sentiments and " seven-footed " words, with which they fill their written work. These have no real meaning, but they look and sound pretty. If a widow of an official asks for a pension, they write pages on the virtues of charity and mercy, and

73

probably end up their report by suggesting a neat way of swindling the poor woman.

Of the officials whom I see this morning, only three are of any interest. The first, Ishak Effendi Benoiel of the Pensions Department, looks like the Jew one sees on the farcical stage. He begins in a snuffling whine. " A sad case, a very sad case, M. le Sous-Secrétaire. The widow of M. Emile Dupuis, an engineer of great merit, asks for the gratuity of three hundred pounds which she would have obtained if M. Dupuis had fulfilled certain formalities before he died. As he did not do so she has no right to a penny, but——"

Here he stops for an indication of my views, and, on my murmuring that it is a sad case, continues: " The Government is ever just and merciful, especially to the weak and defenceless."

I say more sternly that, after all, the law is the law.

" Precisely," he continues; " she has no right to a penny, and ought not to have applied."

Appearing to relent, I remark that, as she is destitute, a small sum might be granted her as a favour.

" What I should have expected," murmurs Ishak, " from your well-known generosity."

" A *small* sum," I repeat, with the accent on the " small."

" Ten pounds would be ample," says Ishak, in a convinced tone.

I look pained and say, " A small sum such as two hundred pounds or more."

" From the purely accounting point of view," says

74

Benoiel, " no doubt ten pounds would be sufficient, but from the more statesmanlike attitude taken up by your Excellency, an attitude that was only to be expected, two hundred to, say, two hundred and fifty pounds would be a very proper sum."

" Very well," I say, " as we have gone so far, I think we might as well give her what she asks— three hundred."

" After all, M. le Sous-Secrétaire is undoubtedly right. Three hundred pounds, though generous, is not too much. Why split hairs in dealing with the widow of so distinguished a man as my poor friend Dupuis? "

And so it is decided. It was, no doubt, a waste of time making Ishak turn round and round, but I cannot help doing it. He waltzes so gracefully.

The next of the three, Ahmed Effendi Murad, belongs to the Treasury, and is a shabbily over-dressed little man, with a superior smile and a particularly noxious brand of scent.

" I came," he says, " to offer my explanations with regard to the unfortunate but necessary delay in payment of the ten thousand one hundred and six pounds due to Messrs. Giuliano and Strozzi, the contractors."

I reply coldly that I shall be glad to hear them as, so far, the delay has appeared to me not only inexplicable, but even discreditable to the Government.

He turns an even more repulsive green than the colour of his tie, but is obviously more hurt than terrified, and is convinced that my remarks are unjust. I continue by pointing out that the bill for

75

the first part of the work undertaken by the contractors was sent in on the 31st of March, and was due then. The payment, I regretted to see, took place in September.

The result of this delay in payment was that the work was also delayed, as the contractors pleaded inability to continue the contract until payment was made.

" I feel confident," says Ahmed, who does not look it, " that when your Excellency has heard my explanations you will be satisfied.

" In the first place, the sum claimed appeared to be two pounds in excess of the amount allowed for the purpose, so we were forced to return the papers with a remark to this effect. We subsequently consulted the Public Works Ministry, and found out that, through a most regrettable mistake on the part of that Department, we were misinformed, and that the contractors were right. We immediately informed the firm by a letter, dated the 8th of June, and invited them to make a new demand for payment, which they did on June the 25th.

" After the necessary formalities before payment had been nearly completed, it was noticed that the new demand had been signed by only one partner of the firm, M. Strozzi, and he had not signed in the name of the firm. We were therefore compelled to write to him to point out that he had committed an irregularity, and to request him to rectify the error. By some mischance this letter was sent to Europe, and we did not receive his answer till August.

" Unfortunately, most unfortunately, the answer was not dated, and this omission was not discovered until the cheque had actually been signed and was ready for despatch. In view, however, of the necessity for the most absolute regularity in matters of business, we suspended payment until we had again communicated with the firm.

" In consequence of these irregularities on the part of the contractors, and the regrettable error on the part of the Public Works with reference to the two pounds, the cheque was not actually transmitted until the 30th of September. But I think that your Excellency will agree that in no respect was the Treasury in fault."

And this is his triumphant justification. The real difficulty in these cases is to keep one's temper. Putting a severe restraint on myself, I ask him if he is aware that the result of all this is that the work has been delayed and that the Government directly and indirectly has lost probably some thousands of pounds. Has it not occurred to his highly-trained intellect that we might have paid the contractors, in the month of May, ten thousand one hundred and four pounds, holding back the payment of the two pounds until we were satisfied that they were also due to the contractors?

No, he must admit, it had not. His business is to adhere to the regulations, and this he submits he has done, and he is very sorry, etc.

I realise it is no use trying to get this type of man to see the relative importance of these matters.

The rest of the interview is unpleasant.

The third official of the three I have selected is illustrative of another class altogether.

He is Morcos Bey Tadros of the Lands Department. He is nearly blind, filthily dirty, and appears to be between three and four hundred years old.

He has come, he informs me with many uncouth gestures of salutation, by the Controller's request, to explain to me the case of the land required for the site of the new hospital. The matter, which I happen to know about, is in reality simple enough, as far as we are concerned.

Three quarters of the new site belong to us already, but the fourth is in the actual possession of four different people, and claimed by a fifth, a princess, who declares (though I think it is doubtful) that it was given her by the Government in the days of the Khedive Ismail, who apparently stole it from some one else.

The obvious and only way out of the difficulty is to appropriate the land, pay the full value into Court, and let the claimants fight for it.

But Morcos Bey won't admit any such simple solution. He carefully and fully relates the histories of the four present possessors and their families, and the exact way in which each of the four *says* he obtained possession of his land, and the method by which he actually accomplished this; the various negotiations and lawsuits which have taken place between the princess and all four possessors collectively and individually; how the princess alleges she obtained her land, and by what arts this was really effected; if, as she maintains, the land does belong to her, what claims her three husbands deceased had during their brief unhappy reigns, and how far those claims have descended to their children.

He then goes into the way in which the land

originally fell into the hands of the Government; whether Ismail stole it in whole or part, and whether he gave any compensation for its seizure. He gives a short disquisition on the usual methods by which that potentate acquired land, and he is starting on an account of the early life of the man from whom Ismail stole the property when I stop him. He is obviously disappointed, as he has only touched the fringe of his subject, so to speak, and he is almost openly disgusted when I tell him what action I am going to take.

What *he* would like to do would be to begin a dozen or so lawsuits, and, after ten years' strenuous litigation, obtain the land for double what it will cost us now; by which time we should have forgotten what we wanted it for. His knowledge is immense, his cunning and resources are of the finest quality, but he only cares for a case while it is in a tangle, and his grimy old fingers are following up the threads to find the ends.

For a man of unlimited leisure who liked playing twelve games of chess at once, and who hoped to live to be a thousand years old, he would be an ideal land agent. For us his chief merit is that we can make use of the mass of knowledge concerning all the land swindles in Egypt for the past forty years which he carries in his frowsy, ill-kempt old head.

He gropes his way out to return to his office and begin on some other labyrinthine question.

The interviews go on, and the last official waiting to see me has just fled from my just wrath, which has been drawn down on him by his insertion of a

79

paragraph in a letter which might form a precedent for deciding the amount of pension due to his aunt's second cousin's husband in a more favourable way than is otherwise likely, when I remember that I promised to lunch with Dorder.

Now I always object on principle to going out to lunch. It always results in an unseemly scuffle at the end of the morning to get things finished up, and causes general discomfort; however, I promised Dorder to go to his lunch, which, he informed me in his own nervous English, is going to be a " corker," whatever a corker may be. It is curious that, though one sternly refuses to accept the lunches one would like to go to, one cannot decline to help a friend who, by his own folly, has succeeded in collecting a number of hopelessly uncongenial human beings under his roof.

Anyhow it is the custom, and he who follows not custom in the East is a fool; so I tear downstairs, upsetting a valued public servant at each turn of the stairs, murmuring apologies in any language I remember at the second, and jump into the nearest cab, which apparently had been retained for a portly notable, who is waddling thitherward from the door of the Ministry of Interior, giving vent to shrill cries of anger and distress at this high-handed act. I pretend to think these are only greetings; and I courteously acknowledge them whilst the driver starts his horses off at a gallop. When I last see the notable, who has at length recognised me, and who is the proud possessor of a land claim against the Government of a particularly nebulous kind, he has changed his peacock-like screams of rage for a torrent of salutations backed by an obsequious smile.

After imperilling the lives and limbs of various liege subjects of Effendina, as well as those of representatives of most of the foreign Powers, we arrive at Dorder's exactly twenty minutes late. Luckily Dorder is not one of the Anglo-Indian or stiff variety of officials, or this unpunctuality would rankle for months.

I drop some piastres into the very filthy hand of the driver, and bolt up the steps into the hall. They have not gone in, as I hear them talking in the drawing-room.

The Berberine servant announces me with severe simplicity as "Sisely," and then adds my office in Arabic. I am sure those who have heard are convinced that my surname is "Malia" (Finance), which is the last word he pronounced.

I was called by this name for the whole of the lunch by an American lady, and I never had the courage to tell her she was wrong.

It certainly looks a "corker," this lunch. I am hurriedly introduced, and we go in. There are twelve of us, including Dorder and myself. Let us see who's here. First, three Americans—Papa, an extinct business volcano; Mama, well preserved, loud, awful; daughter, very pretty, less loud, less awful. From the quality of drawl and the amount of nose in it, I think they come from the North.

Next item, middle-aged gentleman and lady, English, with oldish daughter. I fear the father and daughter take a deep interest in Egypt. I smell theories and statistics.

81

Item, Mollington of the Agency, " roped in " like myself, but next the pretty American, and prepared to make the best of it. Item, Austrian Dip., nice looking, well dressed, and a friend of mine. Item, Mr. and Mrs. Cyril Cruncher of the P. W. D. Cruncher always looks as if he had just escaped from being steamed to death in a laundry, by crawling out through the mangle. Anglo-Indian, full of fever, pains, and etiquette, but a nice fellow and an A1 man at his job. Mrs. Cruncher is, to employ Dorder's language again, " a holy terror." I shall catch it from her for being late. I really think Dorder might have found some one else to meet the Crunchers at lunch; however, I am in for it now.

I find I am between the English lady and Mrs. Cruncher. The Austrian Baron, whose name is Sodisky, is on the other side of Mrs. Cruncher, and the English lady, Mrs. Stanley Merton, has Mollington next her. I see the unhappy Cruncher in the clutches of the American lady, but he is always resigned and, I know, looks upon her as a nervous trouble contracted from living in Egypt.

I hastily turn to Mrs. Merton, leaving the Baron to deal with Mrs. Cruncher. Mrs. Merton begins the conversation by plaintively bewailing that cruel fate, acting through the theoretical husband and daughter, has driven her from her happy home to wander in insanitary places.

"I cannot say, Lord Edward, that I really enjoy travelling perhaps as much as I ought to do. I was never accustomed to travel when I was young, and I am afraid I prefer my home; but my husband and Sophia are so interested in Egypt, that they determined to see it, and, as I could not well stay at home alone, I came too. I am sure it is all very interesting, but, for my part, I think it a pity to leave England in the winter, when I have so many things to see to in the parish. I never really studied Egyptian history, or it might have been more interesting for me Of course one knows a small portion of it from the Bible, though that, I am sorry to say, my husband maintains is of doubtful historical accuracy. How they can possibly tell if this be so or not, I cannot imagine. After all, I hold what may be called nowadays old-fashioned views, and I would much sooner trust the Prophet Moses than a German professor of whom I have never heard, and who is very probably a spy like the rest of his nation. I must also admit that I find hotel life very trying. I am sure that one meets all sorts of people one had much better not meet, and the cooking is so unwholesome and so greasy. After all, our health is most important, whatever they may say, and, though I am sure you may think me very unenterprising, I prefer to be well and happy in my own home to seeing a Sphinx or a Pyramid, and being in bed for a month afterwards—in dreadful pain too very likely." (And so on.)

I feel immensely relieved. She is just the sort of old lady I love, and I think if I can only get her on her own home life it will be quite a pleasant lunch; but I am reckoning without Mrs. Cruncher.

I have just succeeded in finding out that Mrs. Merton comes from Devonshire, and knows a lot of people I either know or have heard of, is an ardent Imperialist after my own heart, and has a good deal to say on all rural topics, when Mrs. Cruncher, who is obviously not getting on with the Baron, opens on my right flank.

"We have not seen much of you this year, Lord Edward. I suppose you are very busy in the Finance —too busy to remember about calling."

I hastily begin to excuse myself, which is just what the old cat is waiting for.

"Ah, I thought you did not leave those cards yourself. I said to Cyril I was sure Mrs. Delaney left them with hers. It is curious how manners have changed. It used to be thought quite the rudest thing one could do."

I try to explain again in a hopeless way, making matters considerably worse.

"Oh, I am sure you meant no rudeness, Lord Edward, but people seem so much more busy than they used to be. Lord Cromer and Sir William Garstin always found time to pay a personal call."

Old liar! I don't believe either ever did more than send a card by an under sub-assistant private secretary, but I cannot say so.

"I suppose, too, it is considered right for a married woman—a young married woman—to leave gentlemen's cards for them. In my day it would have been considered fast, to say the least of it."

Now, hang it all, I shall lose my temper in a moment and be rude, but am saved from this further humiliation by the Baron, who, smiling agreeably, comes to my rescue.

"In my country we leave cards only on old ladies, so there you would be even more unfortunate."

He is a fine liar and a genial one. He races off

before Mrs. Cruncher recovers from the compliment, which must have been the first she has heard for fifteen years at least, and pours into her ears, in very daring and remarkable English, a complete account (imaginary) of social life and observances in a garrison town in Hungary, from which country he comes, whilst I get back to Devonshire and a twentieth-century edition of *Cranford*, but, alas, with all my nerves on edge.

The feeling passes off, however, and by the time the sweet comes round I am fairly comfortable again. Mollington now starts talking to Mrs. Merton about some mutual friends and connections, and is disputing quite warmly whether Mrs. Merton's niece's husband is his second cousin twice removed or not. Miss Merton is extracting information from Dorder, till one expects her to swell up like a spider sucking a fly. The American harpy is parading her titled friends before Cruncher, who is regarding her with patient dislike. Mr. Merton is explaining to the American girl his views on the American Constitution, which she is receiving as dull impertinence, and is actually yawning in his face; whilst the extinct volcano sits brooding over the extra millions he might have made if he had remained active.

There is a lull in the talking, and the Baron's distinct and metallic voice is clearly heard.

" I said to her, you are English, you must be kind; I am uncovered, and when you have no covering in strange what you call routs?—no?—societies, no—parties? yes, it is very uncomfortable."

I dare not look at Mrs. Cruncher, who, I expect, is looking like a horrified cat.

85

" She was very good," continues the Baron
fearlessly. " She showed me round and introduced
some to me, and I was soon very well," continues
the Baron, undismayed. " You do not know her?
Mrs. Gairrner? "

Hooray! If he has been talking like that I expect
Mother Cruncher has had a poor time. She will
never " spot " he means " protect " when he says,
" cover."

The cigarettes now make their appearance, and
we adjourn to the balcony.

I want to get away, as Mrs. Delaney promised
to play golf with me, on condition that I should be
on the first tee at 3.15 sharp. She probably won't
be there till four, but still it is not worth risking. I
edge towards Dorder to tell him, when Mr. Merton
bears down on me with cold determination, and a
sort of your information-or-your-life look on his face.
Confound it! If only that American girl had not
snubbed him so, he might still be talking to her. I
confide desperately in the Baron, but it is too late.
Mr. Merton has pinned me against a Musharabia
screen, and begins.

" I was hoping to have the opportunity of getting
a few words with you, Lord Edward, and I am sure
you will not mind if I ask you a few questions on a
subject which has been recently brought again to
my notice, and that is the relative positions of the
English and native officials in the Egyptian Government."

I murmur something which is happily drowned in
Mr. Merton's sonorous tones.

" Of course you are as well aware as I am of the

86

deep interest that is taken in this subject by all Englishmen who have devoted any time to the consideration of Egyptian questions. Now, frankly, do you not consider that the number of English high officials employed in Egypt is more than is necessary? "

I begin to ask him what he means by necessary, when he continues:

" I quite understand that it must be far pleasanter for you to work with your fellow-Englishmen, but is it fair on Egypt?

" I have talked recently with " (to, I expect, would be nearer the truth) " several quite intelligent native gentlemen, and listened, I trust impartially, to what they had to say, and I must say they make out a very strong case for themselves. Of course you won't mind my saying that they probably speak more freely and openly to me than they would to a man in an official position, like yourself. It is also my good fortune to be able, usually, to extract the views of Orientals on such subjects, and I think that they really meant what they said.

" They said that the want of a greater proportion of natives among the higher officials of the Government was responsible for the very regrettable anti-English feeling which had shown itself once or twice lately.

" For instance, the superintendence of the gathering of the revenue, they declared, would be far better carried out by people who really understand the mind of the peasant than by foreigners, and they also pointed out how degrading to their self-respect this system of foreign inspection and control is.

" As one of them, Mustapha Bey El Masri, said to me, ' I am a member of their clubs, they play bridge with me, they treat me as a man of honour, but they will not trust me with the public money, which, to a true patriot like myself, is as sacred as the fortune of his father.' "

Precisely so. I should like to see old Suleiman Pasha trusting Mustapha with a crooked sixpence.

If this goes on I shall scream. What a blatant ass the man is! I am almost in despair when the Baron, the blessed Baron, marches up with a genial smile, and says:

" My dear Lord, you told me not to let charming conversation make you not remember the Prince waits at three, and His Highness loves not to attend, you know."

I excuse myself to Merton, who is quite non-plussed, and, nodding to Dorder, slip away before any one else can seize me.

" Hold back," says the Baron, " I come too."

When we get outside, I thank the Baron warmly. He waves my thanks aside and says: " It is nothing. With your fat Radical, a Prince is better, so I say Prince. Those fellows, we have them too in Austria. They are devilish bore. I am very fond of Dorder; I have known him many years, in Paris, in London, in Vienna, but I go no more to his lunches." And so we part.

A FAIR description of a great portion of ones' life in the Army was often said to be hurrying to somewhere to wait for hours for some one else, and I think this is true of life in Cairo as well. One rushes away from lunch, tumbles into one's flannels, gallops down to the Sporting Club, to wait patiently for half an hour till, say, Mrs. Delaney turns up. One only hopes that she will not be later than this, as after that the waiting becomes wearisome, and she will probably blame you for her own unpunctuality.

In the meantime, having secured one's caddy and put one's name down, there is nothing for it but to wait and watch the other players start on their " daily round."

The Golf Links is common ground on which all sets meet and to a moderate extent fraternise. The cavalry captain " tees up " with the Inspector of Interior, and the schoolmaster of the Public Instruction exchanges remarks with the Scots Guards ensign.

We are very particular socially in Cairo. There is the swagger military set; there is the smug military set. There is the Egyptian Army set; there is the smart official set; there is the smug official set. There is the smart professional set; there is the smug professional set, and so on. You may move in two or even several of those sets, but you *belong* to one.

The description of Chatham in *Pickwick* is very

like Cairo in some ways. You are either in the Dockyard or the Garrison, or you are not. There is all the narrowness and provincialism of an English garrison town with the Egyptian and foreign elements intruded. The English, unluckily in some ways, luckily in others, don't assimilate a foreign body. If it is noxious it is got rid of; if harmless, it is included but not assimilated; so that the foreign elements which enter into our daily life change nothing in it. Indeed nothing changes an Englishman's life. Jules Verne's description—in *Hector Servadac*, I think—of the English garrison which is carried off on a comet, and which, when the days and nights are reduced to six hours each, continues to eat three meals a day, and live on as if nothing had happened, is a happy caricature of our nature.

Whilst waiting, one watches with amusement the stand-offish manner of the Inspector of Interior, speaking to the young Public Instruction boy, and one knows that presently one will see the latter treat a junior commercial with the same edifying hauteur.

Ninety per cent. at least of the men out here are good fellows and capable men, but they sometimes conceal these facts with wonderful care. Under the nerve-irritating Egyptian conditions all our natural eccentricities assume abnormal proportions. Our vanity becomes childish; swelled head is as common a disease as freckles, and we are as ready to take offence as an Irish fire-eater of the seventeen hundreds. But these defects are mostly on the surface; inwardly we are aware that Egypt is not always of first- or even second-rate importance, and to be of importance in Egypt is like the rank in the

Army which is described as " local and temporary."
If we are haughty at times, the least touch of misfortune, sickness, or the realities of life removes the
childish assumption at once. If we run each other
down in conversation, we esteem one another
warmly in our hearts. It should be a comfort to a
junior if he ever feels aggrieved by the manners of
those farther up the ladder, which leads to retire-
ment at Cheltenham or Tunbridge Wells on a bare
competence, that in the mind of the aggressor the
junior is superior to every foreigner or native that
has ever existed.

Mrs. Delaporte Stokes, who is preparing at this
moment to put her partner into the first bunker,
talks only to the best official set, if possible about the
Peerage. She naturally passes much of her time
alone.

When young Bloggs of the Public Instruction,
who is a frank and refreshing bounder, got fever at
Assiout in the midsummer, " Mother Delstock," as
we profanely call her, packed up her bag without
a word, and went and nursed him like a mother
till she pulled him through. She even discovered a
peerage connection for Bloggs, to that worthy's huge
amusement, which has made social intercourse on
a limited scale between him and Mrs. Delaporte
Stokes possible.

Mrs. Bollinger, whose propriety is as pure, cold,
and disagreeable as driven snow, and who cuts any
one as " fast " on the slightest provocation, took that
little idiot of a Mrs. Dewar, when she got into a real
mess, into her house, and kept her there under the
ægis of her driven-snow reputation until the storm

had blown over, and Dewar could be induced to believe a benevolent and highly improbable explanation of the whole affair.

Of course, with brilliant exceptions, no doubt the women are to a certain extent second-rate; their conversation is not brilliant, and they are inclined to keep up appearances at the cost of comfort. Their personal appearance is rarely pleasing— climate and anxiety have seen to that; and their clothes, well, all that can usually be said of them is that in the daytime, at all events, they are amply sufficient for the requirements of decency. Their qualities that matter are on a different plane. For genuine kindness, real warmth of heart, noble uncomplaining devotion to their husbands and children, they are as a rule above criticism. Poor things! many of them, military and civil, have never had a home of their own since they married; the climate, which is unpleasant for the man, means sickness and pain to them. They must leave the delicate child they love at home, and too often must watch those they love with them wither because they are too poor to send them away. Their very bread depends on the often frayed and slender thread of their husband's life, and their daily existence is one long struggle to make the two ends meet.

And yet they face it all bravely with a smile, keep Jack or Joe going, hearten him up for the long ladder climb, and are as cheerful and fond of amusement as their sisters anywhere else.

The one great idea of both men and women who live abroad is to get a home in England. When

an official of a certain rank asks you with a somewhat sheepishly beaming face, if you happen to
know this or that district of England, you always
know what has happened.

He informs you that he has bought a cottage and
an acre or two of land. Freehold (it must be freehold), with a good garden for the " Sitt " (wife).
It has cost a good deal, and he does not know
whether he was justified in doing it, but still it's
done now, and the " Sitt " is delighted with it.
Of course it is a remarkably charming part of the
country, and the house itself is, curiously enough,
exactly what he has been looking for for years, etc.
With the men this is amusing, with the women
infinitely pathetic.

No, I admit you're not much to look at, Ladies,
and you don't shine at Home, but I take my hat
off with my deepest bow to you all the same.

And, all things considered, if your conversation
is dull, it is rarely empty. You don't talk clever to
talk clever. You have had far too much experience
of the real pain, trouble, and sorrow of life to play
at it. You have often seen a good deal of the
world with its good and bad. You have lived real
lives, not sham ones, and your views and thoughts
are the result of actual experience, and not made
up in a hothouse by electric light.

At this point in this well-beaten track of my
thoughts I take out my watch. I grieve to say
that Mrs. Delaney, instead of, as one might have
expected, being on the tee to the minute, in order
to get as much of my charming company as possible,
is now thirty-four minutes late, and there is no

sign of her coming. At this moment, pretty Mrs. Fitzpatrick, with the inevitable captain in attendance, appears in the distance. She is a widow, and comes out every winter to stay with a married sister of hers who lives here. She has a peculiar attraction for captains. The present aspirant is Bentley of the 30th Hussars. How she can stand him I cannot think. He is like a heavy dragoon on the stage. I rise and greet her, and she explains, with a certain shade of annoyance, that she has been looking for me everywhere. I apologise for not being there, and she explains that Mrs. Delaney has been raided by Towrows (tourist friends have come to lunch) and cannot come, so she (Mrs. Delaney) asked Mrs. Fitzpatrick to play with me, but she (Mrs. Fitzpatrick) told her that she was playing with Captain Bentley, and so she could not play with me, but then she (Mrs. Fitzpatrick) remembered that she had also promised to play with Captain Browning because Captain Bentley had not reminded her, so she (Mrs. Fitzpatrick) had written a second note to Mrs. Delaney, saying that she (Mrs. Fitzpatrick) would play with me and make up a foursome, but her (Mrs. Fitzpatrick's) servant had gone out, and the boy had been sent with the note, and she is not sure if she (Mrs. Delaney) ever got it, and perhaps she (Mrs. Delaney) has made other arrangements, as she said she was going to ask Miss Hopper to play with me, if she (Mrs. Delaney) could get no one else; and now she (Mrs. Fitzpatrick) rather thinks she herself was engaged to tea with the Arlfords at four at Abbasieh, and to go camel-riding afterwards. What had she

94

better do? and is not it stupid of Captain Bentley and that tiresome Captain Browning?

I agree that their action is intolerable, and say that she'd much better play golf, as perhaps her engagement at Abbasieh is for another day. I am glad it's not more complicated than that; to try to follow Mrs. Fitzpatrick's arrangements would undermine the strongest intellect. She never keeps more than one out of every three engagements she makes, but she is very pretty, and has a happy-go-lucky, sunny nature which pulls her out of all the tangles she weaves round herself. Her general attitude is a sort of amazed contempt for the stupidity of people who are so dull as not to be able to follow the straight and simple course of her life. She is quite charming, but I am not sure Fitzpatrick's death after a month's marriage was not due to his finding out what he was " in for."

At this moment Browning turns up with his best smile on, and it has all to be explained to him again. He is a dull fellow, and after a feeble effort to resent the way he has been treated, sinks into a sort of mazed condition. What obviously beats him is why he is to blame.

I point out politely that we must start if we want to play even nine holes before dark, and Mrs. Fitzpatrick agrees with some warmth, implying that it is very unfair for inconsiderate people to keep a hard, even over-worked woman like her waiting.

She decides, with feminine acuteness, to play with me, so that the other two are treated equally badly, and there can be no grumbling. The decision is received in gloomy silence by the captains, and we start off.

She would play quite a good game if she ever thought of it for two minutes together, but she enjoys it all so much, and looks so nice while she is doing it, that she quite disarms all criticisms even on her interpretation of the rules of golf. I am not sure, on reflection, if it is an interpretation at all. I think it is rather a substitution of her own rules.

A few of the more salient are:

If she moves the ball less than five yards, or misses it altogether, she did not mean to, and it does not count.

If she is not satisfied with a longer shot, she may have it back on the formal—purely formal—consent of the other players being obtained.

If a ball lies badly, the ground should be carefully scraped away till the ball is teed up.

All grass, branches, etc., that are in the way of herself or her dress must be torn away.

Extra strokes in a bunker don't count.

The maximum of strokes she can count at any hole is six; if the opponents are playing well this figure is liable to reduction.

If you have no morals and understand the game it is quite interesting, but it shocks Browning terribly.

To soothe his injured feelings, Mrs. Fitzpatrick makes an appeal to him to coach her as we go round, " as he plays so well "; and he looks better, while Bentley sinks into a more stolid gloom.

I am playing well, and Mrs. Fitzpatrick amuses me hugely. She and I always enjoy everything we do together, so the game progresses very comfortably as far as we are concerned. With the others it's different. They both play badly, and are inclined to " snick " at one another. " If you had only taken the iron to play your second at the last hole we should have been up in three," from Browning. " My dear fellow, how could I when your shot was unluckily sliced into that awful ground? " etc., from Bentley; and so on.

At the fifth hole we have our first serious *contretemps*. Mrs. Fitzpatrick, who is advisedly not satisfied with the way in which she is driving, asks Browning to come and put her right. Browning gives her a short lecture on driving, and ends up by deciding her feet are in the wrong position. " You should turn the left toe out more," he says, moving round behind her, with the intention of showing where exactly it should be. Mrs. Fitzpatrick rightly thinks that she has had advice enough, and wrongly that the lecture is over. Before I can say anything, up goes her club, and the Captain reels back a stricken man. Well, it is lucky it only touched him above the eye, but he will have a fine black pair to-morrow, I expect. He takes it very well, though, of course, it does not exactly cheer him up. Mrs. Fitz is cut to the heart, and apologises so prettily that it would be almost worth getting a black eye for; but the effect wears off in a few minutes, and at the next hole she confides in me that it was very stupid of him to get in the way, and that, although she is sorry she hurt him, he really almost deserved it, as he entirely spoilt her stroke and put her off her game. Browning's woebegone look as he stumps along, dabbing his eyebrow with a handkerchief, also makes her laugh so that she can scarcely conceal it.

At the seventh hole a worse fate befalls another of the party. Here we cross the big ditch, which is six feet deep and half full of water. Browning's stroke does not quite clear the ditch, but sticks on the inside of the further bank about a foot from the top. Bentley does not want to try to play the ball, as he says it is impossible, but Browning maintains that if he puts one foot here and one foot there, and digs his heels well in, he can stand all right and get the ball out. Bentley at last grudgingly consents to try, and with much difficulty gets himself into the paralytic position indicated by his partner. Mrs. Fitz is watching the proceeding with intense interest, because, owing to certain mishaps which have occurred to us, our only chance of winning the hole is that Bentley should fail to get the ball out.

" I hope he won't," she murmurs; " oh, I hope he won't! Perhaps he will fall in," she suggests, with a radiant smile. The next minute the unhappy Bentley, still unwisely following Browning's directions, makes a wild slash at the ball with the niblick, loses his balance, throws his arms up in the air with a gesture of despair, and falls with a mighty splash flat on his back in the middle of the ditch. Mrs. Fitz gives a wild scream of triumph, which is changed into expressions of alarm, and again, when the unhappy Bentley crawls out covered from head to foot with a rich brown mud, into burst after burst of uncontrollable laughter.

Bentley stands, trying to look dignified, while Browning and the caddies make ineffectual attempts to scrape him with bits of wood. No human dignity can withstand, however, a bath of brown mud. Mrs. Fitz, after mastering her mistimed expression of amusement, condoles with Bentley with much skill, but rather spoils it by suggesting that he should run home to avoid a chill instead of driving. I can see the immaculate Captain trotting past the Savoy, with all the smart tourists looking on, in his present condition.

He retires sadly to the club-house to make himself as presentable as he can for his homeward drive.

We try to play the next hole; but as Browning can now only see with difficulty, and will explain how Bentley ought to have played the fatal stroke, which reduces Mrs. Fitz to nearly hysterical laughter, our efforts are not very successful, and we decide to abandon the match, which by the ordinary old-fashioned golf reckoning is divided, though by Mrs. Fitz's method we are five up.

When we reach the club-house Mrs. Fitz suddenly asks Browning if he would mind taking her driver to the professional, and asking him to rebind it and put a new grip on, as he, Browning, understands just what she wants. Directly he is gone she says we must have tea in the back verandah, where he won't find her, because he is so tiresome, and she is so cross with him for wetting poor Captain Bentley through. "It was very tiresome of them both," she says, "to spoil our afternoon in the way they did." I feebly remonstrate on her perfidy, but meekly follow her to tea. Here I look

99

at the clock, and see I must be getting back to
change for my committee. Mrs. Fitz is outraged.
She says she has never heard of such an idea as
asking a lady to tea and then pretending that one
has a committee, which she is sure will get on much
better without me. I am just beginning to argue
this point when she asks me what the time is.

I reply, " Five-thirty."

" Good gracious ! " she says, " I asked a whole
lot of people to tea at five; we must go at once.
Why did you not tell me it was so late? "

We hurry out of the club. Mrs. Fitz casts her
eye round, and then walks straight to a motor
which is standing near.

" Would you like a lift? " she says airily.

˙I thank her, saying it will be very convenient, as
I am so late, and off we go.

" Whose motor is this? " I ask casually, as we
turn out of the gate; " surely it is Browning's."

Mrs. Fitz laughs softly to herself. " Is not it
fun? " she says; " we've left him behind ! "

" Well," I say rather blankly, " of course it has
its humorous side, but what will he say? "

" Oh, nothing much; besides, I can tell him
you wanted to get home quick, and persuaded me
to come."

We pull up at my door as she says this, and
I feel that it is no good remonstrating with any
one of so little moral sense, so I go up to change,
and she drives away gaily to meet her starving
guests.

CONTRARY to my expectations, I find, when
I arrive at the Ministry, that I am the first
member of the committee who has reached the
meeting place. We have a mania in this country
for committees, and we have them of all sorts and
kinds. There are standing committees, special committees, interdepartmental committees, departmental
committees, and so forth. They all waste time, but
are not without their compensations for those whose
sense of humour is properly developed.

The members are usually of different nationalities,
and business is conducted either in the tongue each
one knows best, or in what we call " French." Our
" French " is the most remarkable language, except
perhaps pidgin English, in the world. It should be
spoken with a strong accent of your own to show
your independence, and is a literal, or as near
literal as one can manage, translation into French
of the words of your own language in the order
they usually occur. If you don't know the French
for any word, you can either say it in your own
tongue rather loud (to help the benighted foreigner
to understand), or you can use any French word of
a somewhat similar sound, if not meaning; or again
you can simply gallicise the word itself by giving it
what is here believed to be a French pronunciation,
thus enriching that restricted language with a new
word.

Each sentence becomes, under this system, a most
interesting riddle, and the conduct of a discussion

on highly technical matters a task worthy of the quickest brain.

Our committee this evening is one of the standing variety, and is for the nominal purpose of considering and advising upon the granting of concessions to individuals and companies by our illustrious Government. Our President is Mohammed Pasha Ahmed, Minister of Arts and Crafts.

Placing him at the head of that particular Ministry was one of those subtle strokes of humour for which this Government is justly famous. He is by origin the son of a small landowner, and entered the Government service at eighteen. He climbed laboriously up one of the Government Departments, into which he got in some mysterious way, until he was created a judge.

His reign was brief, though, it is said, very lucrative. He reduced the system of criminal justice in the country to a simple tariff of prepaid fines to himself.

Though this was well known, as nothing whatever could be proved against him, amid the tears of the criminal population, he was promoted to the Director-Generalship of the Department of Charity and Trust Lands. This was a stroke of genius. Elsewhere, even among his fellows, his tendency to reduce all transactions of the Government to equivalent cash payments must have excited the envy of his fellows, and laid him open to carping criticism.

In the Trust Department he was scarcely, if at all, remarkable. This Department, which has a semi-religious position, has been kept clean of all Christian contamination, and is personally managed by the highest in the land. It is thought to be grasping and avaricious to hold the appointment of Director-General for more than a few years.

When the last new Ministry but three was formed, an idea got about that the large landholders must be represented in it. His Excellency, who, as I have hinted, is an excellent man of business, had invested his hardly gained savings in land, and was now full of riches and honours. He was very well looked upon in the highest quarters, having always been careful to leave to them their proverbial share in any little profit that accrued from the administration of the Trust lands.

Unluckily, all the Ministries but that of Arts and Crafts were filled. It was at first sight not an ideal appointment, but it was remembered that often the head of a Department is rather hampered than otherwise by technical knowledge, and he was duly appointed. He certainly came to his duties with an open mind.

Personally, I have a sneaking affection for him, as he has the rough, rather jolly way of the peasant, which contrasts very favourably with the oily, snake-like manner of the town-bred Egyptian, and he has a sense of humour of an elementary kind. His philosophy of life has been to judge all men, irrespective of race or creed, by what service they can be to him in carrying out his life-task of adequately providing for his numerous family and his own old age. This makes him less antagonistic to the Christian dogs than his compatriots usually are.

He confided to me once (for we are rather friends) that undoubtedly religion was a very good thing, but very expensive, and that he personally disapproved of people building mosques at their own expense in an ostentatious manner. These things, he said most wisely, should be done by the subscription of many, so that many may participate in the good work.

He is, in fact, a shrewd, ignorant, jolly ruffian, with a kind heart and no conscience.

Our next member, Morcos Bey Wissa, is a very different person. The dark colour, woolly hair, wooden expression of countenance, and want of personal cleanliness, proclaim him a Copt of the Copts. He bears all the marks and possesses the vices and virtues of a race that has been oppressed for ages. The patient manner, the mixture of servility and dignity of deportment, and the absolute concealment of his personal wishes and feelings, are all characteristic of his people. The Copts are liars because for years it has been dangerous for them to speak the truth; crooked and cunning because by those qualities alone could they get a living; proud in their contempt of the Moslem, servile in view of his power to oppress them, careless of their personal appearance from ages of concealment of their riches by this means.

The third, Du Chalons Bey, comes of a Napoleonic family, and traces his descent from a once-famous colonel of Chasseurs of that date. He still wears the imperial and pointed moustachios of the Second Empire period.

Trim, capable, prolix, amusing, emotional, charming in private life, intolerably formal in business, he was a valuable official once, but has long since ceased to take an interest in anything but his pension and his great work on the French influence on horticulture in Egypt, of which the fifth volume has been in preparation for the last ten years, and which goes through endless vicissitudes, and needs as many exceptional measures and irregular favours as a royal *protégée*.

The fourth is a hard-headed Scot, with all the business capabilities and combativeness of his race; and the fifth is myself.

Our secretary is a little Syrian, whose nerves are unable to stand the strain of dealing personally with high officials. Sitting once a week for an hour with men who might in some way affect his promotion, or give him more or less pension, is very trying for him. He is consequently continually making mistakes, for which he is rated by the Minister or reproved in the best Glaswegian by Macnab.

His Excellency is the last to arrive. Rolling his enormous body through the door, he shakes me by the hand, in what he conceives to be the English manner, and which is, in fact, the kind of handshake which one might give a much-loved brother after ten years' separation.

His Excellency, having complained of the heat and mopped his forehead, sinks into a chair, and we seat ourselves in our appointed places.

The secretary, after dropping all his papers several times, owing to the agitation of his mind, proceeds to deal out to us the *ordre du jour*, which consists of the list of cases submitted for consideration.

This is a formality, as we are all aware what cases will be brought before us at the meeting, but we look at the paper with interest in our various ways.

The Minister looks as it as if it were the menu of a poor dinner. To do his Excellency justice, he never even pretends to have any morbid or unnatural love of work.

Macnab examines it as if he would like to criticise it and argue with any one who did not share his views. Du Chalons peruses it in a strictly official manner, as if he were just going to be rude to the general public; and Morcos Bey, the Copt, fixes his eyes on it with that cold, expressionless, snake-like stare which gives no indication whatever of his thoughts.

There are mercifully only three questions submitted to-day.

The first is the petition of one Galipoli, a Maltese, for permission to construct, at Mansourah, mooring quays with a market attached, and to charge a regular scale of fees for their use. He also asks that no similar permission shall be given to any one else in that town. For these advantages he proposes to pay a certain rent to the Government, as well as thirty per cent. of the net profits derived.

The second is a request that the wording of the terms of a concession of land, for reclamation and sale, granted to an English company ten years ago in Behera Province, may be slightly altered to meet an administrative difficulty which has arisen.

The third is a petition from one Charles Dumourier, a Frenchman, to establish and exploit salt-pans on a portion of the sea-coast, in the province of Gharbieh, with exclusive rights to extract salt from

COMMITTEE

sea-water within that province, the Government to share in the profits of the business.

The Minister, having declared the fare is very inferior, fixes his eye on the secretary, and says, " Let us begin! Come now, be quick! "

The secretary begins in quavering tones to gabble out the explanatory note or *résumé* of the first question.

" Is this," says Macnab in his most deliberate manner, " the first, second, or third question which the secretary is reading out? I have no objection to taking the questions in any order your Excellency may think fit, but I should like to know in what order we are going to take them. It is quite impossible to tell what the secretary is reading when he speaks so fast and so indistinctly."

" Quite so," says the Minister. " How often, Khalil Effendi, have I told you to read slowly and distinctly, so that we may be all aware what we are doing. *Sapristi!* You pay no attention."

The unhappy secretary, who looks as if he were in a vapour bath, begins to read the document over again in funereal tones at the rate of one word a second.

" I venture to remark," says Du Chalons, " that if we proceed at this rate, we shall not finish our task before nine in the evening. If your Excellency wishes it to be so, I have nothing to say, but I draw your attention to the point."

" *Sapristi!* " says the Minister. " Why cannot you read properly at a decent pace, neither too fast nor too slow? "

The wretched secretary, now having completely

lost his head and his place, remains silent, where-upon the Minister orders him to bring the paper to him, which he does with his knees knocking together.

" Read like this," says the Minister, with paternal dignity. "'One shirt and two pairs of socks, one piastre.' What is this? This is not the *ordre du jour*. Are you by chance mocking us?"

The miserable secretary, in a shaking voice, points out that it is the back of the paper which his Excellency is looking at, on which he had written down a private memorandum—in fact, a portion of his washing bill. He is very sorry, he did it without thinking. He hopes his Excellency——

" A most improper proceeding," says his Excellency. " Washing lists are kept in a washing book, not on the back of the *ordre du jour* of a committee of high officials of the Egyptian Government, thus causing me, a Minister, to read out ridiculous nonsense about shirts and socks before the whole committee."

" The secretary will find it better to keep things in their proper places, I am thinking," says Macnab.

" The affairs of official life should never be mixed up with those we treat of in our private capacity," announces Du Chalons sententiously. This, from all one hears about his private life, is perhaps as well.

The Copt regards me with his expressionless eyes. I understand, and say to the Minister that we all make mistakes at times, and that I venture to intercede. . . .

His Excellency, who is really the soul of selfish

good nature, says, " Well, well, my dear Lord, let us now proceed; and perhaps you "—turning to Du Chalons—" will not mind reading out the explanatory notes, as they are written in French."

Du Chalons bows stiffly, and, taking the paper, reads it as if he were giving us French dictation. When he has finished the note or *résumé* of the first case, he stops and looks at the Minister, and again bows.

The Minister smiles genially at the members generally, and asks us what we think of it. It seems fairly simple; we want a market, and here is a man who will build one. He will himself express no opinion, but would like to hear what we think.

Macnab would like, before expressing any opinion, to ask a few questions, and then off he starts. He wants to know, in the first place, what a concession is, and if this falls in with the definition accepted. Secondly, what is meant by a market, whether the question of a market and a mooring quay are indissolubly connected or not, and so on, point by point.

When he has at length terminated his remarks, which have lulled the Minister into a state of abstraction, Du Chalons says that he, for his part, considers the question a dangerous one, very dangerous, and one that demands long and careful reflection.

The Copt says he is not favourably inclined to the request.

" But why? " says his Excellency.

The Copt says he does not think it a good plan.

Macnab again starts off, and we enjoy another

lecture of ten minutes' duration on the merits and demerits of the proposal.

The Minister now looks at me, and I ask the Copt if he knows the would-be concessionaire.

It is a lucky shot. The Copt says he has heard of him.

And what has he heard of him?

That he has had trouble and misfortune.

" But that is no reason for rejecting his plea," says the Minister. " We are all liable to misfortune."

The Copt agrees with humility.

" Perhaps these misfortunes were due to his own actions," I suggest. " What was their nature? "

" He had trouble with the law-courts." Then, turning suddenly on the secretary, he says, " Khalil Effendi knows about it better than I, I think."

" Well, what do you know? " says the Minister; " what were the troubles of this poor man? "

" He had five years' imprisonment for embezzlement and fraud, I have been told," stammers out the secretary.

" And why did you not tell us so before, *imbécile?* " thunders the Minister.

" I did not know! I did not think! I was not sure! " bleats the secretary.

I propose the question be adjourned to the next meeting, and that further inquiries be made about the character of the applicant, and especially if he has been convicted of a criminal offence.

" It was 1905—March 1905," murmurs the Copt quietly.

We pass on to the next question, in spite of an

obvious tendency on the part of Macnab to argue
the question as to whether we should be influenced
by the testimony of the secretary, who is not properly
a member of the committee.

I open the next question after it has been duly
read out by Du Chalons, and explain that this is in
reality a formal matter.

The concessionaires wish to alter the wording of
Clause 9. The Finance and Public Works have no
objection to the alteration, which does not pre-
judicially affect the interests of the Government.

The Minister says, with an obvious air of relief,
" Good, then we can agree to that."

But if he hopes that we are to get through it like
that, he is mistaken.

Macnab discusses the exact meaning of the
alteration, which, he declares, is highly technical.

As the concession is in English, all this has to be
explained to the Minister and Du Chalons in Arabic
and French, and his Excellency gets thoroughly confused over the words " herein and hereafter," which
he repeats to himself, murmuring " Now, what does
that mean? " He is also firmly convinced that
Macnab is a bitter opponent of the alteration.

Du Chalons first of all repeats his invariable
formula, that he considers the question a dangerous
one, and one that requires full consideration, and
then launches out into an indictment of all the
British land companies.

To this Macnab takes exception, and there seems
no prospect of finishing the question for an hour or
two.

Finally, his Excellency suggests that the Copt

should give his views. Morcos Bey replies humbly that he is not clear who is favourable and who is unfavourable to the project.

"Then," says his Excellency, "you have not understood. Lord Cecil Pasha is favourable, and these gentlemen"—indicating them with a wave of his pen—"are against it."

"Pardon me, your Excellency," says Macnab, "I never said that. In fact, I think the alteration is not only desirable, but absolutely necessary."

"*Tiens!*" says his Excellency, and, "M. Du Chalons, what is your view, then?"

"I will remind your Excellency that though I have warned the committee, as it was my duty to do, that the question is a dangerous one, I have never expressed an unfavourable opinion on the proposal, which I approve, with the reserve which I have made," is the reply.

"Then," says the Minister, "we are all agreed, eh, Morcos Bey?"

That gentleman gives his usual dignified and respectful inclination of his head, and we proceed to the third, and happily the last, question.

"I should never have understood that part about 'herein and hereafter,'" murmurs the Minister to me, as Du Chalons clears his voice with an official "ahem!" as a preliminary to giving us our third dictation.

He takes this question in hand, after the usual ministerial preliminaries, and at great length expatiates on the merits of the scheme.

Macnab attacks it on the ground that all monopolies are bad, and I side with him.

His Excellency agrees with us in turn, to show his impartiality, and gives vent to the following statements. That salt is a necessary of life. That the sea is salt. That a monopoly grants certain advantages to the holder, of which the most conspicuous is an absence of competition. That salt is sometimes dearer and sometimes cheaper, it is also different in quality, etc.

Du Chalons perorates about French enterprise, the French connection with Egypt, Napoleon, and so on.

Macnab delights us with the opinions of political economists on monopolies, the price of salt, and its commercial value.

Matters are getting a little too warm to be pleasant, especially since Du Chalons spoke slightingly of something or some one Scottish.

My eye falls on the secretary, and I see he is in a state of fear and perturbation bordering on insanity. He is trying to screw up his courage to do something which he knows will bring down the wrath of the united committee on his devoted head.

In a temporary lull, I address Morcos Bey and ask him kindly to look at the papers of the case, which are lying on the table between him and Du Chalons, as I fancy there is some addition or rider to the note which he, Du Chalons, read out to us. This produces a calm, during which the secretary's teeth chatter as Morcos Bey very deliberately examines the documents.

"Your Excellency is perfectly right," he announces, in his passionless voice. "The law officers of the State, to whom the question was submitted, are of opinion that the demand is inadmissible, as the ground in question lies within the concession area of the Salt Company of Egypt, under their lease of twenty years since."

We all look particularly foolish. We are inclined to blame Du Chalons, until the Minister, who has been glaring at the idiotic remnant of what was once a man who called himself our secretary, demands, in tones suggesting a tidal wave and an earthquake, why he did not tell us of this. The poor man is long past any explanation; he can only gibber about his poverty and the size of his family. If he could speak it would make matters worse, because he would have to admit he did not dare interrupt either Du Chalons or Macnab.

" First," shouts the Minister, " you make me read out about your miserable socks. You then let us give markets to thieves, and you finally let us discuss for a very long time a concession which does not exist. You make me late for important matters of which such as you know nothing. Go away! Go!"

The secretary gathers up his papers and flies out of the room, dropping fragments of correspondence as he goes.

We then roundly abuse him till his Excellency grows calmer, and says he is not as bad as he used to be, and the poor fellow has a large family. This means that it is time to cease hostilities, and after a little desultory conversation we break up.

CHAPTER VIII   OFFICE, CLUB, AND DINNER

WHEN I regain my office I set to work to clear up the odds and ends of business which were left unfinished this morning, rough out the memorandum, and write a short report on the pension case for the Agency. I can work twice as fast in the evening, when there is no one to interrupt me, and I get through what I want to do pretty quickly, and find I have still time to write a letter home.

The main difficulty in writing to one's family in England is the choice of subjects.

If you write about what is happening at home or in Europe, the matter has probably been forgotten before your letter reaches home. If you write about that which is going on here, they have either already seen it in the telegrams or newspapers, or they don't understand it. Politics in Egypt are such a web of personal intrigue and counter-intrigue that unless you are intimately acquainted with the subject they are impossible to follow.

There are numberless parties and groups all working more or less against each other, and forming alliances or quarrelling every second day.

To have any clear comprehension of what is going on, you must know the present value of each individual. Men become important and cease to exist politically in the space of a few weeks. The changes of opinion and intention are bewildering. The Khedive's attitude on the first of the month gives you no clue to what his attitude will be on the fifteenth. Politics with scanty principles and

115

wherein the chief mainspring of action is direct personal advantage, are impossible to follow unless you are in constant touch with all their developments.

The result is that one's letters bear strong and rather painful resemblance to those one wrote many years ago, which contained the information that you were well, that you hoped that your correspondent was well, that you had chops for dinner to-day, but that yesterday you had beef, and so on.

However, it cannot be helped, so I do my best and finish my letter.

Now there is just time before I must dress to get to the club, find Bartley, and ask him to share a taxi out to Heliopolis to-morrow night, as I believe he is going to dine with the Lacrosses there, to whose feast I am also bidden.

I say good-night to Mr. Tomkins, who is quite affable, possibly at the prospect of getting rid of me, and drive off to the club.

I have said that our club is a " pot-house." I must add that it is also a " bar." It is the custom that before dinner every one should come to the club and have a drink and talk with his friends. I really don't know which is the worse habit of the two. The first injures your nerves and stomach, but the second the reputation and well-being of your friends.

Of course, I don't mean that they only talk scandal at the club. They discuss games, make future arrangements and plans, argue about politics to a certain extent, and do not a little useful business at times. I admit that the custom of meeting at this hour has its uses, but I still believe that more harm is done in the hall of the Turf Club than in all the other rooms occupied by Englishmen in Cairo.

When I arrive the hall is crowded, and finding Bartley is no easy matter. Apart from the ordinary difficulty of pushing through a crowd, I have to stop and exchange a word of politeness at every second step, and as often refuse the inevitable offer of a drink.

It is an extraordinary thing that directly one gets abroad, this habit of standing one drinks at clubs becomes prevalent. At home you would never think of going into your club and offering every one you met a drink. I should like to do it once, just to see the expression on the head waiter's face.

If one could saunter into the Athenæum and say, "Now then, Bishop, give it a name"; "Archdeacon, what's your fancy?" "Professor, have a damp?" and get out alive, it would be worth doing.

Anyhow, here it is the custom, and though one is not forced to drink, one must refuse civilly, which takes time. I am also delayed by avoiding people who I know want to talk business, which I have not now time to discuss.

At last I see Bartley in a group of five or six who are discussing cocktails and the latest scandal, and elbowing my way towards him, reach him just as he is saying, "Well, all I can tell you is that that is the story as it reached me. I never liked the man myself." So I know another good reputation has gone under. I wonder what the story is. It is quite marvellous what stories can be started and *believed* in Cairo.

I remember we all treated an old American

gentleman with great respect for the whole of one winter because we had been told, and we believed, that he had burnt his whole family, whom he disliked, in his country house in America. It turned out afterwards that he had only saved his mother-in-law from being drowned in a canal in Holland, and we treated him thenceforth with indulgent contempt.

Cairo is a small place where there is not much to talk about outside one's business, and there is a considerable mixture of ethical standards, which renders every scandalous story possible, if not probable, so it is perhaps not to be wondered at that the most unfounded rumours obtain credence.

I arrange matters with Bartley; and as I see by the clock that I have no time to spare, fight my way to the door, jump into a cab, and tell the coachman to drive to my house.

When I arrive there and reach my rooms, I find that, *of course*, Suleiman has not got my evening clothes ready, and as he invariably loses his head when he is hurried, my dressing may be fairly described as a concatenation of disasters. First the underclothing, which he takes out of the wrong drawer, has so many holes in it that one wonders how any human being could ever hope to get into it without a chart and a compass. The socks he provides are odd ones. There is a prevailing absence of buttons everywhere. My shirt is frayed to the extent of apparently needing shaving, and just as he has, at last, after many objurgations, corrected a fair percentage of his blunders, he upsets the hot water over my only tidy white waistcoat. He is now in tears, but produces another from the bottom of a box. It is yellow with age, and obviously was not made for me, borrowed probably at some time, put away to be returned, and forgotten. The last owner was, I notice, a short, stout man.

There is, however, no time to waste, so I struggle into it and my coat, and descend the stairs to the taxi. The Burnhams live somewhere in Giza—of all places to choose. They have taken a new house there, so Burnham told me, somewhere off the Pyramid Road, just before you come to the tram station. It must be a good two miles, I should think, so I order a taxi. I wish I knew where the house is exactly, but luckily, as for a wonder I am early, there is plenty of time to find it.

I therefore tell the taxi-driver to go to Giza, and off we start. Driving in a native-driven taxi on a dark night is a very fair test of nerve. The streets in our suburbs are lighted on strictly economical principles. You can just see one street lamp from the next. They no doubt give one a line as to the way the road runs, and prevent one's entering some one's garden, or, worse still, a canal, in a hurried and undignified manner, but except in their immediate vicinity, they show no part of the road itself.

This would not matter so much if the taxis carried good headlights, but they don't. The one I have to-night has two things like policemen's bull's-eye lanterns tied on to it in front. Even these modest illuminations are bent by previous collisions, and only show about two yards of road in front of us. Beyond conveying when it's too late to do anything that there is going to be a nasty accident, they are of restricted utility. They might give one time to utter one's "last words," but there would be no one to hear them except the chauffeur, who would probably not be able to repeat them, even if they were of a nature to bear repetition. A trifle like lack of illumination, however, does not disturb the driver, who as long as he goes fast enough and keeps his horn sounding the whole time, has every confidence that all will be well. In my cab of to-night, even our horn is not up to the usual Cairo level, and makes a noise like an asthmatic puppy trying to bark.

We spin across the bridge, which is well lighted, and plunge into the darkness beyond.

Wow, wow, wow, goes the horn, as we miss an elderly peasant by the fraction of an inch, swerving as we do so very nearly into a cart laden with passengers on the other side of the road. These carts, on which one may ride for two miles for the modest sum of a farthing, are bound by law to carry a light, but for convenience the driver usually carries it in his hand; so if he stops to talk to a friend *en route*, a not unfrequent occurrence, the cart light is only visible some time after you have passed the cart. The law does not specify either what sort of light the carts must carry, and the most fashionable pattern is a tallow dip in a home-made red paper lantern. It looks in the distance, if you can see it at all, like a fine specimen of glow-worm or fire-fly. But you do not often see it, because, as it is apt to blow out or gutter to a wasteful degree in the wind, it is usually kept sheltered inside the driver's cloak or with his hands.

We continue our wild career, swerving from side to side, catching glimpses of terrified faces and flying limbs as we pass. Occasionally matters are diversified by a camel suddenly shying from the side of the road into the middle, this necessitating on our part an extra swerve, accompanied by a half-skid, with all the brakes on. Camels don't carry lights because they are not carts, and are quite as easy to see without them. At least this is the best reason I can think of for their unillumined condition. The only other incident worth recording in an unavailing and Canute-like endeavour to make a steam-roller, which has apparently been left out to cool in the middle of the road by our energetic Road Department, get out of our way by barking at it with our dilapidated horn, the attempt ending in an unusually perilous emergency stop, with the usual skid accompaniment. I admit the red light looked like a cart-light at a distance, but when we got nearer, we should have chucked the attempt— nervous steam-rollers are so rare, it is not safe to reckon on them.

When we arrive at Giza, I am not in a condition for cool thought, but I fancy that the house must be down a dark turning I see on the left, and impart my views to the driver, who twists his machine in that direction, through a flock composed apparently of children and goats mixed.

When one wants to find a house in this country, the only method is to ask one's way at a house which has been standing for some time, as there is more chance of the servants there knowing the district well.

I select a big, old-fashioned-looking house, and tell my driver to stop there. When we have pulled up and found the *boab* or doorkeeper, who, according to immemorial custom, is sunk in a deep and, we trust, refreshing slumber, he is, on being awakened, divided in his mind as to whether the house is on fire or we are professional burglars. When his normal state of mental vacuity has been re-established, I ask him for the house of Burnham Bey—a new house. He asks what Boughan Bey. I reply, not Boughan, but Burnham, Bey, of the Ministry of Justice. He asks if he lives here in Giza. As if one would drive out two miles, at the peril of one's life, to ask the way to a man's house at the other end of Cairo! But I answer, with that forbearance for which the British official is so well known, " Yes, here at Giza, a *new* house, Burnham Bey." The *boab* repeats what he understands to be the name with variations, and finally says he does not know him. While this colloquy has been going on, a small crowd has collected, and now begins to join in the conversation. The predominant opinion is that the house is a hundred yards farther down the road, on the right, though a strong minority say it is on another road in the opposite direction.

Following the principles of modern government, I side with the majority, and we proceed down the road and stop at another house. Here apparently all the servants, including the *boab*, are out, but at last a house servant is fished out by the chauffeur. Our new adviser is of a different type, and is an intelligent but untruthful person who professes to know Burnham intimately, and tells us to go back past the house of Stobbs Pasha, which is apparently the house at which we made our former inquiries, turn to our right, then to our left, and behold the house—a small new house of a yellow colour. Off we go, and after nearly smashing the car twice or thrice owing to the fact that the road has been pitted for some obscure reason with little holes such as one makes to plant shrubs in, we arrive at the house in question, to be met by a sad disappointment. The house belongs to an Italian lady, whose name sounds like Silly Billy. Signorina Silly Billy's domestic, a small and very dirty boy, suggests our making inquiries at the house of Stobbs Pasha, and only escapes braining through my marvellous self-restraint. On being pressed further, he suggests another house in the vicinity as the sort of house we want, but with no conviction, and taking up the safe but unhelpful position that Bining Bey (his variation of the name) might live there, I agree to draw this likely spot, when it occurs to me that Stobbs no longer lives at Giza, and I wonder who has taken his house. The likely house is inhabited by a large family of Syrians, who are partaking of the evening meal apparently in the front hall.

In despair we return to the house of Stobbs, to see if there is no one there of a higher mental calibre and a wider local knowledge than the respected doorkeeper. On arriving back he welcomes us with interest, and at our request summons another servant, who, he mentions in excuse for his non-appearance, is making ready the dinner. Idiot that I am! I see it! In this country a house is always called by the name of the original owner, or, anyhow, of the last owner. I ask the doorkeeper who lives in his house, or rather the house in front of which he enjoys his well-earned repose. In the intervals of shouting for a mysterious Ahmed, he informs me that Stobbs, or, as he pronounces it, Estobbs, Pasha used to live there (which I knew), but that now there are new tenants, whose name he has forgotten. He, however, on the appearance of Ahmed, asks that worthy, who replies, " Birnim Bey." " Ah, yes," says the doorkeeper, " Birnim Bey."

Well, it is no good saying anything, so I get out and enter the house, reflecting on the inconveniences of employing the word " new " in so loose a way, and determining to speak severely to Burnham about it. Luckily I started early from my house, so I find to my joy that, in spite of my wanderings, I am not the latest guest to arrive, as Burnham's own servant, whom I know well, informs me whilst he takes my hat and coat from me. Burnham receives me with the air of one who has a painful and rather degrading duty to perform—but that is the Englishman's normal attitude towards social functions. Mrs. Burnham, whose colour has come out in the wash of life, is depressedly glad to see me, but is obviously nervous that I may bite her, and extends her hand in a tentative manner.

The party, which continues to arrive, is official, distinctly official. There is Wandle and Mrs. Wandle, of the Irrigation; Judge Blore; Colonel and Mrs. Boomley, Army of Occupation; de Cosson Smith, of the Antiquities; and M. and Madame de Loriot, of the Suez Canal.

My stars, what a lot! and I might have been dining at the Delaneys'!

Judge Blore, an English judge of the Native Court of Appeal, breaks an ominous silence with the remark that he has not seen the Reuter's telegrams this evening. We none of us care a bit, but Burnham, who is a painstaking host, repeats the substance of them to him while we listen. Mrs. Boomley, who is very downright, asks Mrs. Burnham if she takes any interest in politics. Mrs. Burnham murmurs she does, though she's afraid she does not understand them. "I don't," says Mrs. Boomley, with a vindictive look at the Colonel, who does; and we sink into another silence which can be felt.

A laconic servant now opens the door, puts his head in, and says loudly, "Dinnaire serve." Upon which we gravely file into the dining-room—Mrs. Burnham, whom I take in, keeping me as far off as she can. To my joy, I find I am next Madame de Loriot on the other side, who is amusing and very well dressed, and as talkative as most of her race. Her husband has a chronic asthma, and never speaks if he can help it.

I know the dinner before I look at the menu. Messy and bad. *Mousse de jambon* is the classical dish one always gets, and it is typical of the rest.

Now I must talk to Mrs. Burnham, who has the Colonel on the other side of her, for the first course or so, and then I can talk the rest of dinner to Madame de Loriot.

It is no good waiting for her to begin, as she is

only thinking of what sort of muzzle I ought to wear in order to be safe, so I turn on Sudan and deluge her with floods of dreary experiences in that country, she murmuring, " Oh, really! " " Did you? " " Only fancy! " at intervals. Blore, on the other side of Madame de Loriot, begins to lecture her on the iniquities of French law, which evidently amuses her. Presently she turns on him and abuses English law, which she says she has read all about. " What works on the subject have you read, may I ask, Madame? " says Blore in his most ponderous manner. " Dickens," replies Madame, with an innocent expression, " and I also saw a play called *Trial by Jury*." Blore, who looks pained and shocked, says, " Oh, but, Madame, those are not serious works on the subject."

" What are they, then, because they are certainly not funny? " says Madame.

She will have rather fun with Blore, I expect.

The Colonel, having finished his soup, decided the fish is not worth eating, though it might have been once, sampled and left alone the sherry, and drunk his first glass of champagne, fixes his eyeglass in his eye and opens fire.

" Terrible condition of affairs in England," says the Colonel. " The fact is, there is no discipline anywhere. Now, what we want is a thorough change. I really believe the only thing is a war.

" These people don't understand things, but they jolly well would if they were invaded by Germany. We should not hear any more of this d—d rot. And then we should get the two things we want, which are conscription and Tariff Reform. Drill the people and get them back to the land, that is what we want."

Yes, he is well off now, and in two minutes he will draw the Judge, who is a Liberal. I can see the Judge's attention is wandering from Madame de Loriot's painful remarks on the absence of humour in the English and the archaic condition of her laws.

I thought so; just as the Colonel, who has a certain dramatic sense, has explained why he would shoot Lloyd George, hang Churchill, and put Asquith in the pillory, to Mrs. Burnham's obvious terror, the Judge, with what is meant to be a conciliatory smile, but is really an unfounded claim to a higher mental standpoint, breaks in with, " I think I perfectly understand, Colonel, your irritation at the policy of the Government, but don't you think perhaps that you are ascribing to them motives and intentions which they cannot be quite fairly credited with? " (and so on).

I turn to Madame, and we soon get off into a comfortable conversational channel on the recent plays and books of France, and then on to her experiences and travels; a short account of her life at Ismailia—her garden, of which she is justly proud, and other people's gardens, of which she is less justly critical, and so on. Not much in it all, perhaps, but what a comfort, rest, and pleasure it is to listen to somebody who can talk well, as she can! The lightness of touch, the cunning and careful mixture of grave and gay, the foreseeing tact which enables her to glide away from the subject before it has ceased to interest and amuse, the apparent absence of egotism and the delicate *soupçon* of flattery and interest in her interlocutor, fill one with admiration and well-being. All my irritation disappears, the world lights up again; the birds of one's mind begin to sing, and I wish, as I often have, that it was good manners to break into applause, or purr, or do something to show one's gratitude and approval. One sense so quickly affects another, that I am rapidly becoming convinced that she is a really good-looking woman, in spite of a mouth of abnormal size and a complexion which does not bear discussion.

Meanwhile, from the outer world the sounds of battle occasionally obtrude their presence. The booming of the heavy batteries of the Colonel replies to the sharper field guns of the Judge, and the rest of the table, who have been drawn into the struggle, add to the thunder of the combat.

It is that bane of existence, the fiscal question, in its most acute form. They will all argue and bicker, and go over the same ground again and again, and will arrive no nearer to a conclusion.

They will get heated, unreasonable, discourteous, and disagreeable. They don't know what they are eating or drinking, which is perhaps lucky for them at the moment; but they will suffer all the more afterwards, for they will forget to be cautious. As if Burnham's food were not a sufficient strain on their digestive processes, without the additional burden they are casting on their, owing to Egyptian food, already impaired digestions, by exciting themselves in this way! I believe in a way they enjoy it, though, for the sake of the noise, as children like banging a tea-tray with a poker.

The two people who suffer the most are Mrs. Burnham and de Loriot, who, as one does not and the other cannot, speak, are used, as the Speaker is used in the Commons, to address, with the disadvantage that they cannot stop their interlocutors all speaking at once. Mrs. Burnham has obviously relinquished the idea of muzzles or cages, or even lethal chambers, while the Frenchman's sense of humour comes to his aid, and I can see, by the occasional twinkle in his eyes, that his is not unmixed suffering.

As the dessert is put on, the fire slackens, and one is sensible of that feeling of quietude one has in a factory when they stop the machinery.

Mrs. Boomley, who has been pounding Wandle in a pitiless fashion, announces she hates politics and arguing, and, resting on our oars, we glide on to the time when the ladies rise and leave us.

With the port and cigarettes, we split up into groups: the Colonel, de Loriot, and Wandle discussing the iniquities of the various steamship lines plying between Egypt and Europe, and deploring the general increase in the expense of living; whilst the Judge, Burnham, and myself talk shop about the relative scales of fees in the Mixed and Native Courts, and the cost of litigation generally in Egypt. They both talk well on the subject, especially Burnham, who has the transcendent gift of clear expression; and I am quite sorry when we rise to join the ladies.

These we find already prepared to leave the

house, as there is a party at the Agency, to which we are all going except the de Loriots, who are in mourning.

I say good-night to the de Loriots, and agree to lunch there on Friday, dine and go to the opera on Monday, stay at Ismailia next month for a Thursday to Saturday, and send Madame two books I have freely quoted from during the evening, but of which I have only read the reviews (I hope they are fit for her reading), and then, having taken my leave and woken up the chauffeur, I start for the Agency.

CHAPTER IX   EVENING PARTY

BY common consent of all reasonable humanity it has been decided that an evening party is the most trying form of social function; it is also the most senseless.

If one is of a sociable nature, one likes to meet one's fellows and converse with them in peace and comfort. If one loves one's fellow-human, one wishes him to be happy and comfortable.

An evening party certainly allows you to meet, and even bump, your fellow, but under the most adverse conditions for comfortable conversation.

It can be described as a brutal social observance in which the upper classes play at being a mob.

Everything must in essence be good or evil, and that essence can be detected by result. An evening party obviously comes from the nether world, where it is probably a regular institution.

However, it is in our own hands to turn evil and suffering to good account, and if one goes to an evening party in a spirit of fortitude and resignation, I don't believe that it does one any serious harm from a moral point of view.

Physically it deteriorates your body from the outside by undue pressure, applied either to the body or to the feet, and inwardly by an almost total absence of oxygen for the lungs and an acute form of nervous strain.

Whatever its origin (probably a form of sun-worship by making the night or sunless time unpleasant), it is at present kept going either by the medical profession or the bores.

The mental position of the doctors, though sordid, is easy to understand.

They look upon evening parties as a source of income, and I have seen them at these assemblies gloating over the rich harvest they will reap in the next few days.

If you are sufficiently near to one you can hear him mutter, " Aha, there goes Mrs. Jones with the influenza still on her. She is infectious all right. Mrs. Tomkins looks pretty bad. This ought to send her to bed for a fortnight. If Smith's lungs can stand this I will eat my hat. Robinson is bound to get that bad foot of his trodden on, with any decent luck, and if he does he is good for six visits at least," and so on.

Besides the doctors, the bores are the only people (except a few eccentrics and neurasthenics) who enjoy an evening party. In all other positions of life either their energies are restricted, as at dinner or in a railway carriage, to a few people, or the victims have a reasonable chance of escape.

In a party their victims are driven to them in herds. They are hemmed in in a narrow space from which there is no escape, or are forced through doorways and past corners behind which the bore lurks, ready to leap on his victim as he or she passes.

One sees them go away at the end of the evening gorged with the good temper and peace of mind they have sucked from their prey.

Yes, on the whole, I believe it is the bores more than the doctors who keep up this inhuman practice.

In books one reads of brilliant men passing through brilliant rooms saying brilliant things to their fellow-guests; in real life you see men with worn, angry faces fighting their way through a seething mass of overheated humanity to the refreshments, under the hope that alcohol will make them forget their sorrows.

How can you be brilliant with a man standing on your toes, another with his elbow deep in your ribs, whilst a muscular and impatient lady urges you on by prodding you in the back with her fan, which she subsequently accuses you of breaking? Far from being brilliant, one's difficulty is to refrain from coarse profanity.

However, to-night I really mean to try to add to the gaiety of the social life of Cairo.

Mrs. Delaney, Mrs. Fitz, and, I regret to say, many others of my friends have told me that my mere appearance at a party depresses them terribly, and I have determined to make an effort to-night to enjoy myself and amuse my friends.

As my thoughts reach this point, an unusually terrifying swerve of the car informs me that I have entered the Agency gates and have arrived at my destination. Thank Heaven! Mrs. Fitz has asked me to go on to the Savoy to supper, so I shall escape fairly early from this scene of tumultuous delight.

It is important to watch where one's coat and hat are put away, first because, there being no racks or shelves to put them on, they are put down anywhere that is vacant, and, secondly, the servants cannot, as a rule, read the numbers they pin on them, so if you trust to these worthies to find your garments at the end of the party you will probably never see them again. Mine on this occasion are placed on the coal-scuttle.

The portion of the Agency devoted to what is by courtesy called entertaining was designed by a humorist or a misanthrope. A not too wide passage leads from the hall to these rooms, and through it all those arriving, departing, or seeking refreshment must pass. It is here that the crush is usually most painful. At the end of the passage three doors open—one on the right, one in front, and one on the left. The centre door admits you to the ballroom, where the crowd is the densest, the other two into smaller rooms which communicate with the ballroom by other doors. Here there is less crowd, but, as a set-off or compensation, more bores.

In the ballroom even bores are too busy jostling one another to fix on you with any tenacity. In the small rooms they get you into a corner and really enjoy themselves. I determine to try the ballroom to-night, and plunge into the centre of what is called technically the " scrum " at football, I believe. I find myself jammed up against Torper, who smiles at me rather sillily, and I grin back. I often wish there was some other way of greeting men in a crowd. To a lady one can make a sort of bow, or, anyhow, a sort of paralytic convulsion which indicates that if you were a free man in the open you would bow to her, but to a man you can do nothing but grin and nod, a kind of gesture which should imply " Well, you do look an ass ! "

Every one is talking, and as I am ground forward I listen in vain for the brilliant conversation.

Four phrases will carry one through any party. " How are you ? " " Is not it hot ? " " Did you go to X to-day ? " " Are you going to X to-morrow ? " You need not bother about the answers, which very likely you won't hear. At this point I am shot into the ballroom like a cherry-stone from between a finger and thumb. Here, though it is densely crowded, one can turn round. One keeps up the paralytic bows and the nodding grins, and tries to make up one's mind what portion of the room one will make for.

I join an easterly current, which should eventually land me near the window, where very probably one can breathe. Here comes old Madame d'Haricot, crushing her way through the crowd.

" Ah ! milor, where 'ave you been ? I nevare see you. It is no good to tell you my day is Friday, I suppose ? "

I cannot think of anything brilliant, or, in fact, anything at all, except that I thought it was long past, which obviously would not do. I at last murmur something about being so busy.

" What? " she screams; " on a Friday? "

Just so—of course, I have put my foot in it. I can only say, " Alas, Madame, Friday as well as other days."

" You work too hard," she says; " you look tired, older."

Confound her! Who can be brilliant under such circumstances?

I very nearly say, " With you that appears to be impossible," but luckily don't, and change it for, " We none of us get younger," which is, on reflection, a shade worse. Happily at this moment Madame sees Sir Arthur Gibbs, our great irrigationist, who is a few yards off.

" Sir Arterre, Sir Arterre," she screams, and crushes forward in his direction. Heaven help him!

I next run into Pontingly, who is three foot six high, and correspondingly important and mysterious. " Have I heard about Molloy? " I say, " What? " He looks as if the rack would not make him indiscreet, and says in a stage whisper, " It's out," and drifts on. I wonder whether it's a scandal, an engagement, an appointment, or a tooth, and find myself opposite Mrs. Larg, the bank manager's wife, who is a blaze of brilliant brocade and jewels. She greets me with the great manner of Surbiton. I suspect Larg, who is a very capable and efficient man, is there too, but at parties he gets hidden behind her resplendent skirts. It reminds me always of the power behind the throne. We talk the correct platitudes which two personages of finance should do, until I find myself resistlessly impelled forward by the impact of some unusually heavy mass of flesh, which from its size and softness must, I think, be a Minister. I look over my shoulder and find it is so indeed: it is his Excellency of the Arts and Crafts.

"Aha!" he says, as I apologise for his hurting me, "we find ourselves together again. *Sapristi!* how hot it is! I could drink willingly a glass of champagne," and with a seraphic smile he rolls off in the direction of the refreshment-room.

I look round to find I am now opposite to Mrs. MacWhirter, the wife of the American judge—at least I think it's she, but no living soul can remember which is she and which is her aunt, who lives with her. They are not really alike, but their faces are so uninteresting one cannot remember them. As we make again our original remarks on the crowded-ness of the room and the heat, I rack my brain for something better to say. MacWhirter has gone down to Alexandria on an arbitration case, so I say:

"Well, I always said your husband was a very lucky man. He must be chuckling when he thinks of us."

She looks furious and turns away without a word. Good heavens! It was the aunt, and she is separated from her husband. There is nothing to be done. If it gets out I shall never hear the last of it. I must pretend to think it was Mrs. MacWhirter, and trust to the aunt not repeating it.

I am now simply boiling, but another surge of the crowd deposits me near the window, where I find Mrs. Delaney, looking cool and as neat as if she had just stepped out of a bandbox. She will, at all events, be sympathetic. I don't think I ever saw her looking more beautiful and charming. Apparently this sentiment is not reciprocated, because her first remark is:

" Please, Lord Edward, don't try to smile at a party again. It is really terrible to see your face."

This is discouraging, but I tell her of my good resolutions, which I regret to say she receives with unconcealed merriment.

Just as I am feeling happy for the first time since I entered the room, that creature de Courcelle, the French Consul-General, comes up and says he has been told that he is to have the honour of taking her to have some supper, and off they go. She tells me to come to tea to-morrow as a compensation, which takes away some of the bitterness of the disappointment.

This move to the supper-room means that the royalties, princes, consuls-general, etc., are going, and we can slip away. I turn in the direction of the door and slowly fight my way towards it. Once in the doorway one is shot forward by the tide of hungry guests, and I find myself in the hall, where I run straight into Camberley of the Agency.

" Oh, look here, Cecil, they want you to take in Countess Swartzenberg—you know, the Duchess's lady-in-waiting; have you seen her anywhere? " I murmur " No," cursing royalties, ladies-in-waiting, and the Agency under my breath. We search the now empty rooms, and find nothing but two engaged couples, a well-accepted scandal, and his Excellency of the Arts and Crafts fast asleep in a large chair behind a door.

137

I suggest some one else has taken her in, and we regain the hall. Now for a dash before they think of some other little plan for my happiness.

At this moment a hand is laid upon my arm.

I turn round, and realise with horror that I am in the hands of the enemy. Maudely has me in his clutches.

Maudely was, in prehistoric times, a journalist of note, and he has been left stranded in Cairo by the receding tide of his life. Some people declare that a leading newspaper proprietor of enormous wealth pays him a generous stipend on the express condition that Maudely is never to come within one thousand miles of this magnate's office.

" How are you, my dear fellow? " I say with forced cheerfulness. It is like trying to joke with one's hangman.

" Pretty well, pretty well, thank you," he replies. " That reminds me of a certain occasion when I asked the same question of Lord Henry Fitzherbert, who was then ambassador at Rome in 1873—no, I am wrong, I know; it was 1875—and I'll tell you why, because that was the first year in which I left off wearing the old spring-sided boots—Jemimas, they used to be called, you know. They were then still quite fashionable, for only a couple of years before that I can remember as well as possible crossing St. James's Park with Sam Barley—old Sam Barley, as we used to call him, though, as a matter of fact, he was not old a bit. Let me see, Sam was then three- or four-and-forty, not more, because he was the same age as the late Bishop of Blackhampton, who died five years afterwards of a very curious accident.

He was opening a bottle. I don't know what of. I hope not brandy, for that would not do for a cleric, would it? I have been told what it was, but I forget. Arthur Clouston, who was his nephew by his second or third wife, used to tell me about it, as we were both members of the same club, the Stuffington, when it was in Berkeley Square, a beautiful house, which had belonged to Lord Harpendale—not this man, of course, but his grandfather. A fine old boy. He used to wear a blue coat and buff waistcoat till the day of his death, and drank his two bottles of port every day ' to keep the gout off,' he used to say; but of course he was before my time," etc., etc.

There now, what have I done to deserve this? He scarcely ever even finishes one of his infernal stories, and if by any chance he does, one wishes he had not. I wonder if I shall ever grow to be like that; if I do, I hope they'll give me prussic acid or something as deadly.

There is no known means of stopping him, and any attempt to keep him to the point is like cutting off the heads of the Hydra.

Ah, here comes his wife, of whom he lives in dread. He sees her, and, mumbling something about telling me about it another time, he drifts quietly away, and disappears with the ease born of long practice. Judging from her appearance, he has probably been avoiding his wife for the last forty years; ever since he married her, in fact.

I move with the rapidity of the hunted rabbit to the cloak-room, where I find an angry mob objurgating three or four demented Berberine servants who are handing every one some one else's coat and hat. In the confusion they even " break the sets," so to speak. I see a timid youth with two large wide-awakes, one in each hand, bleating vainly for his cap, whilst an irritable tourist has been given three walking-sticks and nothing else, which is certainly insufficient clothing for a cold night.

Knowing my way about these affairs, I slip under the counter, go straight to the coal-scuttle, where I am lucky enough to find my hat and coat untouched, and, casting myself into the crowd, I fight my way to the door.

With a little trouble I find my taxi and start for the Savoy.

CHAPTER X   SUPPER—PART I

AS I drive away, I feel that delicious sense of relief which only comes, with the cessation of severe bodily pain, at the termination of a long illness, or after an evening party.

The comfort of being able to move without crushing or being crushed is very great; and even the atmosphere of Cairo seems pure after the air we have been breathing. As it is necessarily very tiring to play a kind of football without the ball or any oxygen, I don't feel in quite the right mood for a supper, and wish I were going to bed. There is, however, the possibility—nay, even the probability—that Mrs. Fitz has forgotten all about it, or thinks that she has asked me on another night

at another hotel, in which case I can go home to my
well-earned rest.

To-night there is a ball at the Savoy, so it will
be crowded. The hotel balls are, I may say, the
leading feature of our society. There are now
very few big European houses where entertainments
are given, and the increased size of our social world
has rendered the small dances and parties of ten
years ago impossible. The result is that nowadays
nine-tenths of the entertaining is done at the hotels,
and usually on ball nights. This is in some ways
rather convenient for the host, as he does not have
the trouble of amusing his guests after dinner, for
they dance or look on at the dancing. By a merciful but unwritten law, too, the host can go away
without giving offence directly supper has begun—
that is, at eleven o'clock.

All the principal hotels give a ball once a week
throughout the season; but the smart ones, to
which all the *Best People* go, are the Savoy and the
Semiramis. [We talk a great deal about the *Best
People* in Cairo. You should accentuate the word
Best slightly when using the phrase, and it is custom-
ary to add the words, " You know what I mean,"
after using it. Who constitute the *Best People* is a
matter of opinion except, of course, in the cases of
yourself and the person to whom you are talking.]
Next, in order of merit, come the Ghezireh, Shep-
heard's, and Heliopolis, and last of all the Conti-
nental, which is much frequented by the *jeunesse
dorée* of Pashadom.

As each hotel gives its weekly ball on a different
day of the week, it is possible to go to a dance six

nights out of seven for the five months of the season; and I really believe there are some people who do this and survive.

Of course there are other entertainments, either of a recurrent nature—as, for example, the opera (which is usually like nothing else on earth except a concert of cats)—or special festivities which are given from time to time, such as garden parties, concerts, etc.; but the balls are the standing dish, of which you can always partake if you can get nothing better.

As might be inferred, dancing is very popular in Cairo. We all, or almost all of us, dance, and we go on dancing up to any age. Grandmothers and gentlemen with grey hair and a lower chest measurement of fifty inches hop round gravely with the rest.

At this point I am rudely disturbed by my chauffeur, who has made a slight miscalculation, attempting (apparently) to drive up the hotel steps. I pay him off with a proper sense of thankfulness, get rid of my hat and çoat, and enter a large hall, out of which the ballroom opens, and which I believe is called the lounge.

Now my difficulty will be to find Mrs. Fitz. The best chance for me will be to stand in the big doorway which connects the ballroom with the lounge. Here I am very shortly afterwards hailed by Bentley, who informs me, with his usual hauteur, that Mrs. Fitz has told him to look out for me, to inform me that supper is to be at twelve—that is, in about twenty minutes—and that it will take place in the private room at the end of the main passage; which instructions I receive with humility and thanks.

As Bentley is never, strictly speaking, a brilliant conversationalist, and as I don't see any one in the vicinity to whom I am exactly pining to talk, we stand in silence and watch the crowd.

I know a great number of faces, for the same individuals come out here for the winter, as tourists, year after year; and one often gets quite interested in people and their affairs without ever getting to know them to speak to. Then Cairo hotel society is interesting as being, I suppose, the most mixed crowd in the world. In it are to be found representatives of almost all civilised nationalities and of every grade of the social scale, from the reigning Prince of Slappenbach-Spitnitz and the Duchess of Axminster to the Levantine Jew broker and the little French actress.

Besides our queer medley of residents and tourists, there are also many specimens of the passers-through who stop for a week in Egypt on the way between Europe and India, Australia, China, Japan, the South Sea Islands, East Africa, South Africa, and Heaven only knows where else besides.

Egypt is also a not uncommon resort for those who have good reason to refrain from stopping in their own country; so there is also a certain element of romance about these people, if one has a touch of imagination. The gentleman from whom you take a light for your cigarette may be anything from a European statesman to a burglar, a wholesale or retail criminal. A very gentlemanly foreign self-styled baron, who was here for some time a few seasons ago, and who got to know quite a lot of the *Best People*, used to show us some very fine diamonds, which he said he had " picked up very cheap." This was literally true, for he took them off some one else's dressing-table in Paris. An immediate interview with a young and very nice-looking couple, who stayed here last year, was, we heard afterwards, earnestly desired by the police of no less than four European nations.

At one time, like most people, I felt sure that I was a good judge of character from the face, but I have modified my opinion.

It is amusing and instructive, as they falsely said of the old Polytechnic, to try to guess who and what the new arrivals are, and having determined this to your own satisfaction, to go then and ask, say, my friend Mr. Wild, the manager of the Savoy, about them. A gentleman who was known to be one of the leading card-sharpers of the day, I unhesitatingly put down as a surgeon of blameless life in full practice; and I mentally consigned to a lifelong sentence in a convict prison an American representative of the Y.M.C.A.

Still, even if you have some severe disappointments, it is quite an amusing game to play. It is better, however, I have found, to keep your opinion to yourself till you have verified it. It seems to make you guess right more frequently.

In the outer room or lounge, groups of those who have dined here together sit round small tables smoking and talking. That large circle of gentlemen, and, I regret to say, ladies, with their backs bent forward in eager but respectful attitudes, is

the court of Sir Benjamin Abrahams, the great
financier, who is making a short stay here, to look
after his interests (emphatically *his* interests) in this
country. No beauty is regaled with so much
flattery, no king is treated with such subservience.
With no one is acquaintance claimed on slighter
grounds. I heard a leading social light here claim
to have met Sir Benjamin before, on the ground
that they had crossed the Channel in the same boat
on a rough day. I suppose frequenting millionaires
is profitable, or people would not do it, but it must
be disagreeable work.

The next group belongs to the mysterious order
of detached limpets. One glance assures me that
neither father nor mother, nor the two very dull
daughters, nor the very bored son, ever wanted to
leave the parental rock. Why they move is a
mystery. They hate travelling, and take no interest
in either strange countries, or antiquities, or even
amusements. They moodily move in silence from
place to place, until the mysterious force which has
driven them abroad weakens, and they can return
to their homes. I have made the acquaintance of
some specimens and asked them why they travelled.
They either would not or could not give a satisfactory answer. One young lady limpet told me
it was " because the drains were up at home." I
felt puzzled. The danger of even the most poisonous drains does not demand that one should be
thousands of miles away.

The next group are Americans of a peculiar type.
They are always the same wherever you meet them,
the low-class, fast-travelling Americans; they talk

more, see more, and understand less than any other class of traveller, and are better not thought about, if you want to be decently charitable.

The next table is occupied by a honeymoon couple, who, if they were induced to come to Egypt in search of what has been called modified solitude, have been grossly misled. Perhaps it is the work of the rejected rival, a cruel but most adequate revenge.

For two people to travel together for long without showing all the worst sides of their characters is very rare. I would not do it with my oldest, most tried and trusted friend; and why people should so often begin married life—which is, Lord knows, difficult enough under any circumstances—by doing that which is admitted to be most dangerous to all mutual respect and esteem, is more than I can understand.

I consult Bentley on the point, but his ducking has, I fear, soured him, as he only suggests that it is better to know the worst as soon as possible and get it over.

Next to the seekers after modified solitude are three dear old English ladies. Two are knitting, and the third is doing crotchet work. They don't talk much, but just sit there and look on in a benevolent way. They look so lovable and yet so helpless, one is tempted to go to their assistance, and offer to guide them through the difficulties and perils of Egypt.

As a matter of fact, they are three of the most intrepid travellers existing. They are the famous Misses Gubb, whose works, or rather the works of

146

Miss Amelia, who is the scribe of the party, you have probably read. *Through Turkestan in Trousers, Black Kings and White Faces, The Secret Shrines of the Wata Lai,* and several more, which all treat of places where the boldest man goes not if he can possibly avoid it.

Under those black silk dresses there are the hearts of heroes, and those grey locks cover brains which would have not disgraced Columbus or Marco Polo.

Savage chiefs have trembled before those reticules; and Miss Jane has, actually with her here in Cairo, an umbrella with which she personally beat, for being rude to her, the son and heir of Umtoompoto, a Central African monarch who simply prefers wallowing in human blood to any other amusement.

I believe there is only one moral force which it is quite impossible to withstand, and that is the force wielded by a nice but determined old lady.

At this moment I catch the eye of a very attractive-looking lady sitting on a sofa against the wall a few yards away, and she beckons me to come and talk to her.

It is Mrs. Dorline. She is what we call a hardy perennial—that is, a tourist who comes to Cairo every winter. She is of good family, has money of her own, has married a rich husband who idolises her, and she has the constitution of an ox. Having practically nothing in the world to grumble at, she has provided worries and troubles for herself. Her chief sorrow is, I understand, that she is not understood.

She is tall, dark, and slight (her enemies say thin), with slender, well-shaped hands and a handsome clear-cut face, with large restless grey eyes. Her appearance is marred by her complexion being too pale, the shadows of her face too dark, her lips too red, and her dress too eccentric. There is also generally an untidy, unhealthy look about her, which somehow suggests that she has been buried and dug up again.

"Tell me," she says, in her low, even voice, as I seat myself beside her, "what brings you to these places. I always wonder when I see you. Surely this "—with a slight circular gesture of her hand— "cannot amuse you."

Now that is the worst of talking to Mrs. Dorline. She starts in this sort of key, and I don't know what to say. One does not want to be absolutely unsympathetic and out of tune with her, but one cannot answer in the same style without feeling either a humbug or an ass.

I say feebly that I have come because I am engaged to go to supper, but that really these balls *do* rather amuse me in a way.

"I wonder," she thrills out. "Do you come to forget?"

Poor dear! if she only knew what my memory is like, she would not ask a silly question like that. If I could only find any form of amusement that made me remember, I should indulge in it every day.

I reply in what I try to make a lighter tone, though I fear it only sounds querulous.

"I think I come to pass the time, to watch the people, and to enjoy the reflection of amusement."

"I can never decide," she says, "when I see

those deep-set, inscrutable eyes fixed on this scene, whether behind them is infinite scorn or pity. I watched you last Saturday and wondered."

If I remember rightly, any peculiarity of expression I may have shown last Saturday was probably due to my collar stud slipping down and finally lodging in my shoe. Infinite discomfort, that was what was wrong with my deep-set eyes, but I cannot tell her that.

" I don't think it is either," I mutter. " I am amused, and perhaps I learn a little."

(That is better. That is more the tone.)

" What is the use? " she asks with sad intenseness; " it is all so purposeless, so meaningless. There is more to be learnt from the leaves dancing in the wind or the ripples on a brook."

Now I cannot dispute this. I don't feel sure about it. All I know is that the dancers here are neither like leaves nor ripples. The only two apt similes I can think of are cattle and football players.

So I merely remark that one can learn from everything.

" And to what end? " comes back the answer. " Why should we learn and learn, when nothing can solve the mysteries of life and death? " (Drop of a semitone on the last word.)

She is positively making my flesh creep. I wish she'd see a doctor about it. I am sure, with careful diet, plenty of exercise, and a little bicarbonate of soda, she would not feel like that.

I confine myself to remarking that as we cannot solve the insoluble, we may as well enjoy ourselves in moderation.

" Enjoy! " she exclaims. " Ah, how can one enjoy when one has found out that it is all false, all unreal? I feel as though I were crying night and day, Give me something real, something true, even if it is sorrow! "

What a wife she must be to Dorline! I have heard he is a depressed man, and no wonder. This sort of conversation makes me so uncomfortable. I feel inclined to ask her to put on a spiritual dressing-gown. The police ought to deal with people wilfully uncovering their souls in public.

I murmur something about its being more real than she thinks.

" Oh, I wish I thought so, I only wish I thought so! " she almost moans. " It is this distrust of all the so-called realities which makes one loathe and despise the petty restrictions of conventionality."

This is getting worse and worse. Is she contemplating an elopement, or merely walking about without her boots, or something of that sort? I don't know what she calls petty restrictions. With this sort of woman it may mean almost anything from having to wear gloves to the Ten Commandments.

I point out (with really disgusting pomposity) that these same conventions are the treaties which individuals enter into to respect the rights and comfort of the many. This anyhow can do no harm, as it means nothing.

At this moment mercifully, as I really cannot bear much more conversation of this sort, she is claimed by a partner, and I take my leave.

" Come and see me soon," she says. " To talk

with some one who really feels, who really understands, is such a help, such a bath for the soul."

Not if I know it. No mixed bathing for me!

As I make this wise resolution, my eye falls again
on Miss Jane Gubb. I wonder what she thinks
about the realities of life and mixed soul-bathing.
I think I can guess.

As I rejoin Bentley, he exclaims in an almost awe-
struck tone: "By Jove!" and I turn to see what
has produced this unusual burst of loquacity.

In the centre of the floor a couple of dancers are
stretched at full length. As I look, they are helped
up, and the lady, whose dress is badly torn, is
taken away to be pinned up, whilst the man dusts
himself and tries to accept the apologies of his
assailants, a tall muscular-looking girl and an infant
in the Rifle Brigade, with becoming civility.

As all sorts and ages of mankind dance in Cairo,
styles of dancing differ very considerably, from the
slow crawl and rock to the dashing swing; with the
result that accidents are fairly common.

"She will stretch some one for good some day,"
murmurs Bentley, with, I think, savage satisfaction,
"that girl, if she goes on dancing like that."

I am sure immersion does not suit Bentley.

The girl in question, Miss Whanger, undismayed
and dancing, passes us at this minute. "If you
would only be more careful about steering, Mr.
Witterly," she is saying rather acidly. Poor Witterly,
who has about as much control over her as he would
have over a steam-roller, receives his rebuke meekly.
He has long since given up attempting to steer.
All he can do he does, which is at the last moment

to interpose his body between the *objet aimé* and the people she is about to fell to the ground. He confided to me last week that he was so sore with repeated blows that he could scarcely walk.

CHAPTER XI   SUPPER—PART II

I AM beginning to feel hungry, as I wisely declined to poison myself at Burnham's, and so had practically no dinner. My thoughts naturally turn to supper, and I begin to wonder of whom the party is composed. I only hope it is a quiet or comparatively quiet lot; but no one, including herself, can tell whom Mrs. Fitz will ask.

Putting ices down one another's back is amusing enough at twenty, but in later life inevitably leads to a bad chill.

At the last rowdy supper party I attended they poured all the champagne over poor old Toomly, the doctor. He was in bed for a week afterwards in consequence, and could only talk in a hoarse whisper for the rest of the season.

At this moment Mrs. Fitz appears, radiant with a seraphic smile which long experience has taught me to distrust.

" Oh, Lord Edward, I know you are going to be an angel to-night, won't you? " she says, in tones she knows perfectly well we, none of us, can resist. I may well be an angel shortly if I am not given something to eat, as I am rapidly starving, but I don't say so. I feel levity would be out of place.

"You see," continues Mrs. Fitz, "I made a stupid mistake. There is a sort of relation of mine out here, and I meant to ask her to supper after the Charity Ball next week, when I am going to work off all the frumps together, and somehow, some one was talking, or something, and I put in the wrong date. Now will you be perfect and look after her?"

I reply that of course I shall be delighted, and ask her with some misgiving who else is coming to supper.

"Well, that is just it," says Mrs. Fitz, with the worried look of a child whose toy won't work. "You remember we agreed it should be rather a jolly supper" (I don't remember anything of the kind, but I nod sympathetically), "and I asked the Tollington girls and Mrs. Chafferly and Mr. Rimington and Captain Bentley and Captain Dasherly and the Baron and two of the Rifles, I forget which, and oh, the beautiful Mrs. Canley Tupper, the American you know, and her sister Miss Blech. Oh, yes, and I asked Mrs. Dorline specially for you, but she can't come."

Good heavens! It is the very rowdiest lot she could have got together. There is nothing they won't do or say at supper.

"Is your relation very . . ." Here I break down for a word. I want to say "proper," but that does not sound quite civil.

"Proper," puts in Mrs. Fitz, with her most charming smile.

153

"No, I assure you I meant—well—stiff," I hasten to say.

"Then you did mean proper," says Mrs. Fitz triumphantly. "It is the same thing, and you are very rude. Yes, she is just as proper as she can be, and awfully particular. I don't want her to go away thinking awful things of us all, so do keep her amused, so that she won't notice it if the rest do make rather a noise."

This is all very well. Of course Mrs. Fitz, who probably poses as a serious person in Cheshire, does not want to be given away to a lot of very severe relations under whom I know she suffers at home; but if she thinks that any conversation in the world will stop her relation noticing that people are braying like donkeys or crowing like cocks, or throwing peaches at each other, she is altogether too sanguine.

"I am putting the Baron on her other side, and perhaps she won't stay long," continues Mrs. Fitz. "It is really too tiresome of her coming."

"Well," I say, "does the Baron know what he is to do?"

"Oh yes, I told him, and he did not really mind a bit: at least not much. Here he is."

As she says this the Baron marches up and makes his most perfect bow.

"Good evening, milor," he says. "I hear we are in nice jobs; but what Madame wishes——" and here he makes a gesture indicating our powerlessness to struggle against Mr. Fitz's victorious charms.

"I am quite sure," says Mrs. Fitz, whose irrepressible optimism is again in the ascendant, "that you and Lord Edward will manage beautifully between you."

" I think it deeficult," remarks the Baron, " unless we make so something, some how say you, plans now."

" I have got it," cries Mrs. Fitz enthusiastically.

" What it? " says the Baron interestedly.

" Why, let us all pretend to be very serious, like a play or a charade, you know."

I can with difficulty follow Mrs. Fitz's enthusiastic remarks after some years of practice. The Baron is completely fogged.

" What shall we make her to play? " he asks tentatively.

" No, Mrs. Fitz means that we shall all act parts," I explain, " like actors in a play at the theatre, and pretend we are a very serious set of people."

" Oh, I see, yes, it is possible," admits the Baron doubtfully. " We can try."

But Mrs. Fitz, once started on one of her schemes, is not to be discouraged.

" Now, Lord Edward, get all of them together in the supper room, and I will tell Miss Sadenham to wait for us all in the hall. That will give us time to explain our plan " (*our*, mark you) " to the others, and then one of us can go out and bring her in."

We hastily adjourn to the supper-room, where we find the " serious " party have already assembled, and are keeping down the pangs of hunger by playing cricket with a poker and a knotted napkin. They have just succeeded in breaking a window as the Baron and I enter.

Mrs. Fitz, who appears almost as soon as we do, explains matters with such skill and enthusiasm that the scheme is delightedly taken up. Each member of the party selects a serious interest on the spot, and in a short time the cast for our impromptu theatrical performance is decided upon, and it is as follows:—

Mrs. Fitz, as she is known in Cheshire	MRS. FITZ.
A Serious Under-Secretary who believes in England's mission in Egypt	LORD E. CECIL.
A Distinguished Foreign Diplomat who emulates George Washington in veracity and is a devoted advocate of women's rights .	THE BARON SODISKY.
Two Sedate Young Ladies who are the chief support of the branch of the S.P.C.A. in Cairo	THE MISSES TOLLINGTON.
A Student of Arab Art, an artist who paints serious and improving pictures	MRS. CHAFFERLY.
A Lady deeply interested in rooting out the slave trade in all its forms from Central Africa .	MRS. CANLEY TUPPER.
A Lady Egyptologist and Antiquarian	MISS NATALIE BLECH.
An Archæologist of very silent habits	MR. RIMINGTON.
Earnest Soldiers, friends of the above	CAPTAIN BENTLEY. CAPTAIN DASHERLY. MR. SANDGATE. MR. WITTERLY.

The cast is hastily written out on menu cards, and one of them is given to each of us, so that we may remember who is who and what sort of things we ought to say to them.

Dick Rimington, whose English is remarkable,

to say the least of it, is warned to be as silent as possible and on no account to use slang.

The Misses Tollington are also cautioned. Miss Dena is specially requested to abstain from what she calls her " Ittifraz " (Idiot English for little phrases).

Mrs. Fitz really is a marvellous woman. I don't believe any one else in the world could have got us even to think of trying to do such a thing. With one last general appeal to us to do our best, she disappears to fetch her relative.

I really feel a certain amount of stage fright, and I can see the others, except the Baron, share this feeling. He remains quite unmoved, as if what we are going to do is an ordinary part of his daily life.

In a few minutes Mrs. Fitz reappears with a middle-aged lady of most forbidding aspect. There is a squareness about her face and a hard look in her little grey eyes which are simply terrifying. We are all formally introduced to her, and sit down in our places at the supper table.

" I confess I very seldom go out to supper," remarks Miss Sadenham as a commencement. " I think that it keeps one up too late, and plenty of good sleep is most important for every one."

The Baron, whose usual bed-time is 5 a.m., cordially agrees with her. He is, he states, in his own peculiar dialect of English, of opinion that suppers are both wantonly extravagant and interfere with the next day's work in a most deplorable manner, but on certain occasions like the present they are certainly very agreeable.

Miss Sadenham then proceeds to put the Baron through a searching examination with regard to the party assembled, and that gentleman gives short biographical sketches. of each of them, which evidently impress Miss Sadenham. Luckily the Baron's English renders these bright little flights of imagination difficult to understand, and the less they are understood the more likely they are to be believed.

Mrs. Canley Tupper, who is very nervous and obviously going to over-act her part, begins by telling me in high-pitched nasal tones that she cannot sleep at night for thinking of the horrors of the slavery in the Sudan, to which I hastily assent, correcting the place to " Congo " as if it were an obvious slip of the tongue.

The rest of the party begin talking in tones somewhat muffled by nervousness, and I begin to feel more cheerful. Things are not going so badly, and if Mrs. Fitz, who is shaking all over, can only control her suppressed merriment, all may yet be well.

My hopefulness is soon checked by Miss Amy Tollington, who has never remained silent for five consecutive minutes since she could speak, attacking Rimington on the subject of archæology, which I am convinced both of them think is connected in some way with Noah. Rimington, conscious of a certain vagueness of mind on the subject, is not to be enticed into displaying his ignorance, but says with great dignity: " Madam, my impaired digestion prevents me talking at meals, and this is the first food I have had since dawn."

" What a whop——" bursts out Miss Amy, and
Mrs. Chafferly starts a cough which is meant to
cover the remark, but which could only ordinarily
proceed from the throat of a basso profundo who
was dying of whooping-cough. It serves its purpose,
however, for it frightens Miss Sadenham so much
that she quite forgets about Miss Amy's outburst.
Miss Amy, who I am glad to see is crimson, is
glared at indignantly by the rest of the party.

At this point Mrs. Fitz, who has been making
heroic efforts to appear to be listening to Bentley's
minute-gun remarks with an interest not usually
accorded to them, suddenly loses control of herself
and bursts into a fit of almost hysterical laughter.

The conversation stops dead, and Miss Sadenham asks her what has amused her so extremely.

" Oh, oh," gasps Mrs. Fitz. " It is only that
Captain Bentley's stories are so ridiculous."

" And are we to be permitted to hear them? "
says Miss Sadenham, unbending slightly. " You
did not inform me that Captain Bentley was a
wit, Baron Sodisky. I thought you said he was of a
serious disposition."

" Take it from me," commences Dick Rimington,
when he catches my eye and stops abruptly.

" Take what from you, Mr. Rimington, may I
inquire? " says Miss Sadenham, still affably.

Mrs. Chafferly explains that the now purple
Rimington was only offering her his bread, and we
breathe again.

Miss Sadenham now returns to the charge.

" Cannot you, Lilian, let the table have the
benefit of listening to Captain Bentley's stories by

repeating them to us, or perhaps he would prefer to tell them to us himself? "

Bentley, who looks as if he had been given five minutes to decide if he prefers to be boiled to death or roasted alive, falters out, " I would rather not," and retreats into silence. Mrs. Fitz is still unable to speak, so the Baron hurriedly explains in a low tone of voice to Miss Sadenham how shy Bentley is, though he is very amusing when not overcome by this defect.

" He is a good fellow, very airnst but witty, what you call serio-comic," ends up the Baron, to Miss Sadenham's bewilderment.

It is all very well in theory to be mixed up in a joke of this sort, and it may be amusing to talk and think about afterwards; but at the moment of its perpetration the suffering of the participators is intense. I do not know what sum I would not give to be sitting quietly at home at this moment.

We talk on feverishly; even the Baron is beginning to get a worn look, while Mrs. Canley Tupper is now babbling about slavery in a style which can only be described as a cross between Daily Mailian and Earlswoodese.

As all the remainder of the party are now talking fast, and as it is necessary for Mrs. Chafferly and myself not only to keep up our own parts, but also to keep our ears open for the slips of others, in order to cover or explain them away as quickly as possible, a terrible strain is inflicted on our nerves.

Owing to the noise of the conversation and the distant strains of the band which is playing in the next room but one, Miss Sadenham luckily misses some of the worst remarks, whilst others, which she has obviously heard, are more or less successfully dealt with by Mrs. Chafferly or myself. The Baron cannot help us so much when it comes to twisting words out of their meanings. He has enough difficulty with the language without that. But in spite of this he is our main support, as he keeps Miss Sadenham interested, and shows a power of invention which can only be termed prodigious.

I can hear, however, that caution is wearing off and the slips are getting worse. Such phrases as " Now grind the oats and go steady," from Miss Dena, and " Pass the pinky Pop for pale people, Pretty Polly," from Miss Natalie Blech, though they may be quotations from our most recent musical comedy, are quite out of keeping with the assumed characters of their utterers; whilst the hopeless confusion of mind both the Miss Tollingtons display in conversation between the S.P.C.A. and the Y.M.C.A. can only be called regrettable. They obviously think that both these societies are branches of the same parent body, and allude to the latter as " a fair blessing to the donkeys of Cairo."

It becomes every moment clearer to me that the deception cannot last much longer, and unless Miss Sadenham can be induced to go away soon we shall be exposed.

My conviction is, I feel sure, shared by Mrs. Chafferly, judging from her almost despairing expression.

The only person who enjoys the whole thing thoroughly is Mrs. Fitz, who, having got us into this awful mess, is now shamelessly amusing herself by drawing out the various members of the company, to their complete discomfort and disgrace and her own infinite entertainment.

Any uncertainty in my mind as to the desirability of our bringing our performance to a close is soon swept away. Miss Sadenham asks the Baron whether it is true that the Arab women are as transcendently beautiful as tradition says, and receives an excellent reply from him, founded on the knowledge he obtained from a child's edition of the *Arabian Nights,* which he read when he was eight years old.

Dick Rimington, interested in the conversation, forgets all else, and fixing his eyes reflectively on the cornice of the ceiling, remarks:

" I had a pal who knew a little Arab Yum once," and then with an expression of sudden anguish, he continues: " I say, steady on, Mrs. Chaff. You've a boatful of floor to yourself, so please keep the Looey Kainzes off the wheatfield."

This, I feel, as Dick himself would say, has " torn it," but the Baron makes one desperate effort to save the situation.

He quickly, but with no sign of flurry, confides to Miss Sadenham the following veracious facts, viz. that Dick and Mrs. Chafferly are brother and sister-in-law by her first marriage, and that Rimington himself rose from a very humble position in life by his great qualities and genius. As the Baron expresses it, " He broomed in the street. He was a street wiper."

" This," adds the Baron in a half-whisper, " makes him funny talk at whiles, but nevare mind, one must excuse. He is the son of peoples from where he rose," and so on, all of which Miss Sadenham seems actually to accept or, shall I say, swallow.

At this moment an inspiration strikes me. Perhaps Miss Sadenham is living at Heluan, and is going back there by the last train. The last train, as a matter of cold fact, does not start for nearly an hour. If I could only persuade her it went earlier! I will try. It is neck or nothing.

I say casually but distinctly to Mrs. Tupper, as if the remark formed part of a current conversation:

" I do think it is really outrageous to change the time of a train in the middle of the month, and I cannot imagine why they have done such a thing. If I lived in Heluan, I should be very much annoyed."

" Did I hear you mention Heluan, Lord Edward? Might I inquire what you were saying about that place, as I am staying there at present? " demands Miss Sadenham.

" Oh, only that they have altered the time of the last train from Cairo from two to one-thirty."

" Dear me! that is most unfortunate, as I am returning by it to-night," cried Miss Sadenham in alarm. " But the porter of the hotel there informed me most distinctly that the time of departure was two."

" Yes, and it was quite natural he should do so. That train has always left at two ever since I can remember, and he probably has not seen the alteration."

" Then, as I have only just sufficient time to reach the station comfortably before the hour of departure, I am afraid I must go now," says Miss Sadenham, rising to her feet. "Lilian, I must ask you to excuse me."

We all rise, and the Baron slips out to see, as he whispers to me, that the porter here does not make any mistakes.

We all take a formal farewell of Miss Sadenham, Dick's adieu being a model of awkward pomposity, and she retires with great dignity, accompanied by the miserable Bentley, who is trembling lest she should revert to the imaginary story.

We wait in moderate quiet until the Baron and Bentley return.

A chorus of "Has she gone?" bursts out, and on an affirmative answer being received, a gay and riotous scene begins.

The Baron, tastefully draped in a table-cloth with a napkin tied round his head, is giving us an admirable imitation of our late companion's manner, whilst amid a shower of missiles of various sorts Bentley at the piano thumps out "The Turkish Patrol" (his only tune), to which melody the words, "The sad old frump has gone away, has gone away," etc., are sung by such of the company as are not dancing a war dance in the centre of the room. I have just been shoved up on to a chair with a cracker cap on my head to make a speech, when the door opens, and, horror of horrors! in walks Miss Sadenham.

Yes, I dare say it is cowardly, but with one bound I try to get behind the narrow window curtain, where I find at least four more of our party who have been struck by the same brilliant idea as myself. The space behind the curtain is sufficient, as they say of the cabs, for not exceeding two, and in the scuffle to crowd in, down comes the curtain with a crash, and we are disclosed holding on to one another in most picturesque attitudes.

Dick Rimington, who is facing the piano, remains quite unconscious of the disaster, bellowing out our " setting " to " The Turkish Patrol," whilst Bentley stolidly thumps the instrument.

At last, however, Dick looks round, and his voice dies away in a quaver, while Bentley with more quickness than any one would have given him credit for, dives down behind a sofa.

Alone the Baron and Mrs. Fitz stand their ground, though they look as if they wished it was any one else's.

Miss Sadenham glares at the assembled multitude with a cold and steely eye.

" I returned," she says, " for my purse, which I unfortunately, or perhaps fortunately, left on the supper table."

The Baron, with as much dignity as one can expect from a man whose head is tied up in a napkin and who has a table-cloth pinned to his back, immediately picks up the purse and presents it to Miss Sadenham with a low bow.

" Lilian," says the voice of doom, " may I ask you to come with me into the hall? I think you will admit this matter needs explanation," and out of the room Miss Sadenham stalks, followed by the unhappy Mrs. Fitz, who rejects all offers of support.

We look at one another in a rather shame-faced

way, until the ludicrous side of the adventure strikes us, and we weep with laughter.

We are just recovering, and have begun to discuss whether a relief column should not be despatched to the aid of Mrs. Fitz, when that lady dances into the room.

" She is an old darling and we are all beasts," she announces. " She is not going to say a word about it at home, and we are to go and dine with her on next Monday, and Mr. Rimington is to explain everything he says. Isn't she an old trump? "

We join in an appreciative chorus of praise, and a slightly amended version of " The dear old trump has gone away," etc., is sung with much spirit; a final glass is drunk to all our healths, and we go out into the hall.

As I put Mrs. Fitz into her cloak, she confides to me :

" It is too awful. Poor Captain Bentley was telling me how lonely his life was, when I burst out laughing. I am sure I shall never be able to explain to him why I laughed, because if I do I must tell him I was not listening to him.

" And now don't you think really, Lord Edward, that it was not quite a nice joke to play on an old lady? Ain't you a little bit sorry you proposed it? I told her I was sure you only meant it in fun, but I don't really think it was quite nice of you," and then, making a face at me like a naughty baby, she is into her carriage and away.

The Baron, with whom I share a cab home, is much pleased with his evening's amusement.

" That is," he announces, " what you call your rags. It is very funny. We will have rags very often together."

He drops me at my door soon after uttering this gruesome threat, and I climb wearily up my stairs to bed.

I hate this going to bed at two—I shall be a mere wreck to-morrow. Besides, I have a theory that I cannot sleep after a rowdy evening, especially, I reflect as I get into bed, with the noise of the traffic going on till four or five, as it does in Cairo. Quite impossible to sleep—sleep, traffic—aughr snorrr !

CHAPTER XII   MY DREAM

IN my sleep I dream a dream.

Instead of lying in my room in the close, dusty air of Cairo amid the ceaseless, sordid turmoil of the city, I am on the bank of the Great River in the country that I love, the country of the Nile, where it is not yet scattered into branches and canals, but untouched and unguided it flows along between the grim desert hills like the promise of hope in a despairing soul.

From the shape of the hills I know where I am, but all around me, save their outlines, is changed.

Magnificent buildings resplendent in colour and tracery fill the places of the desolate ruins of to-day, whilst luxuriant gardens, resonant with the sound of plashing water, occupy the spots we know as dusty wastes.

I wonder little at the change, as one does in dreams, and look around me with a deadened, listless interest.

In the distance across the river I see the peasants tilling their fields with plough and oxen, and the familiar moaning creak of the distant water-wheels strikes clearly on my ear, whilst from at hand rise the sounds of music, laughter, and many voices.

The place on which I stand is a terrace of massive and curiously carved stone-work, overhanging the very bank of the river. Its decoration is of the richest, and its pavement is covered with rich carpets and stuffs of price, the brilliancy of whose hues vies with the shimmering blue of the mountains and the sky, the glowing yellow of the distant sands, and the rich transparent green of the water.

On the terrace stands, beautifully carved in rare alabaster, a kiosk or summer-house, of which the side towards the river is open.

In this kiosk, on a raised dais of gleaming silver, is a great divan or sofa covered with tissues of gold and gems, which glitter and shine in the subdued light of the building.

Many attendants in rich fantastic clothing surround the divan, and on it is seated one whose magnificence outshines that of all the others, as the sun outshines the stars.

It needs not the majesty of his demeanour, the kingly dress or the great crown of Upper and Lower Egypt, to tell me that I am in the presence of the great monarch, Pharaoh, King of Egypt.

By his side is a man whose noble presence is scarcely less striking than that of Pharaoh, though the half-bent attitude and deferential manner show that in the eyes of men he is his inferior and subject.

Though dressed in the rich clothes of a noble of Egypt, the strongly marked features, sad eyes, and heavy lip, make him a man apart from those who stand around him.

As he speaks, I know that his speech is that of a foreigner, though what tongue he uses I know not.

His words smite on my ear as they reach me, as if they were of vital importance to me.

"Therefore, let not the heart of Pharaoh be troubled for the crying of this people.

"Let Pharaoh remember that when it was fore-told him that famine would come on this land, Pharaoh stretched forth his hand and took the fifth part of the land and the produce thereof, and this, by the King's command, was stored in the King's storehouse in the charge of the keepers of the store-houses. And when the famine came upon the land and was very grievous in the land, Pharaoh bought the land of Egypt for the bread which he gave from the storehouses wherein he had stored the produce of the land, even of the fifth part of the land of Egypt which Pharaoh had taken into his hand.

"From that time forth the people have given to Pharaoh one-fifth of all the produce of the land, and now they cry out, saying, ' Give us this also.'

"But let the King not turn his ear to the foolish crying of his people.

"For though this people are as sheep before the King and tremble at his word, they will not regard the morrow nor what it will bring forth, neither will they save of the fruit of the earth to put it aside, nor will they keep of their abundance so that in the year of plenty they waste their substance, and in the years of dearth they cry for bread, and so it will ever be with this people.

" Now through the might of Pharaoh and through his wisdom, the King's granaries and his storehouses and his barns are full, and if so be that a famine come upon the land, then shall the plenty of years serve the leanness of other years, and this people will eat bread and live and not die.

"Therefore let Pharaoh not hearken to this people; for if the corn were given to them they would surely waste it, and when the famine was upon the land, they would cry for bread, and because there was no bread they would die."

As this speech ends, the King makes a sign of his gracious assent, and immediately the scene is obscured by swirling clouds of darkness, through which the water-wheels shrill out their monotonous chant ever clearer and louder.

After a space, the clouds melt, and I find myself in a well-known room in Cairo, where I have so often heard the problems of the Government of Egypt discussed and the policy which was to govern her shaped.

The figure that is sitting in the well-remembered attitude at the table makes me start with surprise. Has he come back to help us, or was it merely an evil dream that he ever went?

As I wonder how it is, I hear one of those with whom he seems to be conferring say in familiar tones:

" To put it shortly, our object is this : To prevent

the peasant from squandering in the years in which he does well, and borrowing in the years when he does badly. This, we believe, our proposal will effect.

" If you, sir, approve and will support us, we intend to put the machinery we have discussed in motion as soon as possible."

The figure gives the quick decided nod of assent I knew so well, and the thick clouds of murky darkness again sweep swirling over the scene, whilst again the song of the water-wheels rises high and clear in the air.

When the darkness is again disseminated, I am in a stately hall, bare and severe in aspect and simple in its richness. My eyes turn towards the windows, and I see that I am still in Cairo, for through them I see the Mokattam " red with the blood of the dying sun " standing out against the azure sky.

A group of men seated round a table in the centre of the chamber I should take to be negroes, from the dusky hue of their faces, did not their refined and intellectual features show me that they belong to some race of which I have never even heard before.

One is speaking in some strange, sweet, liquid tongue to the chief or President of the Council, for so it seems to be.

" The matter of thrift has ever been mismanaged or neglected in this country. Ignorant and barbaric races have made feeble and abortive attempts to teach the peasant to save and put by, or have devised crude and unpractical schemes to do it for him.

" I have already explained that all these efforts were on hopelessly mistaken lines, and even our own measures of reform in this direction have so far met with no great success.

" The plan we now propose is, however, on totally new lines, and if adopted, we may safely predict that it will accomplish, in a few months, what others have failed to bring about in centuries and millenniums; that is, to teach the peasants of Egypt to be thrifty, and while they are learning, to protect them from the results of their want of forethought."

The President signifies his approval amid a hum of applause, and again my view is obscured by darkness.

The whining notes of the water-wheels sound louder than ever, and have, to my ear, a derisive and defiant ring. As the clouds again part for a minute, I see the peasants at work tilling their fields; and though they are attired differently from those of our time, it seems to me that they are the same people; and that, except for their dress, the Children of the Nile have neither altered nor changed since the days of Pharaoh, King of Egypt, and Joseph his Minister.

And so I awoke.

LORD KITCHENER

LORD KITCHENER

[This sketch was being written when Lord Edward Cecil was taken ill of influenza just before he died.]

I AM writing this whilst nursing a bad lung at the top of a Swiss mountain. I have to hand neither my old letters, portions of diaries, nor other documents which might aid my memory. This is no attempt at more than a sketch from memory of those characteristics of the great man which impressed themselves on me in the personal contact with Lord Kitchener I had the honour to experience.

I cannot accurately remember when exactly it was that I saw him first. It was at Hatfield, and my father had asked him down. My mother, I think, had never seen him. My father, who had met him in the course of business, was much impressed with him. That I clearly remember, for my father was not often impressed.

I remember little of his visit except that he got up at what appeared to me then a godless hour— six. The day at Hatfield began at 9.30, if you felt energetic.

He subsequently came to dine with me on guard. I should like to think I patronised him, but I am pretty sure I did not, as one glance from that eye would have put me back in my proper place. I know I asked him to take me as his A.D.C. some day, and I can only explain my temerity by the fact that one drank plenty of champagne on guard in those days.

I cannot call to mind when I saw him again, but I think it was when he came to London after the incident when the young Khedive insulted him at Halfa. " Naughty boy, naughty boy! " he said, gravely shaking his head. He had very little vindictiveness, and when, years later, I told him how I disliked the Khedive, he could scarcely understand me. The Khedive was not important enough to dislike. He might hate some one who wrecked his plans, and he would even have gone (whatever others might think) very far to remove such an obstacle, but a man who merely insulted him did not seem important.

If one could say that there was a key to his character, that there was one predominating salient, it was that he thought of the end of the task he had in hand, the fulfilment of what he had set himself or others had set him to do, before—much before— everything else. Comfort, affections, personalities, all were quite inferior considerations. The aim before everything. He felt he was defrauding the Almighty if he did not carry out his task. This characteristic is mentioned by itself because, on its being understood and remembered, the comprehension of the character depends.

When the Nile Expedition of '96 began, I received a telegram offering to take me as A.D.C. I naturally accepted with enthusiasm. It must not be thought that I have or had any illusions as to the reason of his patronage. My father was Foreign Secretary and Prime Minister, and it was to please him it was done, and for that reason alone. Lord Cromer was not in favour of a forward Sudan policy, and Kitchener was. My father's support was vital to his whole plan, and I, by reflected light, became of importance.

I served with him through the campaign, and cannot truthfully say that I liked him at that period. He was much more uncouth and uncivilised at that time than he was later. He used to have little consideration for any one, and was *cassant* and rude. He was always inclined to bully his own entourage, as some men are rude to their wives. He was inclined to let off his spleen on those round him. He was often morose and silent for hours together. He was an uncomfortable chief, too, as he never let you know when he was going to do anything. He liked to slip away by himself, but he did not like your letting him do so. He would take his meals at any hour, and after a tiring day in midsummer in the Sudan the staff might have to wait till ten for their dinner, which maybe was then eaten in solemn silence. His " nerves " showed in roughness and harshness, and he was playing a very big game. The War Office, who thought the whole campaign should have been turned over to them, were against him, and would not have been broken-hearted at his failure. Lord Cromer openly disliked the campaign, and took a pessimistic view of the situation; and Lord Cromer meant not only the Egyptian Government, with Gorst, who was bitterly opposed to Kitchener, at its head, but also a large portion of Foreign Office opinion. So it was on my father's support and that of those with him that Kitchener rested. He did not know my father well, nor how far he could be depended on, and he had to fight the campaign with a rope round his neck. If he failed, it was absolute and complete failure; no white-washing or glossing over the awkward parts, nothing but failure and a definite end to his career, and all the plans then in his head, which, alas! he never completed—the foundation of the Viceroyalty of the Near East and North Africa.

The points that struck me as a simple onlooker were his aloofness, for he seemed to confide much in no one, and his extraordinary grasp of detail. It was almost true to say there was no department of the Egyptian Army which he did not know as well as the departmental officials; and though as a force it was tiny, a small force has just as many, or nearly as many, departments as a large one.

In his person he was very neat and always scrupulously clean. He tolerated laxity on these points with difficulty. On the other hand, his office was a sea of papers lying on tables, chairs, window-sills, the floor. No one but himself knew where any particular paper or subject was kept or could find anything. He never let any one touch them except Watson, Bailey, if there, and a few others in whom he had confidence. I have heard him ask an officer whom he had sent for not to stand on the Supplies returns.

He would wander off at that curious stalking stride of his soon after dawn to the railway yard, the embarkation place, the store yards, or whatever interested him for the minute. He saw everything —nothing escaped him; but he officially saw or did not see as much as he chose. Sometimes he seemed to like one with him, but more often he liked to walk ahead, plunged apparently in sombre meditation. He usually got three good hours' work done before breakfast. He worked on then, except for lunch, till six in the evening, when he liked very often to have a gin or vermouth and soda and talk. It was his most human time. He would then go back to work till dinner, which might be at any hour, and went early to his room. Whether he worked habitually at night I don't know, but I often saw his light burning late.

In mind, from long experience of the East, he was cynical, and inclined to disbelieve that any action sprang from motives other than those of self-interest —or rather, he affected to be. He had in reality the greatest confidence in those who were worthy of it, and he was rarely if ever taken in. His cynicism was in a large measure a part of the curious shyness which declined to show any inside portion of his life or mind. He loathed any form of moral or mental undressing. He was even morbidly afraid of showing any feeling or enthusiasm, and he preferred to be misunderstood rather than be suspected of human feeling. Combined with this cynicism and suspicion, partly the result of many years' Eastern experience, and partly assumed as a cloak for other feelings, was a natural and almost child-like simplicity, both in his outlook on life and his display of what most of us hide with care.

He had not a trace of the hypocrite in his composition, nor even that quality which merges into the hypocrisy of moral decency. If he was going to break the moral law in any way, he said so. He used to shock and surprise the respectable terribly. This side of his character was naturally misunderstood. It depended on the dominant characteristic I have alluded to. If he wanted subscriptions for an object which he had decided was worthy, he took them or forced them out of people, if they could be got in no other way. If you examined it, he did not go much further than we all do, but he disdained to cover over his proceedings with any coat of obscuring varnish. We all get royal personages to open bazaars because we know it makes the receipts bigger. Lord Kitchener, when he found he had a price, so to speak, as a personage, coolly asked for a subscription to the Gordon College as the price of his being used a a figurehead. In the same way, for his own state and dignity, he needed plate which he could not afford to buy; instead of sending a roundabout message through three or four people that he would prefer a present of plate to a gold casket when he received the freedom of the city of Barchester, he told the Mayor and Corporation plainly what he wanted. His point was that this or that was, he considered, necessary, and the means of obtaining it were of secondary importance.

Another reason for his apparently surly disposition at this time was health. His digestion was bad and he suffered from the extreme heat, for in the summer of '96 we were with but little shelter in the hottest place, so it is said on good authority, on the globe. He was also all through his life subject to a most acute form of headache, which naturally did not tend towards geniality. Again, he had to maintain discipline amongst his officers and staff. The British officers of the Egyptian Army were not a very united body at that period. There was a frontier party, by far the largest, which believed in Hunter and did not like Kitchener, whose severity, and the economy he was forced by circumstances and superior authority to insist on, had not tended towards personal popularity. Very outspoken criticism was not uncommon, and a tight hand was needed to keep matters straight.

We stayed first at Halfa for some time, and then gradually, as the river rose and it was possible to bring up our boats, advanced, till finally we pushed back the dervishes and reached Dongola. It must not be imagined that the sailing was plain. The difficulty of supplying a force of even fifteen thousand men was immense; the only means of communication beyond camels (which then, as ever, died as fast as one could replace them, a camel being as fitted for regular supply transport work as a Bohemian for a domestic life) was a hastily laid railway, passing over very difficult country, with appalling gradients and curves, the rolling-stock of which largely dated from the time of the Khedive Ismail. Thirty miles of this line were washed away in a night when we had only five days' rations for the whole army. Several of our best boats were much damaged coming through the cataracts, and the north wind was unusually late in starting that year, which made our sailing-boats far slower than had been hoped. Cholera broke out, and at one time looked as if it would paralyse the whole operation.

All through these disasters Kitchener's energy and determination never wavered, though he was querulous about them, with that queer simplicity to which I have alluded. He grumbled that he was doing his best, and if the powers above stopped him it was unfair and hard, and so on. The only time he at all broke down was over a matter which was in itself apparently of no really vital importance. We had built a new type of gunboat above the cataracts, and this was—both for its practical value, for great things were hoped from its speed and armament, and also because it was in a great measure his own idea—the apple of his eye. By straining every nerve it was ready in time for the advance to Dongola, but on its trial trip it blew out a low-pressure cylinder and had to be left behind.

This accident made him quite miserable, and affected him as accidents of far greater importance had not. We dared not speak of the matter for a couple of days, until the new parts were on their way up-country. Whether it was merely the pro-verbial last straw late on in a very hot summer and after many trials had been gone through, or whether he attached some importance of which we knew nothing to the presence of this particular boat in the advance, I don't know. It was one of the many points one would have asked him some day on some favourable occasion, but which one will never know now.

As illustrating how little he knew of my father's character at this time, he remonstrated with me for writing in too cold a style a weekly report I sent him by Kitchener's direction. He gave me as a model a piece of prose he had dictated which would have made the most hardened ink-slinger of the *Daily*

Mail blush. He did not insist when I demurred, but I am sure he was convinced I was wrong.

When he got back to Cairo, after keeping me in suspense for three days, he let me go back to England, where I met him later.

I went to Abyssinia in '97, and did not see him again till I joined his staff near Abu Hamed in '98 in the Khartoum Expedition. Though his general characteristics were, of course, the same, he had already softened a good deal. He felt more sure of his position and backing. His team pulled well together, and everything worked far more smoothly. Transport remained his great difficulty, as the stiffening of the force by a brigade of British had rendered any misbehaviour on the part of the Egyptian Army more unlikely. We got to the Atbara, proceeded up that river to dispose of Mahmud, and then went on by boat for the final stage of the campaign—the attack on Khartoum itself. When Omdurman had fallen I had the good luck to go over alone with Lord Kitchener to Khartoum—as usual, he took no escort but his orderlies. He was certainly moved by the historical associations, taking trouble to identify the place where Gordon actually fell and that where his body lay unburied. He was, as he always was to the poor, gentle and kind to an old gardener, who came to him weeping, as he thought he would be sent away, after fifty years' service, but his mind was really in the future. He was already rebuilding the capital of the Sudan, and his eyes were fixed on the south. The task first before everything—the reconquest of the Sudan and its re-establishment—was what he really cared for; and the intense interest of seeing the place to which so much historical and sentimental interest attached could not obscure this even temporarily.

In course of time we returned to Cairo, and I went home to rejoin my regiment. Lord Kitchener came home shortly after, and, owing to the mismanagement of the police, had the greatest difficulty in getting away from Victoria Station. He lived, as he usually did when in London, in Pandeli Ralli's house in Belgrave Square, which he temporarily annexed. He was a dangerous man to go and see in London, as, quite regardless of the fact that you had other things to do, he seized you and set you to work on whatever he thought you could do efficiently. Few—I was going to say no one, and I am not sure it is not nearer the truth—dared refuse; and the result was that the house was always full of the most heterogeneous elements, grumbling over their servitude, but often, if they had any sense of humour, amused at the situation. A very proper friend of mine spent his time in burning, after seeing there was nothing important in them, the mass of love-letters which descended on Kitchener, and which would have offended him. He placed women on a far higher level than is usual in these days, and it really hurt him to hear or see anything which touched this ideal. Another very sensitive man of great natural politeness spent his time in interviewing the most intimidating people, such as multimillionaires, corporations, big banks, and firms, to obtain from them contributions to the Gordon College. He used to come back in the evening, looking as if he had been at a disturbed mass meeting, and gloomily wonder what Kitchener would say to the result.

I saw Kitchener from time to time after this, but not in sufficient intimacy to see anything of his character. I met him for a few hours at Pretoria during the South African campaign, and afterwards from time to time in England, but I was never really close to him again till he came out to Egypt, when a terrified Government were trying to keep him out of the public eye. Whether he was then Inspector-General of the Forces or High Commissioner of the Mediterranean, for the moment I forget. But I remember well how, without saying a word or asserting himself in any way, he took charge of us all and we dropped back into our old places. At Khartoum might be seen the curious sight of a Governor-General being severely spoken to by an unofficial traveller, and very frightened the Governor-General looked because the alignment of one of the streets had been altered.

Except casually, I saw no more of him till he came to Egypt again in 1912, when I saw him practically every day until the War broke out in 1914.

I have set down all these details, as it is necessary to divide any appreciation, however humble, of his character into periods. No man was greater in one respect—he never ceased learning. He had none of that almost universal vanity which makes us conceal or slur over what we do not know. When he came to something he did not know, he immediately looked round for some one who did, and if the matter was one with which he saw he would be concerned in the future, he learnt as much as he could about it.

The Kitchener of 1912 was a genial man of the world, laughing at matters which would have irritated him profoundly in '96. During this time one naturally saw him more closely and under more normal conditions. The stress of a campaign and the magnitude of the immediate stakes temporarily deform the character. You would not say you knew a man, or be able to give a good picture of him, if you had only met him at a fire.

One appreciated more quietly the great qualities of Lord Kitchener when one saw him day by day, as one also became more acutely conscious of the oddities and contrasts of his character. What struck one almost first was the vitality of his mind. He was always doing something, planning something—and something big. He never was for a moment satisfied. No one understood more thoroughly and practically that life is far too short for all you ought to do. His mind was always devising something fresh, some new improvement, some move forward in the path he followed. This continual feeling of hurry was very stimulating, but very tiring. One lived, like the Jules Verne men dosed with oxygen, at a double rate. The mind might be middle-aged, the illusions of youth might be gone and a rough cynicism have taken their place, but the vitality of the young man was unimpaired—there was none of the hesitation or the let-things-take-their-course of an old man.

This energy was sometimes misplaced, and he would assume the personal control of a lot of details which were really not within his province, and which he could not do efficiently. These periods were, as a rule, short, and his inferiors had ever to be ready to pick up the threads where they were dropped.

The second quality he shared with nearly all first-rate men, and that was the accuracy of his mental perspective. Big things only were big to him—to quote the criticism on Bright, he went from headland to headland, and left to others the exploration of the bays and creeks between.

He instantly saw the dangers of the land problem in Egypt, the overcrowding, the land-hunger, the absenteeism, and the inevitable discontent and political trouble that must arise. This led to his enormous drainage and irrigation projects, which had reached twenty-three millions when he left, and would have been nearer forty. He took up a policy like Lord Cromer's of favouring the peasants and constituted himself their protector and friend. He was quite civil to the intellectuals, and entered into any harmless schemes they put forward; but he was firmly convinced that they were of no importance from a political point of view.

He was naturally and ever on the side of the weak and the oppressed. No one was perhaps in a sense more dictatorial, but no one was more truly just or had more reverence for the rights of his poorer fellows. The oppression of the *fellaheen*, and the way in which the half-civilised upper classes of Egypt regard them as little better than animals, stirred Lord Kitchener to the depths of his character. I often used to wonder what the feelings of some of the *pashas* would have been if they could have seen his real opinion of them in his face.

A DAY ON THE SUEZ CANAL
(1905)

[At the time these notes were written, Lord Edward Cecil was in the Egyptian Army.]

ACCORDING to my promise, I write again to tell you the result of the explosion expedition. Unluckily, it was decided to postpone the event until after the British mail had passed through the Canal. In the interval the Suez Canal authorities, who are exclusively foreign, consulted each other and let their minds dwell on the more sombre side of the question. A darker tinge was given to their thoughts by the daily Press, which apparently employed the lineal descendants of Ananias to write up the question; and finally the Suez Canal Board in Paris sent urgent instructions to them to save as many lives as possible, but to die like men and Frenchmen.

During this time they communicated frequently with the Native Governor of Port Said, who at first treated the matter in a most philosophical spirit, until they explained to him that probably his town would be wrecked, but in any case it was his duty to be present on the scene of action, as it was in his province. He then not only took a deep interest in the whole question, but firmly announced his intention of remaining in Port Said to calm the terror-stricken populace.

As we all know, prolonged discussion of a subject

from a pessimistic point of view only increases depression; and when your humble servant came on the scene, "Melancholy had marked them for her own."

I was first brought into the matter by being informed by the Prime Minister that the Canal authorities wanted me to furnish a military cordon round the scene of the cataclysm. This appeared to me to be a wise precaution as long as the Egyptian Army were not allowed to meddle with the actual explosives, but hardly as useful in a desert as in a populous country. However, I asked if I was to make my own dispositions or to take my instructions from the Canal authorities. The answer was that I was to carry out the wishes of the Canal Company, who desired that the cordon should be at least five kilometres from the explosion. A moment's thought showed me that the cordon would have to be thirty kilometres in length, and allowing one man to ten yards, it would take three thousand and odd men, which was rather more than I had in Cairo. But, as I wisely reflected, they would not have any one to stop if they wanted to, and it really did not matter how far apart they were, except for the dullness of the thing. I said I would do as they wished, and after discussing the matter with our only expert, who was once ploughed in a special examination on explosives, we decided that a hundred men would be quite enough to line from the Canal to the nearest sandhill, and that, following the practice of the manœuvres and field-days of our native land, the rest of the cordon should be " imaginary," because, unless the Lost Tribes returned by the way they set out, no one would think of coming in from that part of the desert. Our only danger was that an excited Canal man should take it into his head to inspect the cordon.

I started the troops off at eleven on Wednesday, as the explosion was fixed for dawn on Thursday, and had them camped for the night on the scene of prospective carnage. I had been for the last few days honoured by various communications from the Governor of Port Said, who seemed to have a vague idea that explosives could be kept in order by the military like a disorderly crowd. He had a strong opinion that I ought to do something vigorous to make the dynamite understand that it could not explode as it liked in the Khedive's dominions, but must do so, if at all, decently and in order. I expressed my willingness to assist his Excellency in any way in my power, but generally held that this dynamite was essentially civil, being for mining purposes. This was to avoid any suggestion that the Egyptian Army should have anything to do with the matter, as I have explained above. On Wednesday the Governor began to feel more concerned than ever about his poor frightened populace, and suggested that he should come to Cairo to discuss the matter and stop over Thursday morning. After the troops had left for their post, he wired that it had been decided to make the radius of the cordon ten kilometres instead of five, so as to save what we could of our troops; he added that this was on the advice of the great French experts, who had telegraphed from Paris. At first I was annoyed, as it seemed to me to be a half-measure. Why not really play for safety and let the cordon stay in Cairo? A moment's thought, however, showed me how little it mattered, owing to our great foresight in employing the "imaginary" system. Once you accept this great principle, you can make a cordon of any size you like with any number of men. Here we were providing a first-rate cordon of sixty kilometres in length (which would have needed six thousand men at least under the old-fashioned systems) with one hundred men! It only shows what a lot of nonsense is talked about our War Office when they say that they never invented anything but new buttons. I am sure if the Boers had really grasped that system the war would have been much shorter, but they were stupid folk. So I wired back agreeing cordially with the French experts' idea, and sent telegraphic orders to the Officer in Command to "imagine" another thirty kilometres of cordon of the finest description.

As the O.C. is naturally a truthful man, I thought I had better go down and help him, and also see the explosion. I got there late on Wednesday night, and sent one of our party to find out from the British expert (who had been sent out by Nobel's) what was going to be done.

He appeared to be in a somewhat irritable condition, as he disliked receiving different orders every hour, and I could see was not at all the man to be happy under the Canal Company or our War Office, or any really up-to-date body like that. He was the one grim touch in our farce. He knew that the dynamite had, owing to the action of the sea water and some chemical manure which formed part of the cargo, become unstable and dangerous. The least shock might send it off. He had, knowing this, to go and lay two mines in the ship, and connect them by an electric wire with the firing battery. He was confident that the explosion would be very local in its effect, as the high explosives usually are, and in his benighted ignorance put the danger zone down at one mile, at the outside.

The inhabitants of Port Said disagreed profoundly with him: some left for Cairo, some sat on the beach in sort of bomb-proof shelters, and some actually put out to sea. By order of the Canal Company the ships in the harbour were double cabled, and all windows were to be left open, though the actual scene of the explosion was twenty kilometres away.

On the fatal morning we proceeded to the railway station, where we found the senior officials of the Canal assembled. Only the seniors were allowed to come, on the old Hatfield Station principle that only people of some local importance may cross the line in front of an express, and, accompanied by twenty members of the local Press, we got into a special train that was waiting to run us out. I was glad to notice that we took out two ambulance waggons, but the absence of any coffins struck me as evidence of carelessness on the part of somebody. The Governor was unluckily detained by business of importance, which report says he conducted on his face in a cellar.

On arriving at the scene of action we alighted, and

I was pleased to see how well the cordon looked, and quite regretted that they had no one to keep back. In this I was wrong, as I found out afterwards.

I now devoted myself to answering the various questions of the Canal authorities, which were summed up by the Agent Supérieur, who said, " Then, milor, one can be assured that the military preparations are complete? " I assured him that everything that the most modern science of war could suggest had been done, and we bowed. It was an impressive sight—we two great men having our final interview, surrounded by the members of the Press, note-book in hand. I then was interviewed by the remaining Canal authorities in order of seniority, who each drew my attention to some point they wished me to consider, and after replying in suitable terms we bowed. I now decided to cross the Canal, partly to get a better view and partly to avoid an attack of hysterics, of which the premonitory symptoms had begun. I also was developing a severe form of lumbago : punctuating all your remarks by a bow needs a practised back if it is to be done with impunity.

I got into a small boat and crossed over. The Canal authorities begged me to be quick, and to have the boat removed from the water as soon as I could, as a tidal wave would sweep down the Canal, wrecking all ships, both great and small, in its path. Getting the boat out was a business ; and the Canal Company was nearly a Commissaire-Général, or something like that, short over the job, as in his enthusiasm he lent a hand and had the boat deposited on his toe by the willing but clumsy Egyptian privates. He murmured "*Sapristi!*" in a tone of deep anguish, and sat down in the Canal, producing a magnificent tidal wave on his own account. We helped him out and bowed, and he bowed, maimed and wet as he was.

After a breathless period of suspense, enlivened by the French doctor's reminiscences, which might have been entitled "Operations I Have Performed," suddenly a great column of vapour shot up into the air and then expanded into a great mushroom, from the edges of which we could see tiny black specks (you must remember we were six miles off) falling. Through our glasses we could see the waters seething and boiling in an indescribable way at the foot of the huge mushroom.

We remained listening for what seemed to be an interminable time, and at last we heard a tremendous thud, as if something soft had fallen from a great height. Meanwhile, we had been nerving ourselves for the explosion wind and the tidal wave. We were, so our foreign experts had warned us, to be blown forward on our faces as the air rushed in to fill the vacuum caused by the detonation of the dynamite, and then swept from our sandy bed into the Canal by a tidal wave twenty feet high, which would rush down the Canal at the pace of a galloping horse. I had already selected a position where I should not be crushed under the flabby but massive form of one of the Agents Supérieurs, but at the same time near enough to him to use him as a life-buoy during the tidal wave part of the programme. The maimed Commissaire remained in a prone position in anticipation. He was a kindly man who wished to give as little trouble as possible, even to hurricanes and tidal waves. We waited in constrained attitudes which gradually relaxed as each individual decided in his own mind that he was looking a trifle silly, and we attempted to induce the remainder of our fellow-creatures present to believe that we usually looked on at interesting ceremonies with our teeth clenched and our heads bent. It was a beautiful sight to see successive smiles light up those monumental French faces and the natural ruddy hue steal back to the leaden cheeks. It reminded me of a sunrise in the Alps, when peak after peak catches the golden glow. We re-crossed the Canal humming little songs in a nonchalant manner, as if we had been waiting for nothing in particular. Launching the boat was difficult to do with dignity, but we let the soldiers do it while we looked at the view, and only turned round when she was in the water. It really was a little hard. If only there had been a gust of wind from any quarter we could have pretended it was the result of the explosion; if there had been one ripple our faces would have been saved; but no! I have never seen in Egypt so absolutely still a day, and the waters of the Canal were as smooth as glass. Once over, things went better, and we mounted the train to be carried nearer to the scene of destruction. I was glad to notice that a tactful railway official had got rid of the hospital car.

We were prepared for the worst now, and it was lucky. Mile after mile was passed and no sign of the explosion was visible. In fact, until we came within the danger zone according to the despised Briton, the face of nature was unchanged, except where the Canal Company had pulled things down to avoid their being broken. When we did get close there was much to look at, and it was very interesting. Everything was shredded, after the manner of dynamite. It seems to tear things up into small pieces. Great pieces of iron and steel, torn, not broken, lay about in all directions, and the wood was in many cases literally pulped. We spent a most interesting hour there examining the effects of the shock. A mass of earth two hundred feet long by sixty wide had been blown clean out of the solid bank against which the ship had lain, *and that earth had disappeared.* Where it went to I don't know; but I suppose it was scattered abroad in small fragments. Great fish were picked up in the desert a hundred yards from the Canal bank, and some of the heavier pieces of iron flew a thousand yards before they came to a standstill.

On one thing we—I mean the British portion of the onlookers—congratulated ourselves, and that was that the *entente cordiale* had been preserved unclouded throughout the day. I remarked on this with much satisfaction to the English head of the railways, who was with us, as we ran up the line in our " special " to visit the southern limit of the danger zone. He cordially agreed, when, as we slowed down preparatory to stopping at the point where the cordon crossed the line, we heard a terrible sound. There was no mistaking it. It was the voice of a Frenchman hoarse with rage objurgating some one, and the first words we made out were—well, I cannot translate them, but they included the expression *sales Anglais.* I rushed to the window and

beheld a scene far more terrible than any explosion.
About twenty yards from the train stood our newest
subaltern, who hails from the Far West of Ireland,
with his legs apart, with an amused but tolerant smile
on his face, and the general attitude and expression
of some one passing a few idle minutes by teasing
an irritable lap-dog. In front of him, I cannot
say stood, as he was never still for one second, the
most *supérieur* of all the Agents. He was a very
small, very fat and very fussy little man, who had
often made me wonder how he contained such an
enormous opinion of himself in so small a body. At
that moment he was not looking his best. He was a
rich crimson with rage and exertion, and he was
performing a sort of war dance which, though, as I
was subsequently informed, it had begun as a sort
of lively polka, had now from pure exhaustion
degenerated into a kind of negro shuffle. His voice
was nearly gone, and it seemed merely a question
of seconds before he had a fit. As I scrambled
out of the train, I heard my Irish subordinate sum
up the case as follows: " It is no good, monsieur;
I have told you you cannot go through the cordon,
and you're not going; but if you like dancing in the
sun and screaming I shan't stop you." Here he
was cut short by a yell of fury which eclipsed all the
previous efforts of the enraged little man. In the
background stood a mob of Greeks, half-castes, and
natives, who were all jabbering at the top of their
voices like a stage crowd.

I hastened forward, accompanied by my railway
friend, who in the excitement of the moment began
talking fluently in a mixture of French, German,

Arabic, and Hindustani. On seeing me, the Frenchman rushed forward and launched a torrent of hoarse whispers at me. He was nearly inaudible, and when he was not, one wished he had been. As far as I followed, he proposed taking the case into the Consular Court, sending for the French Fleet, driving the English into the sea, and shooting my Irishman at seven the next morning. In the midst of the tornado I had time to be thankful that my Milesian did not know a solitary word of French; as if he had done so we should have probably had to fish the Agent out of the Canal, always supposing that he was not in bits. He (the Frenchman) walked up and down raving, and I perspired after him, never getting a word in; and I began to think we should go on until his fit began or he dropped down from sheer exhaustion. But at last I remembered being told never to give way to a man in this condition. So I bellowed in my best French: " It appears, sir, you forget to whom you are speaking." At first it looked as if my experiment was going to be a failure. He changed from crimson to purple, but luckily he was quite unable to speak. At this juncture a less *supérieur* Agent rushed forward and murmured that I was the Minister. It was not true, and seemed to me an absolutely futile contribution to the conversation; but I had forgotten a Frenchman's respect for a Minister. By an effort which must have permanently strained him, he recovered himself, and muttering that I must excuse him, as he was outside himself, he fled into an adjoining hut. After a decent interval I followed, and we made speeches to each other and were very dignified. Keeping in front of the window in order to prevent his seeing the culprit, I pointed out that he, the offender, was cut to the heart at the way he had been treated for merely doing his duty and obeying the orders, not of myself, but the Canal Company, etc. I could hear the young ruffian whistling airs from *The Little Michus*, with variations, and my only hope was the Frenchman would not hear him too. However, all went well, and he admitted that he had misunderstood my officer, which was luckily quite true. The culprit was called in, and shook the Agent by the hand with a bright smile in which no form of penitence appeared. We then drank weird drinks together, and parted full of mutual esteem and with as many compliments as my exhausted French could put into words. So we fared gaily back to Cairo and agreed, as my Irishman said: " Rum beggars, those Froggies, but quite decent when you get to know them and they keep their hair on."

A WELL-MANAGED CEREMONY

I AM just getting over the effects of a funeral which I attended the other day.

I received a message from the Governor of Cairo that one Ahmed Izzet, ex-Minister of War, etc., in the year one, was dead, and the funeral was at four.

I cursed heartily, but I felt I ought to go, with which all my subordinates, who had received no invitation, cordially agreed.

It was literally the hottest day of the year—108 degrees in the shade; but I, with heroic courage, put on a frock-coat (black, but the only one I have), and a tarboosh, and arming myself with a large green-and-white umbrella, proceeded to the house of deceased at 3.45.

It is the custom on these occasions to sit round a room in the house of the defunct for some time before the funeral actually begins, and (nominally) discuss the good qualities of the deceased, the shortness of life, and other cheering topics.

When I arrived, already, saving your presence, dripping, I was ushered into a tent (instead of the usual room) which had been pitched in the gentleman's garden, and on which the sun beat fiercely. From mere force of habit I very nearly undressed and asked for a towel, as the temperature was that of a Turkish bath.

I was installed in a nice " cool " red plush armchair with yellow tassels and gold braid. I wanted badly to put up an umbrella, but I felt even the high position of a Financial Adviser, combined with the well-known lunacy of my race, would scarcely have protected me from ridicule.

I looked round on the company, and found I was the only European. On my left was an official representing H.H. in an even gayer and hotter arm-chair than mine; and on the other side an old gentleman who has indefinite claims on the Government for a large pension.

The official, who is, I think, the greatest rogue but three in all Egypt, is an old enemy of mine, so the conversation was rather sparse on that side, whilst on the other I heard again the purely imaginary story of my old claimant. As a work of fiction it was admirable, but very complicated to follow and containing things one does not like to think about on a hot day, such as, if a man's service begins according to his story at a date when you know he was only two years old, is it likely that he was, as stated at that time, the most trusted Inspector of Customs? or can one by an effort believe that he was dismissed from the service by a series of plots which were carried on by all the high officials of the Government, with Lord Cromer's assistance and the countenance of all the judges of the Mixed Court? or to say that he stole was a lie, for there was nothing to steal, and he replaced it on the next day, when the accounts were found correct, but his chief stole largely.

I bore it and they bored me. (Joke.)

After the usual twenty minutes I began to feel uncharitable towards the family for not going on with the funeral. What were my feelings when the official explained that at the last moment it was decided to give the deceased a military funeral, and a battalion and a gun-carriage had been sent for !

Of course, I knew what that meant. We sat for one hour and a quarter waiting in that temperature. As it is Ramadan the natives were all fasting, and felt the heat even more than I did.

After a time, when the conversation did turn on the deceased, it was not at all complimentary, and the official, who, except for low cunning, has few intellectual qualities, said that this man always mismanaged everything, alluding, I suppose, to his dying during Ramadan, or mismanaging his own funeral, which I thought hard.

At last the welcome sound of English blasphemy in the street announced the arrival of two British officers followed by a semi-mutinous battalion which looked as if it had dressed *en route*. But no gun-carriage. This apparently had been ordered still later.

We waited on, and I amused myself by nodding and smiling to various extreme nationalists who were glaring at me from the other side of the tent. It is an amusing pastime, as their friends immediately edge away from them, believing they are spies. I made one man so miserable by my cordiality that he got up on the plea of illness and left. I caught him at the door and thanked him for his services, and he has been, I believe, explaining it away ever since, but he will never get them to believe it was my form of humour.

Even this soon palled; and, besides that, I felt

that by continued deliquescence I was like a Boojum Snark—vanishing away.

The official, who for the last ten minutes had been interspersing deep groans of heat and exhaustion with Arabic oaths of a most unsuitable nature, looked at his watch. From crimson he became black. " My dinner," he gasped, " I shall be late for my dinner." And, rising to his feet, he announced that the deceased must be carried to the cemetery on men's shoulders, as the gun-carriage, it might be by the will of Allah, would never come. A sound nearly resembling a cheer arose from the mourners, and in a jiffy the deceased, slung on two broom handles and a clothes prop, started down the road to the solemn strains of the Funeral March (imperfectly executed in rather quick time because we were late).

The official and I, at the head of a motley crowd of exhausted mourners, followed through the stinks and dust of old Cairo.

The official, recovering his self-importance, which I really believe is larger than his waistcoat, kept on marshalling the procession and sending advice to the military officers on how military funerals should be run.

The messengers he sent returned with the air of men who had seen affliction.

I myself had wisely avoided speaking to the British commandant, and I am sure if the Pasha had heard how his messengers where received, he would have reserved his advice for another and cooler season.

His Excellency, full of military ardour, now made a frantic effort to keep step to the music, giving a sort of little hop whenever he thought he was out of step, which averaged out at about once in four steps. The unsophisticated mourners thought, I suppose, that this was part of the ceremonial of a military funeral, and religiously imitated him. I only looked back once, as after that I dared not, for fear of disgracing myself and hurting people's feelings, but I shall never forget that fat and superheated body of men hopping gravely down that sun-scorched road with agony written on every feature of their broad but expressive countenances.

Another incident occurred which again nearly destroyed my character.

An aged Mullah or Turkish priest announced that he wished to carry the deceased. He meant, poor old man, to lay his hand on one of the broom handles in a ceremonial way.

Not so was it understood by the dirty and perspiring gardener who had been pressed into the service. He quickly placed the handle on the old man's shoulder, who immediately subsided into the roadway and was carried home, whilst I and the official rushed forward just in time to save a catastrophe.

The official, in tones which pierced the music, announced his opinion of the gardener and his family, and amid murmurs of applause from the mourners resumed his hopping with moody determination.

We then mercifully arrived at the Mosque, where, according to custom, I left them.

AN OFFICIAL CORRESPONDENCE,
1916

January 1st.   F.O. to Cairo.

101. Greek Prime Minister wishes to import grain. Can you do this?

January 4th.   Cairo to F.O.

416. Your 101 not understood. Where does he want to import? Is it into Egypt?

January 8th.   F.O. to Cairo.

103. Greek Prime Minister wishes to import grain into Greece. Can you do this?

January 11th.   Cairo to F.O.

420. Your 103. We have done it several times.

January 12th.   F.O. to Cairo.

108. Regret copy mislaid. What is gist of my 103? If possible, repeat.

January 14th.   Cairo to F.O.

Regret copy to your 103 mislaid here. Believe it concerned Greek Prime Minister.

January 16th.   F.O. to Cairo.

108. Greek Prime Minister wishes to import grain into Greece. Can you do this?

January 19th.   Cairo to F.O.

428. Your 108. We have imported grain into Greece several times. It was believed to go to the German Army.

January 22nd. F.O. to Cairo.

112. Your 428. If you import grain to Greek Prime Minister, can you suggest measures to prevent its reaching the German Army? Would Prime Minister's personal guarantee be sufficient?

January 24th. Cairo to F.O.

430. Your 112. Which Prime Minister's guarantee do you suggest? Prefer M. Briand, if still in office.

January 27th. F.O. to Cairo.

114. Your 430. We alluded to Greek Prime Minister. Please let me have your views as soon as possible, as matter is urgent and delay to be avoided.

February 8th. Cairo to F.O.

435. Your 114. To avoid delay, suggest the personal guarantee in writing of Greek Prime Minister countersigned by British Consul at Piræus, with documentary assent of British Government and approval Director General Customs Administration, Alexandria.

February 10th. F.O. to Cairo.

118. Your 435. Have agreed to accept joint and several guarantee of King of Greece, Archimandrite and Greek Prime Minister, countersigned by leading British merchant at Piræus, Mr. Carl Sonnenschein. How much can you send?

February 13th. Cairo to F.O.

440. Your 118. Will reply as soon as possible, but some delay inevitable, as uncertain what Department of the Egyptian Government deals with these questions. Have so far unsuccessfully

inquired of Main Drainage, Public Instruction, War Office, Agriculture, Public Works and Wakf. Will wire again later.

March 23rd.   Cairo to F.O.

150. Regret delay answering your 118. Matter very complicated. Your 487. Naval authorities object export of seed, as many seeds contain oil suitable for submarines. Can you arrange with Admiralty?

March 26th.   F.O. to Cairo.

495. Your 150. Have arranged with Admiralty.   Seed will be escorted by two destroyers.

March 28th.   F.O. to Cairo.

499. My 495. Have ascertained seed question less important than at first considered. Greek Prime Minister has written explaining seed is needed for his favourite parrot, who is of great age and delicate. Two pounds of selected will be sufficient. Please obtain and send. Admiralty consider escort unnecessary under circumstances.

March 31st.   Cairo to F.O.

161. Your 499. Am obtaining seed at once. Can you inform me of approximate size of parrot, as understand from inquiries that there is a direct relation between size of birds and size of food seeds?

April 7th.   F.O. to Cairo.

506. Your 161. Stop seed.

April 8th.   Cairo to F.O.

165. Your 506. Seed stopped.

April 12*th.   F.O. to Cairo.*

510. Your 165. As information has reached me that the Greek Prime Minister's parrot died last week of indigestion, no further action in matter is necessary.

GOING ON LEAVE

THANK goodness nowadays nearly all we Anglo-Egyptian officials get our leave every year.

The old Indian anti-annual-leave school are happily nearly extinct. I believe that they thought that no one ought to have any leave, merely because they were in their long past and misspent youths so unpopular at home that they were forced to stay for ten or fifteen years on a stretch out of England. At one time they were painfully influential, but luckily for us the Government doctors took a very strong and altruistic line about the question, prophesying the most ghastly results, personal and departmental, if annual leave was not freely granted to all, including themselves. So it has now become the fashion in Government circles to say that it does not pay in the long run to take no leave. If you don't, it will come home to roost one day, and will find you out later on, and other cryptic and mysterious sayings, obviously depreciatory of the no or rare leave system. It is true that old Blatherly, the P.M.O. of the Egyptian Army, did tell me that the year when he did not go on leave his work was indifferent, but he is an optimist, and, besides, I don't think that he was really trying to support the old anti-leave theory. Jenkins, our principal hygienic authority, who is incidentally a crank and lives on parrot food, will, on the other hand, tell you, if you can bear it, that the year when, according to his own account, he simply could not be spared from his work and had to stay here, he had a curious swimming sensation in the head, and lost his appetite so completely that even a Carlsbad rusk did not tempt him, and stewed prunes excited no enthusiasm in his jaded internal organisation.

Though, as I have said, going on leave is now quite the correct thing to do from the earnest official's point of view, still we like to profess that we do it rather for reasons of health, and for the public good, than because of any personal predilection on our part. We therefore, according to our temperaments and the extent to which we have adopted Egyptian ideas of truth, advance in public various reasons why, though we ourselves don't particularly want to go to Europe, we are practically obliged to do so.

Jones, who, by years of carefully graduated incompetence, has got himself placed on a nice warm shelf with practically no duties and a comfortable salary, finds leave necessary to relieve his brain from overstrain, and to enable him to accomplish the strenuous tasks of his official life.

Alfort informs us that he positively must go, as he has to look after his grandmother's affairs, which, it is believed by the profane, he does by ascertaining if the old lady's will is still in an unaltered condition, and in the tea caddy in which she, being eccentric, insists on keeping it.

Capperly deplores the necessity of going, but points out he must personally select the British recruits for the Department to which he belongs. It is hard to believe that this can take the whole of the three months, as the usual number selected is one in every two years. Certainly the people I have occasionally met him with in London and elsewhere, though most prepossessing in many ways, do not look like candidates for the service, and I should say are obviously unfitted, apart from the sex question, for a serious career.

That Maunders goes home solely to see his wife no one who knows either him or her attempts to believe; but many are convinced that Harper only leaves Egypt after, according to his own account, a moving scene with his physician, who is also an old friend, and who apparently invariably makes this annual statement: " My dear fellow, if you don't go at once I am not responsible for what may occur. Your condition is, I am bound to tell you, one which gives me much anxiety." It is most self-denying of the doctor to say all this, as H. is a regular and reliable source of income to him whilst he is in the country, but then I expect, on the other hand, he is a very trying patient. Constantly prescribing for a man who is as strong as a horse and who would never have a day's illness in his life if he could be persuaded that he had a stomach and not a destructor inside him, must be wearisome work. Anyhow, Harper, laden with medicine bottles, goes off to a cure, where he places himself under a noted German specialist, who tells him in confidence (as we hear later) that he, Harper, is only just in time. What for, we have never found out, but I suspect it is meals, which I am bound to say H. faces bravely and punctually, no matter how near he thinks he is to death's door.

Bagley, on the other hand, we are led to believe, does not consult his doctor. He does not believe in 'em. He knows, "My dear boy, when you get that heavy muzzy feeling in the head of an evening, that feeling of repletion after your meals, and that quick, laboured breath after running, it is time to be off if you don't want to snuff out like poor Tommy Muddly and old Simpson;" whom he personally repeatedly warned, but they would not listen, and there it is.

Lamberly, as he has often confided to me, would not think himself justified in taking leave if it did not enable him to study on the spot matters which are of the deepest importance to his Department. This means the question of water supply, in which he has specialised. Not only does he travel all over Europe at Government expense to look at waterworks, but obtains I don't know how much extra leave to do so. Not content with thus meanly taking advantage of his position, he produces on his return a horrible report in his best style of dreariness, which we all have to read and write minutes about. It is impossible to conceive how dry water can be until you have seen it treated by Lamberly. His last effort occupied 112 pages of type, and the things we wrote and said about it were naturally very bitter. So bitter indeed, that we christened the document "Marah," and, of course, some one told Lamberly. Even then the joke fell flat, as Lamberly confided to me, in his most pompous way, that he saw no fun in calling a serious Government question by a woman's name.

Whatever reason we may put forward for taking or not taking leave, the fact remains that it constitutes the great event of the year, the time when the curse of Adam is lightened and when we, the sons of super-heated toil, are temporarily free. For most of those who live abroad leave is almost as important as one's holidays were in one's school days

As it is so important an event, it naturally is the subject of much conversation and discussion. We ask about each other's plans in order that if we wait quite patiently we may get a chance of talking of our own. There are so many points to be discussed. In the first place, there is the question of whether you prefer second or first leave. Do you prefer the soft, enervating warmth of the autumn to the dry, fierce heat of the early summer? Do you want to see your friends in London and " do " the Derby and Ascot, or do you want to shoot in August and September? Then are you going straight to England, or are you going to stop *en route*? Has Monte Carlo or Paris in the off-season any attraction for you? Do you wish to improve your mind with travel? Does scenery or sight-seeing, nature or art, appeal to you the most?

Then the actual route has to be considered, and on this we have very strong opinions. Some people will not go by a German boat, and many more by a P. & O. Every person who has been out here for some time has a favourite line and will defend it hotly against all comers.

Of course the question of expense comes in, but

this needs treating with delicacy, as we do not obtrude our poverty on one another except in a dashing sort of man-of-the-world way, nor do we allude to the cost being a principal consideration unless we are married and senior and wish to impress the world with our steadiness and forethought. It is quaint that men are almost as shy of admitting poverty as cowardice, and in both cases only he who is above suspicion can afford to say what he really feels and thinks.

So we gloss over these sordid considerations, and our young bloods (for we have young bloods) talk of " dropping in at Monte " or " giving Paris a chance," whilst graver spirits argue on the relative interest of the views in Switzerland and the picture galleries of Italy. Great meetings in town, too, to see the theatres, and elsewhere for golf or what not, are arranged. It is strange that people who live all the rest of the year together in a narrow society should like to foregather on leave, but so it is. Perhaps some of us who have been long abroad feel a little " out of it " at home, and like to meet others in the same position. Officials, unlike prophets, have but little honour out of their own country

Such is the train of thought into which I have fallen on a superb evening in the month of April when walking up to the club to dinner. It was started by my receiving a somewhat curt note from my chief to the effect that he has no objection to my starting on leave to-morrow, but that he hopes that this year (underlined) I have arranged for my work being carried out in my absence. I hate innuendo, and pity and despise a man who cannot give save in a reluctant and grudging spirit.

During the hot weather we dine on the terrace of the club, which is cool but not perhaps an ideal spot for the purpose. It is bounded, as they say in the geography books, on the north by a Coptic school, a fine old-fashioned institution with, as one cannot help noticing, a mediæval system of drainage. On the east stands a Jewish synagogue, which is a miracle of ugliness; it was designed apparently by one of H. G. Wells's Martians, who had become converted to the *art nouveau* school. It has a heavy, massive appearance, with queer twisted windows in unexpected places, and it is further disfigured by an irritatingly unsymmetrical scheme of decoration. And as on the south side you have one of the noisiest streets in Cairo, you have, before you sit down to dinner, three of your senses wholesomely mortified, whilst the dinner itself is of a nature to discourage any tendency to deify one's stomach. An Englishman will eat anything if it is served hot, there is plenty of it, and he is sure he knows what it is. The fear that a designing foreigner may one day make him unknowingly eat a cat is still present in some form or another in most British minds.

One dines at our club, as at most other clubs, at small tables, but, for some reason I never have been able to fathom, there are no tables for one, and very few for two. If you come in at all late you are forced to dine at a table for four. This makes it necessary to sit down, so to speak, warily. If you hurry on to the terrace without thinking, you will find yourself irresistibly impelled by some malign influence towards a table at which are sitting the greatest bore in Africa and your two most devoted enemies in Cairo, and you will have a purgatorial dinner. When bitter experience has taught you to be more careful, you will reconnoitre the tables before emerging from the doorway. One tries to do this as unobtrusively as possible, but it is an awkward business. You attempt to do it with an air of being only too pleased to sit anywhere, but such a choice of agreeable company in front of you makes it hard to decide which seat one prefers. I hope I do it nicely, but I know other members have the appearance of discontented customers at the fishmonger's, and you fancy you can hear them say: " A very poor lot to-day."

Luckily to-night I have very little difficulty in making my choice, for opposite me is a table at which are seated Tommy Dorimer, Harbutt, and Blazeley. Tommy is one of my most intimate friends, and the other two are both good fellows and tolerable company.

Tommy has had a life of varied experiences, and has served both in Egypt and the Sudan, besides many other even less-sought-after parts of the world. He has been in many places and has learned much, but has the grace to keep this to himself. He is youthful in appearance, and rather particular as to his clothes. He has the distinction of being one of the very few men out here who do not take themselves or the country too seriously, and who realise that it is in reality a huge joke or series of jokes, not all perhaps in the best taste, but very humorous nevertheless. It is not, as some falsely hold, a corner of the Empire inhabited by future pro-consuls and the grateful people they govern (as if any one ever did like being governed!), but an enormous and unending *opéra bouffe*. Tommy and I, in days that were much earlier, began to write one on the subject, but we had to stop because we tried to introduce incidents from real life and made it too scandalous. I think we completed the first act, because I know it ended with Tommy's Ministers' Song (with dance), of which the refrain ran:

> " And every one of them has to pay,
>   Pay, pay, pay, pay,
>   Whatever they want and whatever they say,
>   Yes, yea, yea, yea."

It was a brilliant work, but just a trifle too dangerous to go on with.

Harbutt is a tall, old young man, with dark curling hair (which usually wants cutting), clear-cut features and an eye-glass which he drops when he wants to see. He is rather depressingly cultured, and is particularly wearisome on Saracenic art, which I am sure he must really know a great deal about, or he could not make it so hopelessly un-interesting.

Blazeley, on the other hand, is a short, sturdy young man, with a sun-reddened face and straight, plastered-down, sandy hair. He is a budding pundit, and will, unless he checks himself in time, become an authority on the country and do a great deal of harm later on. He is already supposed to know more about a particular district of Upper Egypt than a respectable man should do, and alas! he disseminates his knowledge gratis to his suffering brother officials.

As I sit down, Blazeley is just finishing an anecdote. This pleases me, as I feel as if there was one less of them in the world. Tommy, however, is possessed to-night, as he frequently is, by a mischievous devil, so he says, " How very interesting! Do tell that to C., Blazeley "; and I, of course, have to say, " Please do," which I do about as cordially as one assents to one's dentist's unwarranted assumption that you won't mind if he hurts you a little.

" Oh," says Blazeley, " it is not much of a story really, only rather characteristic of the place, that's all. It would not interest any one who did not know the country, but I'm sure you will like it, sir. I was up at Fareshein the other day, and I happened to be talking to old Mahmud Suleiman the Omdeh—don't know if you know him. He is rather a fine old bird, and a pretty knowing one, too. He says devilish good things sometimes. Well, we got talking about dogs—I really don't know how, but we did anyhow—and he said to me, ' Do you see that dog?' pointing to a great beast of a pariah—you know, one of those big, ugly, yellow devils—and I said, a string of Arabic, meaning ' Yes, O Omdeh, I see that dog.' ' Well,' he says, ' he is the worst dog in the village—ill-tempered, savage, and without manners.' I said, ' O Omdeh, that I can well believe.' ' Do you know what I say of him, Excellency of an Inspector?' says he. I said, ' No ';

and then the old boy smiles, and says, ' I say that he is the worst dog here, but in other villages he might be the best.' Rather good, wasn't it? "

" Awfully good," says Tommy. " Sounds even better the second time one hears it. Both wise and in a way witty, too."

" Yes," says the unconscious Blazeley. " But you know they are very witty in their own way, and jolly wise too."

" Quite so," says Tommy; " I used not to think so, as I was prejudiced against them at first, but a few sayings like the one you have just repeated convinced me that there is much more in them than meets the eye."

" Perhaps so," says Harbutt, " but I confess that their total lack of refinement is utterly repugnant to me."

" Quite true," admits Tommy, " and that is just where they differ so much from other peasants who, I think, all have a strong innate sense of beauty."

" Indeed, that is true," agrees Harbutt, " and though naturally the contemplation of Nature can never produce the same degree of refinement as the intelligent study of art, still it must and does have its effect in every country save this."

" Oh, of course, they are not artistic," says Blazeley, with some contempt. " I never said they were. They have not time for that sort of thing."

I see Harbutt's hackles rising, and that we are on the verge of the deepest abyss into which a conversation can fall—a heated argument. So in order to turn the conversation I ask Tommy, who is travelling by the same boat as I am, if he has finished his packing. This, it is true, leads the conversation away from the value of art as a refining influence, but not in a very fortunate direction, for it appears that the leave prospects of both Harbutt and Blazeley are very gloomy, and that they both have a grievance on the subject. So far their cases are alike, but only up to this point. Harbutt, owing to Algar walking backwards in order to get a better view of his new house and unintentionally descending head first into a dry well, was called back from Florence, where he had just arrived and made a special arrangement for his stay at a little-known and artist-frequented pension. Blazeley, on the other hand, had after three years without leave applied for and been granted it. It was, however, cancelled at the last moment owing to Sopely, who has been always justly unpopular, coming unexpectedly into five thousand a year and resigning on the spot.

We try to smooth things over by abusing Sopely. Harbutt, generously forgetting his own troubles, leads off by saying that it was very inconsiderate. Tommy pronounces it to be a rotten thing to do. I go as far as to say it was scarcely fair, and Blazeley himself declares it to be unsportsmanlike, which finally damns Sopely, whose sporting tendencies, it may be incidentally remarked, have at no time of his life risen higher than a mild satisfaction in killing flies on a window-pane.

We then, led by Blazeley, who wishes, so to speak, to return Harbutt's compliment, condole with Harbutt on his personal misfortunes, with some remarks on the uncertainty of human affairs and the impossibility of foretelling the future. We do all agree that it was a very stupid thing for Algar to do, as he probably thinks himself. Harbutt, however, all but extinguishes our growing post-prandial sympathy by saying that he would not mind so much were it not for missing his annual intellectual bath, and showing signs of wanting to quote Italian poetry, which tendency is mercifully checked by the base and coarse suggestion from Blazeley, that a feminine personality has something to do with his regrets, or, as he more tersely puts it, he expects there is a little bit of skirt in it somewhere. This pains and annoys Harbutt, and nearly leads to recriminations. The conversation then falls, as I feared it would, into two—I listening perforce to Blazeley's views on the condition of the peasants of Upper Egypt, which I have heard several times before and never agreed with, and Tommy being the recipient of Harbutt's ideas as to the position of woman in the life of the cultivated and artistic, which is apparently a cross between a stimulant and a poison. Something, as Tommy says afterwards, like bad whisky.

Maddened by the wearisome iteration of anti-quated fallacies, as Harbutt once said when de-scribing a row he had with his servant about boot polish, I again remind Tommy of his packing, and we leave the dinner-table. Refusing with en-thusiasm a rubber of bridge with Colonel Shuffler (retired) and a visit to a music-hall with Raffington, who assures us, by way of inducement, that the performance ought to be, and will be, suppressed by the police on grounds of propriety, we descend the steps into the odoriferous street and drive home.

231

CHAPTER II   PACKING, ETC.

WHEN I have said good-night to Tommy and ascended to my flat, I am confronted with an imposing array of locked and strapped boxes and bags in a plethoric condition. It appears from this, that Suleiman the Untruthful (to distinguish him from the Wise, the Magnificent, and other minor historical characters) has completed, or thinks he has completed, my packing. I trust he has done it properly, but I am sure in any case that I should not have done it as well. I cannot pack. Packing is, to my mind, under any circumstances, a more or less insoluble problem. If one packs close, in two days' time one cannot shut one's boxes without asking the whole hotel staff, from the manager down, to assist one by sitting on them whilst one tries to lock them. If one packs loose, at the termination of one's journey one's clothes look as if they had been fighting inside the box the whole way, the struggle ending by the hairwash committing hari-kari over the shirts, and thus by its death destroying its enemies. I suppose there is a golden mean, but I never found it; and I have now wisely abandoned attempting that which I have no natural bent for, and confine myself to giving the Untruthful general instructions on the subject, which he interprets in an eccentric and broad-minded way.

After years of objurgation and remonstrance, I have got him to understand what I may call the theory of packing for this particular journey. The principle is that what I shall require during the voyage must be quite separate from what I shall require when I get to England. This principle he has at last understood, but where he fails is in its application. He cannot grasp what I do want for the voyage.

I once crossed Europe with half of my only trunk taken up by a typewriting machine, of which no part could be used as clothing. Even the ribbon could scarcely be regarded as a sufficient costume by itself, however cunningly arranged, anywhere but in Central Africa.

Though this took place in early days and he undoubtedly knows better now, he still thinks that I want to play golf *en route*, presumably on the steamer, and that I make my official entry into London on horseback. This latter idea is firmly fixed in his mind. Even if I succeed in preventing him packing my long boots and khaki breeches of an ancient date, I am sure to find a pair of spurs or some spare straps concealed among my socks and ties.

Suleiman in some other respects, it must be admitted, cannot be regarded as a perfect travelling servant. The prospect of a journey, whether he is to accompany me or not, always upsets him. In old days I used to have to go to Khartoum several times a year, and often had to start at a few hours' notice. When I told Suleiman that we were starting, let us say, that night on our journey south, he always burst into tears. He sat overcome by grief for some time, loudly lamenting his hard fate, which compelled him to pack in a hurry, and thus of necessity forget things, drawing down my wrath on his poor innocent head. After a time he partially mastered himself, tottered to his feet, and, blinded by his tears, began to pack by placing a frying-pan and a tall hat, or some such weird combination, in my portmanteau.

Nowadays he gets more notice, which is better for him, but even worse for me. The moment I tell him that I propose to start that day month for England, he packs up every single thing I am not actually wearing at the minute, and then promptly forgets in which box each article of clothing has been put. The result of this is, that dressing for dinner entails repacking the whole of my luggage. The Untruthful is always deeply hurt at this, and remains in a condition of chronic sulks until I start.

There are several other crises of a minor nature which have to be also gone through before starting. One of these is when Suleiman, with a wild look in his eye, informs me (usually the day before I am to leave) that all the trunks are broken, and none of the keys fits the locks. It is, of course, no good reminding him that I had asked him weeks ago if they were all in order, and that he had replied, with a readiness I should with my experience have mistrusted, that he had already seen to the matter personally. These alarms are, however, usually more or less false, and the one this year proved to have no greater foundation than that Suleiman in his condition of high nervous tension had been trying to use on my boxes a bunch of antiquated keys which must have belonged to the grandfather of a former master of his.

This all occurred this morning, and after order had been restored and a suitable admonition had been administered, I proceeded, according to my annual custom, to question the Untruthful one on what articles he had put into each bag, case, or box. The object of this is to try to make him think rather than to obtain trustworthy information, for the answers he gives bear very little relation to the truth. There is a chance, however, that after he has finished lying and I have gone away, he may correct some of his more salient errors. To-day he was not lucky, as he had only just assured me that all my clean linen was packed with even more than his usual skill and care at the top of the several boxes, where I could get at it with a minimum of trouble, and that this had been done the day before yesterday, when a perspiring washerman arrived with three baskets of the said linen and excitedly demanded extra pay, on the ground that it was only given to him to wash this morning. Comment was useless, so I left the two worthies to fight it out, and went off to my office.

I must now pack my despatch boxes, which is the only part of the operation which I see after personally.

I begin by carefully arranging their future contents in two little piles. There is stationery, telegraph forms, pens, ink, and pencils, which are always very useful for marking at bridge. There is my travelling inkpot, the pride of my life, which never lets out a drop of ink unless properly opened, which can only be done by jamming it in the crack of the door, as the screw is rather stiff. There are half a dozen reports and some serious works on finance which I shall not read, and some novels which I shall. These I have chosen with great care. First, there is *Dorinda of the Alameda* (a sentimental One), by Wason; *The Fatal Tiara*, by Le Snob (highly sensational); *The Mystery of the Wry-Faced Girl*, by A. Blight (ditto); *Dripping with Gore*, by Tedious Still (ditto, ditto); *Coupled in Chains*, by Elinor Streatham (a marriage muddle); *The Death Cough*, by Whitestone (mystical horrors written by a man with a kind of spiritual D.T.); *The Duke Rides Out*, by Pluffington Blobbs (historical, with lots of fights). I like them all except *Coupled in Chains*, which I thought when I bought it was about the chain gangs in the Australian convict settlements. On examination I find, however, that it is two hundred and odd pages of the crass mistakes of two or more congenital idiots, and I expect it ends badly, which I don't like. I'll look. Ah! I thought so! The last paragraph gives the show away. "'Yes,' she said, 'I am free at last, but, like the victims of the French tyrants when released by the sovereign people from the gloomy depths of the dungeons of the old Bastille, I cannot use my liberty. The freedom of my spirit died long since. I can only sit and patiently wait until the end.' And she did." If she talked like that I should have given her any amount of freedom at once. Perhaps I can exchange the book on board the boat for something rational.

Next I collect that mass of odds and ends which one always thinks one will want on a journey and never does. There are medicaments, safety-pins, pen-knives, cotton wool, travelling candlesticks, a small tape measure, some drawing-pins, and a patent thing for holding needles and thread. Then there are a certain number of confidential documents to be got in, and, finally, a little space must be left for the small articles which Suleiman, according to the law of probabilities, will forget to pack elsewhere. This finished, I find that I have mislaid my keys; I search my pockets, turn out both the despatch boxes, and find them, on a re-examination, in the pocket into which I thought I had put them, but in which they had somehow escaped my searching fingers. I notice again with regret the misplaced activity of inanimate objects. No conjuror can make small articles disappear with the rapidity with which they move themselves out of sight and reach when bent on annoying you. Keys particularly will slip from pocket to pocket with a speed far higher than the human eye can detect. They will move from table to chair and chair to table without making a sound or apparently a motion.

I feel greatly relieved. It is a great thing to have finished packing and got everything in. One nearly always forgets something, but this time, what with forethought and long habit, all difficulties have been overcome. But at this point my smug self-satisfaction is rudely shaken by a terrible thought. Put into words it takes the form, " What about boots?" I don't remember where my "spare" boots have been put in. With a sinking heart I go to the small cupboard under the bookcase where they are kept. When I open the door, there appear to my horror-struck gaze my heavy walking-boots covered at least an inch deep in a nauseous dubbing which S. insists on using on them, two pairs of evening shoes simply dripping with a new and lavish coat of varnish, my spare slippers, my golf shoes, my golf boots, my tennis shoes, etc., etc.

I summon Suleiman, thinking over a suitable form of blessing to salute him with on arrival, but my summonses are in vain. He has obviously gone for the night, and I now remember with horror that I told him to execute various commissions for me to-morrow morning and, as all the things were to be packed to-night, to come to my lodgings only just in time to take the luggage to the station. This means that I must pack these beastly boots myself.

After reflecting on what I should like to do to the Untruthful, I resign myself to my fate. First, I must open the boxes to see which one will best bear the extra strain. I left my keys on the table, I am sure, but, of course, they have moved, and I search the room, first perfunctorily and then systematically, until I feel thoroughly discouraged, when I find them on the table hiding behind a book in, as far as I can judge, almost the exact place I put them down. I open the boxes, which apparently have been packed under hydraulic pressure, and decide that there is the most hope of getting them into the big brown portmanteau. The next step is to remove the superabundant grease from the shooting-boots, a filthy process, and then wrap them up in an old towel before packing them, so that they may lubricate as few of my personal effects as possible.

Then a worse task is before me. I must remove

the wet varnish from the shoes, as they will be for ever ruined if I pack them wet. This has to be done with spirit, and I produce in the process some gallons of a fine, clinging, black spirit-paint, which gets gradually distributed over everything, including myself, till I feel like the ark pitched within and without. It is, I am sure, due to want of enterprise that a self-distributing paint has not been put on the market. The text-books always say that one should take advantage of natural tendencies, and the self-spreading power of black paint, tar, or varnish is extraordinary. A very convincing experiment to show this can be carried out as follows: Take of black paint as much as will cover a threepenny bit. Place it in a room with a small boy from seven to ten years old. In a few days you will notice that a thin but quite perceptible coat of black paint covers everything in the house. The same experiment can be tried with honey, but a little more must be used, as the boy eats some of it. Though inferior as a distributor to a boy, I expect I shall find black varnish lurking about this room for years.

However, at last the shoes are dry and packed, and I can go to bed with the pleasant thought that though, as the train does not go till eleven, I need not really be called till eight-thirty, Suleiman's lieutenant, Ali, who will in S.'s absence perform this duty for him, will no doubt, from excess of zeal, have me out of bed at six-thirty sharp.

CHAPTER III   CAIRO TO PORT SAID

THE morning one starts on leave is a time of trial and tribulation.   First, I am always called much too early, then I dawdle about until I find I am in danger of being too late, and have finally to dress as fast as possible, a thing which always upsets my equanimity for the day.   The bath is, of course, cold, and my washing becomes a pharisaical ceremony.   My razors on such occasions, for some obscure reason, refuse to cut anything except incised flesh wounds.   My clothes are always put out wrong and I cannot find anything.   If the article required is not packed up, it is put away.   The laces of my shoes break, the buttons on which the whole stability of my dress depends are either broken or missing, and my very socks have so many holes in them that it is nearly impossible to find the orthodox entrance.   Of my breakfast (taken at home to save time) it is impossible to speak kindly.   The tea is lukewarm, the butter salt, and the eggs predynastic.

My fate this morning is no different in these respects from what it has been on similar occasions, with the result that when I finally reach the station I am what is termed ruffled.

Here I find Mirsal, my *shawish* or orderly, waiting for me.   He is in many ways the apple of my eye, but memory is not his strong point.   He has, according to custom, forgotten my railway pass, so I am obliged to take a ticket. The ticket clerk, who is a villainous-looking Copt, is apparently adding up the monetary results of his last night's murders, and dislikes being interrupted. To mark his disapproval of my doing so he gives me a wrong ticket and some change, of which the amount, as far as I can see, bears no relation to any previous transaction between us. Just as I am drawing his attention to the point and beginning what I know will be a long and wearying discussion, Mirsal, who has been fighting the cabman about his fare outside, appears and lets loose such a torrent of thumbnail word-portraits of the clerk's family that, used as I am to his powers in this respect, I am struck dumb with admiration.

The clerk, realising from Mirsal's uniform that I belong to the sacred official class, merely bows his head to the storm and, following the advice of the old saying, pays up and looks pleasant; that is, as pleasant as one can with a criminal cast of countenance thickly encrusted with the dirt of years.

I now proceed to find my carriage. We higher officials are given reserved compartments when we travel, and these are for some reason always in the front first-class carriage of the train. Whether this is to give us our proper precedence in a collision, or whether it is from a tender solicitude on the part of the railway authorities that we should take enough exercise for the good of our health, I don't know, but it is so, and it means one has a long walk before one gets to one's place. The railway officials, when they travel, I notice, have their service cars hitched on to the back of the train. This leads me into a gloomy train of thought on the selfishness of humanity. At last I arrive and am greeted by my secretary and the man with the feather brush, no one else having yet arrived as it is so early. However, the man with the feather brush is there. The man with the feather brush is indispensable in the highest ceremonials, and is present on the most ordinary occasions. When you call on a friend, he dusts your boots. When you enter a railway compartment, the seats are dusted by him. When the Khedive goes anywhere in state, the last touch before he arrives is given by the man with the feather brush dusting the red carpet. The operation itself is usually purely formal, and only just stirs up enough dust to make you cough a little, but it is a sign that you belong to the higher or fit-to-be-dusted classes. I believe the man with the feather brush is the present-day representative of the slaves who waved the sacred feather fans over the head of Pharaoh. I am sure there is something in this theory, because not one of the archæologists will look at it. Anyhow, I think I should feel hurt nowadays if I got into a railway carriage without coughing and sneezing.

One of the results of living alongside Orientals is that you catch their inertness. The consequence of this is that we have many customs, especially social customs, in Egypt which are generally execrated, but which continue to flourish nevertheless because no one will take the trouble to do away with them. Among these one of the worst is the ceremony of one's friends assembling to see one off at the station. It dates probably from the time when Egypt was much further off in time from Europe than it is now, and when the return of a departing friend was a matter of more uncertainty. Anyhow, whatever the original source of error, we still religiously see each other off at the station when we go on leave, so that one cannot even leave this thrice-blessed land in peace. A deputation of one's chief clerks, petitioners, and friends crowd round one at the last moment, and distract one's mind from the really vital problems of whether one left one's cheque-book on the writing-table, and if one did or did not lock up one's keys in the spring-lock despatch box which is registered through. It is idle mockery wishing a man who is on the brink of brain fever and without a handkerchief in the wide world a happy journey, or offering flowers, which is in itself a custom most repugnant to the self-conscious Englishman, to one who feels that he and his keys are parted for ever. It is a gruesome ceremony, only lightened by the arrival of one's servant in a frenzied condition carrying a pill-box in his right hand and a selection of intimate articles of dress and toilet in his left, which he insists on giving one, quite regardless of the presence of one's lady friends. A man who wore a wig confided to me that he was so used to his servant giving him his spare one on these occasions before every one, that he had quite ceased to feel embarrassed, and would not now feel comfortable if this were not done.

At last, however, we are off, and I sit down to

collect my scattered faculties and mentally draft a letter to the Archbishop of Canterbury, suggesting the inclusion of " he who hindereth the wayfarer on his way " in the suitable portion of the Commination Service.

I had intended to start this journey with a minimum of hand baggage, but on looking round the carriage it does not appear that my intentions have been perfectly carried out. Amongst those present we notice (as the society papers say) golf clubs, hold-all, valise, hat box, two despatch boxes, rugs, book net, deck chair, luncheon basket, tarboosh case, paper parcel (contents uncertain), two bouquets, and a basket of fruit.

Why Suleiman will send my tarboosh case and luncheon basket with me when I go on leave is one of the insoluble mysteries of the East. Perhaps on the White Knight's principle. Anyhow, they will be left with a friend at Port Said and probably forgotten, so they don't much matter. The bouquets can go out of the window, and the fruit will do to give to Mrs. Despard, who went down by the early train this morning, and who, with Mr. and Mrs. Hester, is travelling home with us. I am very glad Mrs. Despard is going, but I could have spared the Hesters.

I notice that the porters, as usual, have made an ingeniously balanced pile of my old despatch box, luncheon basket, and hat box on the rack. It is evident that it is only a matter of minutes before they collapse. I have no intention of playing at being Damocles with an Egyptian-made iron despatch box, which weighs as much as a small safe, hanging over my head, supported by a single luncheon basket, so I take it down. My despatch box is a marvel. I got it in the days when I still believed one ought to patronise native industry, and I had it made at one of the Government model shops. It is made, I should think, of half-inch plate, and is too heavy for any one but a trained athlete to lift. Its only other faults are that it holds less for its size than any other box I ever saw, and that, owing to the fact that a cheap lock was put on it in the interests of economy, it is liable to come open at any minute if you are rough with it. So it needs careful handling.

I then make a compo. of the golf clubs, hold-all, parcel, and rug. Now, if I register the hat box and one despatch box through, all will be well.

Tommy, who got in with some friends of his in another compartment but is already tired of them, now joins me; but after saying gloomily that there are the deuce of a lot of people from Cairo going with us, he is obviously not inclined for conversation, so I let him be, and open the newspapers with which Mirsal has provided me.

We are not exactly in the forefront of civilisation as regards our press. There is nothing in England quite on a level with our European papers. They usually consist in a leading article which is scurrilous but witty in the French papers and respectable but soporific in the English, Reuter's telegrams, *faits divers*, some articles or extracts from European papers, Bourse news, cotton quotations, and advertisements. There is also a column headed "Personal," which is supposed to give one the fashionable news—movements, births, deaths, and marriages. This column in the English papers is sometimes funny, as it is occasionally written by some Syrian sub-editor with a very imperfect knowledge of our tongue. Thus one reads with amazement that "Mr. Untel goes off his leafs on October the 2nd," which sounds serious, or that "Wahid Pasha is condoled with on the gloomy decrease of his father."

Owing probably to paucity of material, our papers, especially the British ones, will put in almost anything you send them. When we were all younger we used to take advantage of this to get up bogus correspondence on really dreadful subjects, and the perfectly serious editorial comments on our letters were worth anything.

Perhaps the best joke we ever played through the press was when Gorley and I wrote an indignant letter signed "Matron," to say there was a poster on a hoarding in a distant and dirty part of Cairo which was an outrage on common decency. We followed this up the next week by a powerful appeal to have it removed, signed "Englishman." We sent these to the editor under false names, and he accepted them. The letters sent many respectable members of the community on a most unpleasant expedition, and we had a most entertaining afternoon down there, meeting most of our friends, who, curiously enough, were all called there by various forms of business, or had wandered there by chance.

At this moment the engine starts whistling more

vehemently than ever. I once asked one of the younger station-masters why the engines whistled so much in this country. He replied, " Sir, the law says if you don't whistle he is murder or manslaughter, but if you do he is a total accident." Our engine-driver is evidently out for a total accident, whatever that may be. Tommy says that we are just running into Zagazig, which proves not to be the case, for we soon pull up at a wayside station. All the native officials are apparently in a state of great excitement and are rushing about feverishly. The station-master, who is a portly gentleman of unusually dark complexion, is gravely proceeding at a sharp trot up and down the platform, accompanied by a shambling, one-eyed Coptic clerk, who is trying to hold a green-lined white umbrella over his chief's head to protect him from the sun. The station-master is obviously under the impression that he is doing something important, but unless it is for a substantial wager I cannot imagine why he is taking this unwonted and dangerous exercise. The panic increases, and the remainder of the station staff are now gesticulating and shouting in groups, whilst the ticket collector is sobbing in the corner. Tommy selects one of the sanest of the officials, and demands sternly to be told what the matter is. The man with an effort pulls himself together, and replies in voluble what he thinks to be English, " Sir, there was accident. This train has run down, so line is block." "Any one hurt?" asks Tommy. "Station-master know, sir, I not know. Station-master very sorry. He like this one hour." "When shall we go on? " I inquire, it dawning on me that we may possibly miss our boat. " I not know, sir; two, tree hours; not long. Station-master telegraph all round as per regulation. He very sorry and upset."

At this point that worthy trots by with his faithful umbrella-bearer. He, the station-master, is purple in the face, and his eyes are starting from his head. He stops for a second, issues two or three contradictory orders, and gives verbal instructions, of a kind which are bound to be misunderstood, for another sheaf of telegrams to be sent off. Tommy tries to reason with him, but he is incoherent, and starts off again down the platform to the accompaniment of the wails of the ticket collector. At this moment the signalman rushes up and announces that a train is coming down the line from Cairo and won't stop though the signals are against her. The station-master would scream if he had any breath left for the purpose. He murmurs, " Tell the engine-driver of this train to start and to go on fast." " But," urges the signalman, who has remnants of sense left, " the line is blocked by the accident." " Then what am I to do? " whimpers the station-master, turning to the telegraph clerk who has joined the group. " Telegraph at once to Cairo for instructions." " It is too late," says the signal-man; " in five minutes the train will be here." " They will see the express and stop," suggests the telegraphist, who is obviously of a hopeful disposition. " No, no, they won't," groans the station-master. " If they won't stop for signals, they won't regard an express." "That is indeed the truth," says the signalman. "Every one must get out of the train," says the station-master, struck with to-day's great thought. "Do not alarm the passengers, but say quietly that they will all certainly be killed if they don't get out of the train at once."

The officials rush off on their mission, and in two minutes every one is scrambling out of the carriages, flinging their luggage ahead of them. The platform becomes a sea of furious, scrambling, yelling, fighting humanity, through which the station-master starts on his endless trot down and up the platform again.

After this scene has lasted for some ten minutes, a peculiar-looking train appears from the Cairo direction, whistling fiercely, and stops just behind ours. It is the breakdown train, cranes, jacks, and all.

From it steps a burly-looking individual of a certain portliness, dressed in those peculiarly ill-fitting white clothes worn in summer by our railway-men, from our general manager to the stokers on the goods engines. It is Larkins, whose special business is this sort of work. His imperturbable countenance is carmined over by the pink cast of desire to kick some one hard. He is, however, far too old a hand to show his irritation in any open way. On his appearance there is a distinct change of attitude on the part of the station staff. They quietly assume that, to most of us difficult but to them from long practice almost normal, position, the top of the fence. If the station-master is commended they will appear as his faithful servants and adherents, and get their part of the praise; if, on the other hand, they find he is blamed they will dissociate themselves altogether from his action and openly bewail his folly, giving information against him if necessary, especially if there is any hope of reward.

Larkins speaks to the station-master in a polite and business-like manner, but his first dozen words reduce that official to a cold perspiration. I expect Larkins is suggesting to him the things he ought to have done, and pointing out that unless he can keep his head on occasions like the present, it is possible that in the interests of public safety it will be necessary to transfer him to a smaller station in a feverish district at a reduced salary. He listens with patience to the station-master's halting and improbable story, gives a few short recommendations, which that official translates into orders to others, and in five minutes order is restored; the crowd of officials and staff have melted away, and every one is with superhuman assiduity attending to his own affairs.

Meanwhile the breakdown train has got on to the other line, and Larkins, after pouring into our sympathetic ears a few bitter remarks on the life of a railwayman in this country, and a short sketch of what the station-master's future career would be like if he, Larkins, could do what he chose, gets into his car, and the breakdown train starts off for the scene of the disaster. He told Tommy before he left, that from information received from another station, he did not believe there was much damage done, and he would probably be able to clear the up line at all events in a short space of time.

As there is nothing to do but to wait, we wander up and down the platform, which is now empty, as the rest of the passengers have been put quietly and unostentatiously back into their carriages.

We fall to discussing the effect of that weirdest of all human phenomena, panic, on the natives of the Delta, and the way in which an Oriental crowd passes in a few seconds from an indifferent, good-tempered, docile mass to a collection of raving maniacs with strong homicidal tendencies. The Northern Egyptian is a curious mixture of apathy if things are done for or to him, and mad excitability if he himself has to take an active and responsible part in anything that needs action.

Gradually the time slips away and we have just exhausted all our conversation, and are about to re-enter the railway carriage, when a message comes that we can proceed by the up line. This is communicated to the engine-driver, who seems doubtful of the wisdom of the proceeding. We join the improvised council, composed of the station-master, the signalman, and the engine-driver himself, who are discussing the affair. The station-master says: " It is an order. See thou, it is quite clear. It reads thus, ' Up line clear, but use caution after passing the bridge over the canal.' "

" But," says the engineer, advancing his principal argument, " there is an express due from Ismailia shortly."

" I tell thee, O brother, it is an order signed by
Salesy Bey himself, and thou canst go carefully
with due precaution."

" But," says the engineer, who is obviously an
obstinate fellow who hates collisions, " the order says
truly that the line is clear, but it says nought of
the express.   What if we meet it? "

" That," says the station-master piously, " is as
God wills.   But thou must go on."

And on this comfortable footing we resume
our journey. I rather share the engineer's point
of view, and my admiration for the station-master's
simple faith is a little weakened by the reflection
that he is remaining comfortably in his office, while
we have to go on to meet the express or not as it may
happen.   In fact, I am not a little relieved when,
after passing the canal bridge, we glide slowly by
a couple of wrecked waggons and turn over the
points on our own line again.

After this Tommy and I naturally fall to discussing accidents, and I tell him of the last accident
which I was in.   It was on a suburban line near
Cairo, on which, at that time, I had just begun to
travel daily.   The rolling stock in those days was
decidedly antiquated, and used to make any old
railwaymen who came out as tourists to Egypt quite
sentimental.   I remember Sir Andrew M'Gregor,
ex-manager of the London, Bristol, and East Coast,
sobbing like a child over one of the engines, saying
he had never hoped to see the old days come back
again.   It carried him back fifty years and more,
when he and his lamented wife started on their

honeymoon dragged by just such an engine, possibly the same one.

Of course, one had to be careful with the carriages, as one always has to be when dealing with genuine antiques. Many careless men got nasty falls by something giving way when they were trying to get in or out of the carriages. Sometimes, no doubt, it was a little inconvenient, as when an old lady I knew had to hold the door to all the way, owing to the latch having dropped off.

The express by which I usually travelled went at the maximum speed considered safe, taking into consideration the state of what was ironically called the permanent way, and this was nearly twenty miles an hour on the flat. One travelled usually in a venerable saloon of vast proportions, which had the peculiar earthy, musty smell of extreme age. Everything in it was very old—even the fleas only walked about; their hopping days were over.

One night I travelled out of Cairo in this mobile vault with but one companion, a fat old Frenchman with a capacious white waistcoat and a discontented expression. We were swaying along at our maximum speed, and I was just trying to find out what time it was by my watch and failing, owing to the oil lamp not being quite as bright as usual, when I felt the jolt of crossing points, and the Frenchman turned to the window and said in a tone of concentrated bitterness, "Animal!" Then all the brakes were suddenly put on, and directly afterwards we stopped with a very sharp shock. I suddenly left my seat and flew through the air, alighting in the centre of the capacious white waistcoat with considerable force. The proprietor and I did rather a complicated joint somersault, and finished up sitting on the floor. As soon as I felt sure I was not dead, I attempted to apologise to the poor old man whom I had so wantonly assaulted. He had recovered his breath, and having raised himself with difficulty into a kneeling position, he shook his fist towards the side of the carriage and exclaimed: " *Imbécile ! Imbécile ! Voilà ce qui arrive tous les quinze jours !* "

When I had helped him up, he explained that the native pointsman at these particular points was a man whose memory was deplorable, and he could not ever be sure in his own mind whether the lever should be pulled one way or the other. About once a fortnight he made a mistake and turned the express on to the siding, with the results we had just experienced. He, the Frenchman, had a family, and alas! was too poor to live in Cairo, so he had to bear it as best he might. It was a pathetic picture, this excellent *père de famille* doing his fortnightly somersault in the interests of economy.

There are, of course, many stories of the doings and sayings of our railway staff and the passengers, from the old gentleman who, when he was asked if he was *abonné* (season-ticket holder) by the collector, replied with heat and severity, " No, O dog Mahommedan "; to the porter who slept with his head on the rails in order to be sure to wake up in time for the first train. So we have plenty of material, and with this to discuss and with gossiping, reading, and an interval for lunch, the time soon passes, till we find we are slackening down to run into Port Said. Tommy points out that we shall have none too much time to get on board the boat.

This is a comfort, as it will shorten the time during which I shall be in the grip of the sub-governor (the governor is away), Ahmed Bey Murad, whom I see waiting to welcome me on the platform, and who is not a bad fellow, but a little trying, especially to any one who has a difficulty in controlling his countenance.

Where he learned his extremely voluble and singularly incorrect English, of which he is inordinately proud, is a mystery, but his teachers cannot have been very refined as to accent or substance.

He, like most of the governing classes in Egypt, is of Turkish origin, with the large face and build of his race. He is very nattily turned out, wears his tarboosh well on the side of his head, a pink satin tie with a pearl pin, a brocade waistcoat, an immaculate, heavily braided frock coat, light grey " weddingy " trousers, and yellow leather spring-side boots with imitation buttons on them. On his hands are lavender kid gloves, under his arm a presentation walking cane, and in his mouth a gold cigarette holder picked out with amber, in which is burning an enormous cigarette. He disseminates an odour of perfume which would be strong enough to run him as a " drag " with a pack of hounds.

" And how are we? " he says, welcoming me

255

cordially. " I hope your Excellency is pretty bobbyish, eh? Excuse half mos, but you have what you call sky-skippers in your train, and I am told to look at him."

At this moment the station-master bustles up with an elderly and portly cleric of the ultra-serious description, and presents him to the sub-governor, who makes him a rakish, lion comique sort of bow, and says: " Delighted. Hope feet and well, reverend." " Thank you for your kind wishes. I am very well, I am glad to say," graciously replies the cleric.

" An' all at home? Your fine lady, kids, and so on," continues Ahmed Bey genially.

The dean (I am sure he must be a dean) draws himself up, and replies with pained toleration, " Your wishes are most kind, I am sure, but, ahem! I am not married."

" Oh dear, how bad, reverend," says the sub-governor jocularly. " But quite right; women are deuces and all."

I feel I had better interfere, as Ahmed Bey's views on women, though interesting, are slightly astonishing to the untrained western mind.

" Well, Ahmed Bey," I say, " I think we ought to be getting on board. It is nearly two o'clock now, and we shall not have too much time."

" I'm afraid your Excellency quite right," says the Bey regretfully. " I had hope you would have had time what you call glass of fizz and nice bit of lunch."

This is partly addressed to me and partly to the

clerical gentleman, who is looking a little astonished. An Oriental never misses noticing a change of expression, though he may be too civil to let you know it, but he often, as in this case, puts it down to the wrong cause.

" I don't mind," continues the Bey, addressing the cleric, " what you call a nice drop of wine, reverend. That no drinks business is all what you call tommy rot. The Pasha here drops on my little place some time and we crush bottles of bubbly."

I wish he would leave me out of his remarks. I feel sure that I am now looked upon in the clerical mind as a roysterer.

The Bey, thus talking, leads the way down to the landing stage, where we get into a motor launch, for our ship is lying further up the harbour.

I strive in vain to persuade Ahmed Bey that he need not come on board with us, but he won't hear of it, until, with a flash of genius, Tommy remembers that I ought to send a telegram (perfectly unnecessary), which we write out and the good-natured little man rushes off to send personally, and we proceed quietly to the ship, I trying on the way to remove from the clerical mind the false impressions which Ahmed Bey's eccentric conversation may have left there.

CHAPTER IV   GOING ON BOARD

IF you see two Anglo-Egyptians in deep conversation, you will find that five times out of ten they are discussing steamship lines, their virtues and iniquities. If you get within earshot you will hear, "Yes, dear, right at the bottom of the hold, and not a stitch to put on till I got to Port Said. Oh, they were rude"; or, "I ventured to point out to the purser that in law he had not got a leg to stand on," and so on according to the sex and profession of the individual. I am no exception to this rule, and hold very strong views on the subject. To my mind any one who knows and does not prefer a blue funnel to any other steamer is simply either stupid or wrong-headed.

This year, however, I am going by the Island and Far East Line, not because I like it, but because the date of sailing happens to suit. I mind less going by it in the dead season, because one is almost sure of a cabin to oneself, which I must have, and which this line won't ordinarily give you. That any one should be so barbarous as to put two or more people who are liable to be attacked at any time by a painful and disgusting illness to live together in a box ten feet by six or seven, is really amazing. The foreign lines are gradually doing away with this uncivilised practice, and are providing a sufficient number of roomy single cabins, but on English steamers we still tolerate this outrage on decency and comfort; we don't even seem to mind it.

When we arrive at the ship, which is lying close to a quay but not touching it, we find the ladder crowded with boats from which passengers and their attendants are scrambling with that haste which every one uses when travelling, whether they have got heaps of time to spare or not. As, after a desperate struggle, we get on the gangway, we are reminded of another curious trait of the Anglo-Saxon traveller, which seems to be in direct contradiction to his willingness to share his cabin with a stranger. This is a tendency to regard as his own any temporary habitation he may occupy, and to resent any intrusion upon it. If an Englishman is in a railway carriage or a steamer or a hotel, he immediately regards it as his own, and is prepared to discourage or even resist any trespassers to the utmost of his powers. One is never more acutely aware of this than when one joins a steamer *en route*.

As Tommy, the dean and I crush forward up the ladder, we are greeted by a hum of muffled disapproval from the passengers above on deck. I can hear portions of frank opinions which are obviously hostile to our travelling by this steamer anyway. As we reach the deck, I, who am leading, am trying to find my ticket, which, though I know I put it in my left coat pocket, I find in my right waistcoat pocket (for tickets, like needles, once they get into you work about all over the place), when I hear a clear female voice say, " Well, thank goodness, there are only a dozen of them." To which another answers, " Yes, but I suppose we shall hear nothing but *mafish* and *malesh* now. Why cannot they go by one of their own lines?" These are obviously Anglo-Indians. We in Egypt profess to despise Anglo-Indians as people who are out of touch with Europe and essentially provincial, whilst they, on the other hand, talk with contempt of our size and village politics. One method of showing this lofty hostility is to pretend not to understand anything about the others' country or language.

At this moment my attention is turned to Tommy, who has a theory that you should always carry your most cherished possessions yourself, and who has now assumed the memorable position of the young lady of Norway, owing to his golf clubs and sticks interlocking in some mysterious way with portions of the ship, whilst a determined-looking lady's-maid is jamming the sharp corner of a mysterious tin case into the small of his back. I feel deeply relieved for the dean's sake that Tommy is, in the hurry of the moment, expressing himself in the vernacular and only making the boatmen blush. He is freed by a strong sailor, gains the deck and disappears down the companion, knocking off bits of the woodwork as he goes.

I now begin to make inquiries for my cabin, but as usual no one pays the slightest attention to me.

If you took a French post clerk, a German police officer, an American customs official, and an English road hog and rolled them into one, you would get a being who, as far as manners went, resembled faintly the ordinary officer of this revered line. In army parlance, the passengers on these boats rank

in the minds of the officers with, but after, black
beetles. Passengers are regarded as a sort of un-
savoury pest with which a ship becomes infected
whilst lying in port. Restrained by regulations they
profoundly disagree with from throwing you overboard or stamping on you, the officers are forced
unwillingly to tolerate your existence, but no more.
They used to make me mad with anger until I
travelled with Tommy, but he taught me how to
combine justice with amusement. He makes it a
practice whenever an officer is rude, to ask him in
mellifluous tones to come and look at the dirt in his
cabin, or to get him a clean pillow-slip, or some
such request. On the officer turning indignantly
away, he explains loudly that he thought that he
was the chief steward or the purser, because he was
so civil to the passengers. He looks so innocent
when he does this that his victim is not sure if he
means to be rude or not, and retires crimson, amid
the titters of the audience.

I wearily continue my inquiries till at last the
chief steward or the assistant purser or whoever it
is feels that I am becoming a nuisance, and fiercely
tells a steward to take me to number 47, as if that
place was the proverbial alternative to Connaught.
The steward sulkily complies, and takes me up and
down into a very narrow and evil-smelling passage,
where, murmuring something about this not being
it, he leaves me and disappears.

Here I remain very much in the way of a lot of
irritable stewards, who seem to be taking exercise
by carrying piles of dirty plates backwards and

forwards, till another steward appears and asks me suspiciously what I want. I explain that I want 47. " But that ain't on this deck," he says gruffly, with the air of a policeman moving an undesirable on. I say humbly that I don't know where it is; can he tell me? He replies shortly that it is not one of his cabins, and I had better go up on to the deck above.

This I do, and find myself in another passage equally dark and almost as odoriferous. On examining the numbers of the cabins, I find that I am opposite number 122, whose owner, a drab-coloured Indian lady, coming out suddenly, looks alarmed and calls to the stewardess to lock her cabin up, as there are dreadful-looking people on board. Suffering under this unmerited harshness, I wander on and meet another official whom I consult. He replies stiffly that he doesn't know. (I find out subsequently that he is the seventh officer, or something which hates passengers.)

At this moment when I am undecided whether I will seize a cabin by force, demand to see the captain, or write to *The Times*, my original steward appears. He is very indignant with me for having moved from where he left me, and says he has been looking for me nigh all over the ship. The prospect of obtaining a more or less permanent resting place on any terms induces me to curb my natural desire to keelhaul him, or whatever you do to people you dislike at sea, and I follow him without a word. He takes me to a totally new part of the ship, which is deeper down in the darker bowels of the ship and gloomier than where I was before.

The smell is different, but equally unpleasant. It seems to be compounded of decayed funguses, hot engine oil, and onions. I expostulate, and point out that my cabin was in the plan of the upper deck. The steward looks at me with hatred and contempt, and asks in tones of suppressed irritation if I ain't 297. I, speaking with difficulty through my grating teeth, reply that I have told him already that I am 47. He then mutters fiercely that he wishes people would give him their right tickets.

This is more than I can bear—as if I should take pains to exchange my upper-deck cabin with some unhappy person who is to live in the noisome cell he is showing me! I am just looking round for a capstan bar, or a belaying pin, or a marling spike, or whatever the proper thing is to use in exterminating a mendacious and uncivil steward, when round a corner comes the portly form of Mr. Tarlington, the agent for the company at Port Said. I explain matters to him, and in two minutes we are on our way to my cabin, while the steward retires in a cowed condition, to wreak his vengeance on some unfortunate passenger who has no friend at court to protect him.

Tarlington promises to send my luggage along, and beams away on his mission of mercy and protection to the unhappy Anglo-Egyptians on board.

In five minutes or so some luggage turns up, though, of course, not the right luggage.

When one announces directly, or through Messrs. Cook, to this steamship company that, in spite of the dangers and disagreeables of the proceeding, you are going to embark as a passenger on one of

263

their steamers, they give you a lot of incorrect information, charge you large sums of money, and supply you with a sheaf of assorted luggage labels. There are some of all sorts. First, there are some with nothing on them but a big capital letter which is the same as the first letter of your surname, so that in the case of your getting complete amnesia, it will help you to remember who you are. Then, secondly, there are labels on which is printed where you come from and where you are going to. The idea of these is excellent, but in practice I don't think they pay much attention to them, as they often send Egyptian luggage to Bombay. Thirdly, there are labels marked " Not wanted on voyage," which I have so often longed to paste on the backs of several of my fellow passengers. These labels work well, almost too well. Putting one of these labels on a trunk has much the same effect as sending a man to exile in Siberia. It sends it away for a time for certain, and, with any luck, for ever. I believe they cast luggage marked like this into a bottomless hold, from which some adventurous sailor may rescue it; or it may just stay there till the ship is broken up. The next sort of label is that with " Wanted on voyage " printed on it. These condemn your luggage to detention in a hold from which it can be produced at any time if you know exactly the right official to ask for it and they don't send some one else's instead. I struck up quite a friendship with a lady years ago through always getting her luggage when I asked for mine. Finally, there are labels marked " Cabin," and these are

the really useful ones. I never waste anything, so
I paste the other labels on the inside of my box
where they can do no harm, and put a " Cabin "
label on each of my packages, even if they are as
large as grand pianos.

If you do this, all your luggage is put together on
board in a place where you can see it, and handed
over to your bedroom steward, who, from venal
motives, is more or less devoted to your interests.
You can then select the articles you really do want
in your cabin, and have the rest put away in the
" Wanted on voyage " place under the eye of the
said steward, who can then always find it again if
you want it.

My bedroom steward now appears, and with his
aid my luggage is found and dealt with, and I think
I had better go on deck and see how my companions
are faring.

When I come on deck I am met by Mrs. Despard,
who is apparently going to catch a train. " Oh,
Lord Edward, I have lost my bag." " Not *the*
bag? " " Yes, *the* bag. What shall I do? All my
money and jewels are in it." I ask where she saw
it last, and she says she put it down in one of the
saloons, and when she looked round it was gone.
I rush to the saloon which she indicates and search,
with no result.

Mrs. Despard always reminds me of the hero in
Jerome's *Stageland*, only he is always in trouble about
his title deeds, and she about her bag, and consequently her keys.

The adventures of the bag, if properly written,

would be as exciting as any romance. It has travelled by itself, hotly pursued by telegrams and letters, all over the world. Every transport official knows and dreads that small oblong of blue morocco. Chiefs of police and even Ministers of State have passed sleepless nights during its periods of fugue. It looks innocent enough; in fact it is prepossessing, but it contains more original sin, according to Mrs. Despard, than its limited cubic content renders it possible to believe. It was, unfortunately for all of us, the gift of a deceased friend, who probably had a weak heart and died of the anxiety it caused her. It is therefore sacred, and even in one's moments of most deadly hostility one dares not think of destroying it. In virtue of its sacred character, it is still trusted by its would-be keeper as if it had not already on countless occasions betrayed its trust. It invariably, when lost, contains Mrs. Despard's keys, her most private letters, some addresses which (though not wanted) she can never get again, and a variety of small feminine possessions, I fancy not unconnected with resisting that, to the female mind, greatest disfigurement, a shiny nose. When tele-graphing a description of its contents, these are included in some general term. I usually describe them as " other small articles," but every acting aide-de-camp has used a different phrase, down to poor little Parley in the Lancers, who boldly described them in French " *des poufs pour poudrer la contenants*," thus giving the finishing blow to the already impaired sanity of an overworked station-master.

In addition to its truant characteristics, it has a power of self-concealment I have never seen equalled. It gets behind chairs and under seats—a newspaper affords it cover, and I have known it completely blotted out by a book half its size. Anyhow, it is not in the saloon nor the music room, nor on the upper deck. I feel a wild idea of searching the engines, when Mrs. Despard gives vent to a cry at once joyful and vindictive.

"There it is!" she says excitedly, pointing to the bag. "Do you see that man is carrying it away? Oh, Lord Edward, do run after him and stop him!" I dash down the wrong companion, tear madly round, and emerge, after severely injuring some of the less agile passengers, at the top of the ladder. I rush down and, accompanied by X and a stray customs official, jump into a boat, gain the quay, and give chase to the robber, who appears to be a respectably dressed old Jew. I am not as young as I was, but in the excitement of the chase I do my two hundred and fifty yards in a very creditable time. As I come up, the old gentleman is tottering into one of the houses of business fronting the harbour.

I touch him on the shoulder and pant out, " I want that bag, please."

He turns half round and his face goes a greyish green horrible to see, and he begins literally squealing for help. Three or four more Jews of various ages rush out of the house, and, as the old gentleman falls back in the arms of the stoutest of them, I realise with horror that, though like it in a superficial way, it is not Mrs. Despard's bag.

"What you want? Who devil are you?" says the second stoutest Jew in rather a nervous way.

I say lamely it was a mistake. I thought the old gentleman had taken my bag by mistake as I had lost it.

"You have no right playing silly things on my father, who is very rich and does not steal bags," says the fattest Jew sternly, as he places his father in a chair which has been brought for him. "My father is a weak heart, and if he die you murder him and be hanged for damages," says the youngest and least podgy scion of Israel excitedly.

This is too awful. I, crimson with shame, produce my card, which I hand to the fattest, again apologise, and walk away with the air of a detected card-sharper, followed by my mystified myrmidons, who, I think, now share the obvious view of the Israelites, that I have been imbibing too freely at an early hour. I arrive back at the ship, to find Mrs. Despard sitting comfortably in a chair in the cool breeze, with the bag beside her. She reproaches me with having been too hasty, as the moment I started she saw it was not the bag, which, it appears, was found in her cabin on her bed, though who put it there, as she says, is a complete mystery.

And here I briefly note the adventures on this journey of—*The Bag.*

Lost at Port Said.

Lost on ship under Mrs. X's skirts.

Lost to Apache, Marseilles.

Left behind in Paris.

Lost on boat.

Goes on to London alone.

CHAPTER V   DINNER ON BOARD

DINNER on the first night on board a ship is always trying. It is, as it almost always is, rather rough off the Egyptian coast, and we all, so to speak, come to dinner making our reserves and without prejudice to any future action on our part. Tommy and I are unlucky enough to arrive early, and therefore have to take a more or less active part in the acrimonious discussion which takes place between Mrs. H. and the head steward with reference to our table, which, though it was the one she chose originally, does not meet with her approval. In vain does the worn-out and perspiring head steward explain that it is impossible to change it now. She says she will *not* sit at a table where she will get all the smell of the kitchen, be in a draught, and served last.

The steward limply points out that it is nowhere near the kitchen, that there is just the same draught elsewhere, and that it is not served last. Mrs. H., who, I feel sure, prides herself on being firm, says that it is practically in the kitchen, that one cannot keep one's seat for the draught, and that it is not served at all; and she appeals to us to back her up. Tommy and I care, in the first place, not a scrap where we sit, and, secondly, rather like the table, and, thirdly, would sooner sit anywhere than stand up before two hundred people as the supporters of a shrill-voiced woman who is obviously speaking to the steward in rather an unpleasant way. However, she prevails, and some wretched people who have done nothing wrong are hustled out of their places to make room for us on the ground that there was a mistake, which no one believes.

As a matter of fact, we are no better off than we were, and there are distinct signs of a brewing row with the huge family whom we have dispossessed.

Mrs. H. is, however, triumphant, and I think gloomily that it will be like this the whole way to London. Taking a journey with Mrs. H. is like travelling with the Flying Dutchman; one moves in a perpetual storm of small unpleasantnesses.

I manage, however, to sit next to Mrs. Despard, and the two other seats besides those occupied by our party are filled by Mrs. Somberley and her sister, Miss Harlane. Mrs. H. makes a desperate attempt to place me between the sisters, but I am firm and say that this is my place. H. is placed between the sisters, and he deserves it for marrying Mrs. H.

Mrs. Despard, of course, comes late. It appears she mislaid her bag, and it took her a long time to find it. She then inquires, as a matter of course, who Sophy has been having a row with, and is mildly amused at my account of it.

Meanwhile Mrs. H. has been letting H. have a bad time of it. She won't have any food, as it is so ill cooked; she cannot get the brand of champagne she wants, and she cannot remember its name, and she finally rises to her feet saying she has such a headache, and goes on deck, where H. has to accompany her. However, she goes, which is the main point, and the dinner ends better than it began. We then start talking about ships and their virtues and vices. Mrs. Despard has always something original to impart, and now tells us all about a ship which is, as far as I can make out, rather too big to navigate anything but the Atlantic, which the Germans are building to invade England with. She explains to a breathless audience that it draws thirty-five fathoms, is four hundred yards long, and is only kept steady by turning round and round. I know better than to question her facts, but I think I recognise the gyroscope in the last description. Tommy, who does not know her well, is impressed, and asks her quite seriously if the turning round is not uncomfortable. She replies serenely, " No, it is just like a rifle bullet," which settles him, for if you come to think of it, one has never heard if a rifle bullet is comfortable or not. At this point H. returns. His dinner consists to-night of soup and fruit, which is a nice light diet.

He immediately launches out into one of his anecdotes. It is about ships, at least a ship he once travelled on. It appears he once went from Malta to Athens in a boat which was built of steel and had two masts and two funnels, and went about 12 knots, and there was a deck on the top and cabins below, and there was a bowsprit in front and a rudder behind and engines. In fact it would form an excellent article for a cheap dictionary, explaining the word " steamboat, see also steamship." He crushes the conversation, as he usually does. In conversation, unless it is the dialogue of a smart play, each remark must or should have some bearing on the last; and if you tell a story or make a long remark about which nothing can be said but profane oaths which are not admissible, conversation must cease.

After a pause Tommy starts on " Stewards I have known." Of course, the first day at sea one is always near the subject of sea-sickness. I am sure in the prisons in the Terror the conversation wavered between knives and necks.

We get on very well at first, and Mrs. Despard says stewards are nearly all old firemen who lose their nerves and become stewards, and the companies prefer it because they can always put the passengers out if necessary, which is of course true in a sense. Tommy, more impressed than ever, says it must be rather difficult to get so many firemen, but Mrs. D. with her usual skill says, No, because it is safer and the pay is better, which crushes Tommy again. Mrs. Somberley tells us about a mad steward who shaved a nervous old gentleman by force all night, and he came to breakfast next morning as bald as an egg and nearly mad. Miss Harlane, who is romantic, tells us of a Sir Somebody Something, who became a steward and married a millionaire's daughter, when H. flattens us out by telling us of a steward he had going from Gib to London, who was an ex-soldier and was five foot six high, with brown hair, and he was quite a decent valet and kept the cabins quite as clean as one could expect, and ate meat and drank a little beer and said "thank you, sir," when you tipped him.

After this even Tommy can think of nothing more to say, so we go depressedly on deck. After a dreary struggle up and down the deck, we assure one another that the weather is getting better and that the wind is dropping; which is manifestly not the case. We then reel below to our stuffy cabins, to pass the night as best we may. I order a stiff brandy and soda, drink it, and get into bed as quickly as I can, wedging myself in with the pillows to avoid literally taking a leap in the dark, and sink into a heavy sleep.

CHAPTER VI   AT SEA: MORNING

THERE is no sensation more luxurious than the feeling of rest and freedom which comes when one first starts on leave; and it is in the morning when one first recovers consciousness that this feeling is sweetest. For the first few moments one is not sure where one is, and then one begins to realise that one is in a ship and that leave has really begun. I can only compare it to the feeling of convalescence. The load is lifted from one's shoulders. One need no longer rack one's brain to find combinations to meet hopeless situations. It is no longer one's fate to listen to endless grievances and complaints, to adjust ever-recurring quarrels, to carry on that ceaseless war against red tape and slackness. One is freed for the time from the anxieties of that perpetual game of political card spillikins one has to play in Egypt. Foreign interests, British interests, Missionary interests, Mahommedan interests, Coptic interests, Greek interests, Jewish interests, Turkish interests, Sudan interests, Khedivial interests, are among the cards one must not disturb as one pulls out the card one wants; and is not there trouble if any other does just get stirred! Moreover, if from long practice and bitter experience one can get through one's own moves fairly well, what about one's subordinates? One never goes to bed without the uneasy consciousness that one may find oneself the next morning in a sea of difficulties, owing to the whole-hearted but misplaced zeal of the newest-joined inspector. The worst part of it is that, to continue the card-spillikin metaphor, it is impossible to see beforehand how many interests one will affect by touching any particular subject.

Then, again, all those awful personal questions are temporarily out of the way—the rows, squabbles, petty jealousies and intrigues in which one lives.

One is no longer a servant, one can sleep when one likes, eat when one likes, and play when one likes.

I can feel, too, on this particular occasion that it is a fine morning. The ship is only rolling very slightly and lazily, just enough to dull the vibration of the screw. The port-hole is open, and the fresh sea breeze is blowing on my face.

At this point the steward enters with my tea, or what is supposed to be tea, and I decide to have my bath at once before the rush, so as to avoid having to wait. My decision is partly due to the fact that further sleep is out of the question, owing to the noise which is now going on on deck just over my head.

It is said to be caused by cleaning the decks, but this is hard to believe. Judging by one's hearing, one man is beating the deck hard with something like a glorified wet towel, another is doing a step-dance of a complicated character to express his satisfaction, whilst others pump on them with the hose. Periodically the rest of the crew get tired of this and drag the two men away on their backs. Then somebody suggests that a race round the ship would be fun, and starts the competitors with a singularly harsh whistle.

I get out of bed, and wrapping myself in my dressing-gown, proceed to my bath, which is difficult to find, as it is well concealed, and none of the people you meet take any interest in the subject. I arrive just in time to see the last vacant bath seized by a yellow-looking Indian colonel, and I resign myself to wait in the narrow alley-way, my only amusement being to avoid having my toes stamped on by passing stewards and others. It is often very hard to find a bath, especially on one of the older boats. I remember a most respectable old gentle-man, a pillar of his parish church, and all that was

275

desirable, telling me he looked for one for three days with no success until, feeling that an exceptional effort must be made in the interests of hygiene, after many wanderings he found a door on which in the Cimmerian darkness he could just discern the word "bath." It was, however, obviously occupied, so he patiently waited. He thought he saw the door open a little tiny bit once or twice, but nothing happened. He was, however, resolute, and waited on till at last the door was flung open and Mrs. Colonel Bolger of Ramnugger flounced out and told him what she thought of him. It was the ladies' bath. He, of course, fled, but was reported to the captain and shunned by the rest of the passengers for the remainder of the voyage.

By this time four other candidates for ablutions have ranged themselves alongside me. We don't speak, but wait in gloomy silence, murmuring occasionally at the awful time people keep the bath. At last an irritable gentleman, No. 2 on the list, rattles fiercely at the door opposite.

A moment later the door opens, and the colonel stalks out majestically. We all feel like schoolboys caught doing something they ought not, and I am sure the man next me murmurs something about its not being him.

However, the bath is cleaned up in a perfunctory way and I get in.

Washing on an old-fashioned boat like this is an art. In the first place, your bath is filled with what is supposed to be sea water, and a small tub of what is in theory fresh water is placed on a shelf across it. As a matter of fact, both liquids, as one's olfactory nerves inform one, contain a good many of the coal-tar and petroleum products as well. The result is that the floor of the bath is like a butter slide, and many a nasty fall has one had by not getting in carefully. I have never quite made out how one ought to wash. I think standing up, with soap and the fresh water first, and then soak in the sea water, but I am never sure. I only know that the complicated arrangement marked "shower douche wave" should never be touched except by a professional engineer. Once in my young and reckless days I gave myself a shower of boiling water, and on another occasion I touched the tap (it was in January) and an ice-cold three-inch jet of water hit me where my thick woollen waistcoat would have been if I had known it was going to do it.

To-day, however, I feel so light-hearted that even a bath of diluted engine oil in an evil-smelling box seems delightful, and I sally forth in the best of tempers.

Luckily I took very careful note of the way I came, and after a brisk ten minutes' walk am back in my cabin, which, by the way, I find afterwards is only 20 feet from the bathroom, if one went by a different route from the one I chose.

Dressing and shaving accomplished, I make my way on deck. It is a perfect morning, with a cloudless sky and a rippling sea of deepest blue. It is fresh, but with that pleasant, indescribable promise of heat in the air.

277

One drawback is that, owing to the mysterious operations I listened to earlier, everything is dripping wet, so one cannot sit down, but I don't want to. To complete my happiness, on rounding a corner I find Mrs. Despard, looking as if she was the very spirit of morning herself. She pretends to be astonished at my getting up so early (she never gets up till ten on land), and declares that we must take a proper constitutional, as it will be too hot to do anything in the middle of the day. This project we carry out with occasional pauses to lean over the bulwarks and look into the swirling, dancing, blue and white water beneath. It is perfectly delightful, and I am just explaining my views on some very interesting subject—Mrs. Despard's higher intellectual self, I think—when I become aware that there is a crumple in my roseleaf, something wrong, something wanting. I analyse mentally, and at once recognise that it is an effect of the body on the mind. It is hunger—not your nice civilised appetite, not that delicate intimation which is sent to your brain that a little light refreshment would be agreeable, but good, honest, barbarian hunger, a craving, empty feeling, an imperious demand for immediate supplies. I have up to now been in, so to speak, the higher mental atmosphere, and this sudden and irresistible tug earthwards is distressing. I hope above all things that Mrs. Despard may not notice it. Women are so quick. After all, the body is subordinate to the mind. Do not faquirs sit on sharp nails for years without losing their outward composure? Though, of course, in such a case one wonders if there is a mind.

Anyhow, by an effort of will I disregard the
" base cravings of the moulded dust." I fear, however, that my conversation is deteriorating. I notice
Mrs. Despard is losing interest, and instead of turning
those wonderful eyes full of inquiry or comprehension
on my humble self, she is looking absently away.
Covertly I look at my watch. Thank goodness,
only three minutes to breakfast! What an insane
idea it is to have breakfast at nine! I believe it is
mere pandering to the tastes of these desiccated,
over-curried Indians. At this moment a bell strikes.
" What is that? " says Mrs. Despard. " I mean
what time is it? " " Nine," I begin, when it strikes
me that one bell is only half-past eight. Horrible
thought! It is that beastly clock; they have been
putting it back. It is an odious trick they have
now to put it back during the night. " Isn't breakfast at nine? " says Mrs. Despard in a detached
way. " Yes," I say, " but I am afraid I was wrong;
it is only half-past eight." " Oh," says Mrs.
Despard, in tones of dismay, " what am I to do?
I am simply famishing." I suggest kindly that I
might get her some biscuits, and, without waiting
for her answer, descend the stairs five steps at a
time. I believe it is against all the ancient laws
and regulations for a prisoner, I mean a passenger,
to ask for biscuits, but my eye is so wild, and my
jaw so determined, that the steward feels that if I
cannot get biscuits I may resort to cannibalism to
assuage my pangs, and hastily produces some, which,
after placing a certain number in my pocket in
case more are wanted later, I bear in triumph to
the deck, and we are soon both munching, in spite

279

of the peculiarly sea-sodden flavour which all biscuits on board a ship have got.

Of course, after this the conversation becomes more material. One cannot be sentimental or highly intellectual with one's mouth full, but we both feel a great danger is overpast.

However, when the breakfast bell rings we are by no means indifferent.

In the saloon we are joined by H. Mrs. H. does not appear till later, still suffering from the effects of yesterday. He naturally destroys conversation, but, as we both want to eat a serious breakfast without being distracted, this is just as well, and even H. has some merits, of which one is not talking at breakfast. The only excitement about this breakfast beyond other breakfasts is that it has certain dishes I have never seen elsewhere. There are things with names like Welsh pie and Smashpot, which are all out of tins and all taste the same, but one takes them out of curiosity. In fact, everything does taste the same, except various excellent curries and the butter, which tastes like what they call on musical programmes a *pot pourri* of the larder.

After breakfast Mrs. Despard declares we must sit down and solemnly read serious works. She has brought a philosophic work. I know it. It is Pluffenheim's *Integral Concepts*. Charles Rainsford, her great literary friend, gave it to her four years ago, and she got to page 28 the first week and has been there ever since; at least she was still at it a month ago. I once pointed out that this page was getting a different colour from exposure to the weather, and we had quite a coolness for a fortnight.

I must go and get my " stodge," which is a new work on currency some one sent me the other day. Bloresby, our expert on these subjects, told me it would startle me, which I am bound to say it has only done once, and that was when it fell off a table.

We soon settle down in our chairs, and I make up my mind to begin Chapter III, " Tokens." I read the first paragraph and look up. Mrs. Despard is not playing fair. She holds the book open, it is true, but she is looking over the top of it with a rapt expression. Is she puzzling out the master's last great thought? She turns her head and says, " Oh, Lord Edward, what is twelve metres at five and elevenpence a yard?" I work it out. " I think it is £3 16s. 11d." " Yes," she says, " it was not really cheap," and looks back at her book.

I resume my reading, and read the first paragraph over again and then the second, when I become attracted by the shape of the sun flecks on the sea. I wonder why they are that shape; is it because . . . I regain consciousness to find H. is shaking me and saying, " Hi! hi! time for luncheon."

When I have washed my hands, I make my way to the saloon. On the companion I meet Tommy, who has a wild look in his eye. " Ned," he says in impressive tones, " I have been having the h—— of a time." " How?" I ask. " That Mrs. H. is a sweet soul. First she wanted to go on the bridge, and pestered me till I asked the captain, who was rude to me. Then she wanted to go on the boat deck, and I asked the chief officer and he was rude to me. Then she sat on a coiled hawser until the third officer, who held me responsible, was rude to me. Then she made me move her chair round and round till people thought I was doing it for a bet, then she sent me to fetch three separate things she had all the time in her d—d work bag. Then she wanted a chop at twelve, and I saw the chief steward and he was rude to me, and if I have any more of her I shall go mad, mad, mad! " This last delivered in a highly theatrical manner, with disastrous results on a nervous old lady who, coming round the corner suddenly on Tommy, gives a faint scream and scuttles away like a rabbit.

We discuss whether we should go after her, but Tommy says, No, never chase a frightened horse, and old ladies are the same; so we go down to luncheon, to find the whole party rather under the weather. Mrs. H. is giving H. what we used to call " socks," because he did not look after her this morning, which makes it awkward for every one else.

The lunch is like the breakfast; the names are wonderful, but the food tastes exactly the same. I am sure that any one who disbelieved in the universal source of matter would be converted by this food. You have galantine and mutton and chicken and ham and beef all tasting exactly alike.

After a time Mrs. H., having said all she has to say about her grievance, goes on deck, and we get into the usual discussion of how long it takes to go from Port Said to the Straits of Messina, about which we are all positive, and all more or less wrong.

AFTER lunch we make no pretence about it, but all retire for a *siesta*. One idiocy which the East breaks us of is the childish shame we have in England of going to sleep in the daytime. Where the idea comes from it is hard to imagine, but all Englishmen regard sleeping in the daytime as an unjustifiable and shameful thing to do. One can understand the popular and universal prejudice against watchmen and sentries sleeping when on duty; but why an idle man, whose most harmless moments are probably passed in slumber, should conceal the fact that he has been asleep, I cannot imagine.

Even after shooting or hunting, men will only admit to a nap in a chair. I suspect it was supposed to show that one was a weakly creature, or perhaps there is some forgotten superstition connected with it. Anyhow, the notion of deliberately undressing and lying on one's bed fast asleep after lunch for an hour or more would shock most untravelled Englishmen profoundly. I love it, if it is not too hot, and it certainly makes all the difference to one's well-being if one can do it.

When I come on deck again the world is taking exercise, which either consists of that weary prisoners' tramp up and down the deck, or of joining in one of those painful games which are inflicted on one on these occasions. Mrs. H. has just been evicted from the place which she had chosen for her chair, across the deck quoit pitch, by an obdurate quarter-master, and has now made H. put it where it is most inconvenient for the promenaders, and is complaining generally of the hopeless selfishness of the human race. I avoid games on board ship as the devil does holy water; so I join X, and we commence our tramp up and down, with that broken, jerky conversation which is produced by having to steer through or round couples coming the other way, like an endless first figure of the Lancers. Detectives say that finding out crimes is dull work as a rule, because ninety-nine out of a hundred are exactly like others one has known. The criminal types are comparatively few, and the individuals resemble each other closely, so that, given similar circumstances, they will take the same line, endeavour to conceal their acts in the same way and make the same mistakes. Steamer folk follow the same law. One meets the same types again and again on these boats, so that even the inevitable boredom of ship life is rarely lightened by meeting new types of interesting people.

I am cursed with an excellent trivial memory. I cannot remember that I have to dine with some one, or that I must write a letter of importance, but I remember for years what an Indian judge tells me of the difficulty of dealing with the Brahmin, or what the Chinese merchant has to tell me about tea. And I never forget the types I meet or the things they say or do, and on this boat there are plenty of amusing ones.

I like Miss Arbutley in theory, and to a certain
284

extent in practice. She is nice-looking and dresses neatly, and she has a nice voice, and is always glad to see one and ready to talk. She has, however, views which, though they have changed often, are not apparently approaching perfection. I gather that her latest conversion is to what she calls a worship of Pan. At first this sounds to my untutored ear disreputable, but on inquiry it appears to mean that we should all be more natural and worship, as she expresses it, great Mother Nature. I cannot picture her as a nymph; she is too eccentrically dressed and puts mauve powder on her nose, a thing no satyr would admire, I am sure. I have always had a sneaking desire to be natural; one could tell people what one thinks of their wine, and seize all the nice things for oneself. How pleasant it would be, too, to hit H. hard, where it hurts him, every time he bored one! Miss Arbutley says it would be a more joyous life for every one to do as they pleased. Now that, speaking altruistically, from H.'s point of view, I doubt. I cannot imagine even the greatest enthusiasm would make him like being kicked by every one who could do so with impunity, and even Miss Arbutley would, I am sure, dislike my scrubbing her face with a wet handkerchief to see if the mauve would come off, or whether it is a dye, which is my present natural longing. Poor dear, her naturalness is like Marie Antoinette's rusticity. She would like mentally to milk well-trained cows into silver buckets, and dance with silken dressed shepherds afterwards. How the mere sight of fierce, cruel, dirty, selfish nature would upset her! However, what the South Sea Island king explained to his people about the bishop—viz.: he talked very fiercely but did not mean what he said—is true of her, for on the arrival of the inevitable H., who, I am sure, belongs to a secret sect for the suppression of human intercourse, she pretends to be pleased, and is led away by him to play one of those thrilling games provided for the passengers, which consists in throwing rings of rope into a bucket. H., however, makes it more amusing than it usually is, by flinging his rings with vicious force at various harmless individuals, who are only very comparatively in the direction of the bucket. I am glad he lands one of the gilt-edged officers a nasty clip on the jaw, especially as he apologises by saying he never noticed him, but I regret his hitting an old gentleman, for whom I have already a deep sympathy, on the nape of the neck. Ever since I came aboard that unhappy old person, who is afflicted with severe lameness, and a bespectacled daughter of forbidding and earnest appearance, has been hunted from pillar to post, or, to be nautical, from funnel to mast. He is moved by his daughter, who does it in a practical and rather violent way, obviously regretting the time lost to her by this function from the study of statistics of the moral condition of India, or whatever deadly subject she is immersed in. On each occasion he says plaintively, " Amelia, I think perhaps I had better move," when he is whirled away to a new scene of helpless suffering with his chair, sticks, cushions, shawls, etc. He came on deck early, and no sooner was he established than they turned the hose on his feet on the pretext of washing the deck. He had scarcely been placed in a safe position on the other side of the deck, when he was again inundated. Rescued from a watery deck, he is no sooner partially dried, than he is moved in order to let an odoriferous gentleman of colour play at polishing some brass work against which his chair is resting. Hardly removed to another spot, when a small boy and an obvious amateur paints him and a piece of iron work in his vicinity impartially. Spotted but unruffled, he next is placed in a position in which he interferes with the putting up of the awnings, and men with naked feet walk about all over him.

CHAPTER VIII   AT SEA: EVENING

THERE is something particularly unpleasant about rough weather at sea when the temperature is high. The only pleasure in, or compensation for, rough weather in the north is that it is bracing and invigorating, and when that solitary advantage is taken away rough weather has no recommendation.

I explain this to Tommy as we shoot out of the companion into the sticky darkness, slip up and sit down in beautiful time, but too loud, like a black

Sudanese band. We struggle to our feet, saying what we think of rubber shoes on a wet deck. Tommy expresses his opinion that two inches of his spine must be projecting out of the top of his head, when the door of the companion again opens and Mesdames D. and H., as the playbills say, bound out and fling themselves into our arms, or perhaps more literally our waistcoats. When one reads of a woman flinging herself into a man's arms it sounds romantic. In real life it hurts. Mrs. D. arrives shoulder first, and in fighting parlance bags my wind. She then says " Oh! " stamps twice on my toe (the sore one), seizes my hat with one hand and my tie with the other, thus bonneting me and strangling me in one motion, as they say in the drill books. Out of the eye which is not obscured by my hat I can see, by the light coming from the companion door, Tommy hanging on to the bulwarks whilst Mrs. H. is apparently trying to throw him overboard. (The deck lights are out, as the electric light has gone wrong.) At this moment, with the inconsistency of their sex, the two ladies suddenly try to stagger backwards, and are only restrained by severe physical exertions on our part; again changing, they fling themselves upon us with renewed energy.

After a few moments of this awful struggle the rolling becomes temporarily less violent, and we get the ladies to the bulwarks, where they can hold on to inanimate objects that we trust don't suffer as we do in the process.

It is decided to get some chairs in a sheltered

spot, and tie them there and then put the ladies into them, and this we do after incredible struggles and suppressed profanity. We then wrap the rugs round the ladies and anchor ourselves in the vicinity, while it is explained to us how rough we are. Tommy meekly agrees, but says the treatment he has received will be a warning to him never to do it again; and asks me what a broken back feels like.

It is rather a fine sight, now that our eyes are accustomed to the darkness, as the sea is semi-phosphorescent, and in the dim light the huge waves look huger and more tumbled and tormented by the howling wind.

Where we are, we are out of the wind and in comparative calm and quiet, and we begin talking.

In the dark one either talks very well, very foolishly, or not at all. In this case Tommy begins telling us of his adventures in the South Sudan, and he lies well. Not that all or even a quarter of what he says is untrue, only the probable parts. That is one of the most irritating things that exist— the improbability of truth. I have had to modify some of my best stories, because you simply could not believe them. In this case, as usual, the audience accept Tommy's flights of imagination with enthusiasm, and question his facts with evident disbelief. It is amusing to watch with what skill women cover their ignorance. They are forced, poor things, to listen to men talking about all sorts and kinds of subjects which they can know little or nothing about, and they become marvellously skilful at appearing to follow with interest a series of words which can mean little or nothing to them. Sometimes I believe they follow your ideas from your expression and manner, as children do, and not by the words you use. It is very likely a surer way of exchanging ideas and impressions than the artificial code we have devised. I don't mean that women are necessarily more ignorant than men, but that they show it less.

Tommy has really a great talent for description, and he makes our flesh creep with his picture of those awful marshes where the steaming temperature never changes night or day, and the extent of your view is always bounded by the high grass round you, and where you hear, not see, the unknown enemies moving round you, and the sullen pools are full of foul reptiles, and the torture of the mosquito never ceases. We are all impressed, when the effect is spoilt by the arrival of H. on all fours. Whether he has been in that position since he came on deck I don't know, but that is how he joins the party. He anchors himself to his wife's chair, and in three minutes has destroyed the charm of the scene.

He asks Tommy what pay one gets there, and if he tried Bolger's syrup for fever. Then, in spite of the obvious disapproval of the company, tells us how he once nearly went to West Africa, and did not, worse luck!

After enduring this, not because we are gifted with any undue measure of fortitude, but because we are averse to moving, we decide mentally that we would sooner face the fury of the elements than another of H.'s anecdotes, and with much difficulty pilot the ladies back to the companion and wish them good-night, whilst in order to pander to T.'s evil habits, as I explain to him, we adjourn to the smoking-room for a drink.

Here we find the usual small gathering of the society of the ship. The Anglo-Indians are exchanging ideas on their respective provinces, and a bridge party are quarrelling over their last rubber. Half a dozen subalterns are discussing their leaves and the meanness of the War Office in that respect. It is not inspiriting, and I am nearly dead with sleep, so I totter to my feet and eventually to bed.

   •   •   •   •   •   •

CHAPTER IX   MARSEILLES

I HATE leaving a ship, other than a Channel steamer. One has usually settled down and got used to the monotony of the life, and no one hustles one or hurries one about. There is plenty of time to do anything, for the longer it takes the more day it fills up. Out of this torpid condition one is suddenly hurled into a French custom-house. Of course the din of unnecessary conversation, which to the Northern ear is deafening, to one used to Egypt seems like the gentle speech of a taciturn woman.

But still it infects one, and we passengers all begin talking in a loud voice about nothing in particular. We also press forward through the throng of officials and others, who seem to be paid by the French Government to hinder and obstruct travellers, for that is all they do. The inevitable Cook's man tries to attend as usual to twelve people at once, and as usual fails. Hotel touts seize weak-minded travellers, and bear them off to hotels which they never meant to go to or even positively dislike. We resign our hand luggage to an elderly and, I trust, reformed Apache, and are taken to the usual comfortless shed where we are to register our luggage, etc. I suggest to my companions, that as we know by long experience that no one will think either (1) of unloading our baggage from the ship, (2) of paying the smallest attention to us when it is unloaded for at least an hour, we should get one of the hotel porters to look after our interests in our absence, and go for a walk or drive to pass the time. We discuss the matter, and I find I am in a minority of one. Tommy has principles and disapproves of walking when he can sit down; Mrs. D. says she is sure they will send off her luggage, when she is not looking, to some awful place; Mr. H. says he never loses sight of his luggage when travelling, which must be uncomfortable for him, as holds and luggage vans must be horrible places to travel in, and an awful bore for the luggage. I restrain myself from suggesting that he might give his portmanteau a rest to-day as it looks fagged and yellow, and meekly acquiesce. I borrow a chair from a customs clerk who has fallen a victim to Mrs. D., and the rest of us sit on the low barrier table on which the customs officials play at noughts and crosses with the passengers' luggage. Here we sit talking while H. does *tours de force* in destroying all human interest in each subject as it comes up, and Mrs. H. groans out gloomy prognostications, like an overfed pythoness.

Time wears away, and instead of increased activity every one seems to be going away. At last Tommy, who is full of latent energy, suggests H. should make inquiries. This is carried out almost unanimously, and he departs on his errand, giving vent to his first *Est-ce que* as he turns the corner of the shed, whilst we settle down to amuse Mrs. D. with considerable success; even Mrs. H. gives a gloomy smile occasionally as Tommy describes his social experiences (purely imaginary) in India and elsewhere.

Such happiness is not to last: a warning *tray biang* from what they call in stage directions " off," tells us of the return of our messenger, and we behold H. being led back by the irate elderly Apache, who is talking volubly in a broad Marseilles dialect, whilst H., who understands one word in twenty-five, is interjecting an occasional *tray biang*, to pacify the irate foreigner and at the same time, so to speak, keep his end up. The Apache, having restored the wandering sheep to his proper fold or shed, with renewed injunctions for us to wait where we are, departs. I notice that he is even more rollickingly murderous than he was, and I feel a qualm.

Supposing his naturally astute mind is obscured by clouds of scented alcohol. I suggest this to Tommy, who replies with decision, " I did not notice any scent, but if you mean that he is very drunk, I agree with you."

Once the germ of distrust is implanted in the human heart it grows fast. Up till now we have regarded the Apache as an uncleanly and dissipated but beneficent person.

Mrs. D. is now sure we are in the wrong place, and may have missed a train and lost our luggage.

We proceed in a body till we find a person of consequence in uniform, but he declines to speak or interrupt the train of reflection which is passing through his mind. He merely points to another shed and turns away. We march on, every one explaining how sure they were that we were in the wrong shed but did not like to say so.

At this moment it all flashes on me : instead, as I thought, of being under the protecting care of one whose past life, though regrettable, enabled him more effectually to defend our interests, we are the sport of the whims of a brain steeped in alcohol. We therefore, that is Tommy and I, appeal to a gentleman in uniform, who characteristically declines to answer and walks away.

We try another and yet another until we despair. We only want to know what to do, but we can get no help. We are pariahs. It is an excellent instance of the results of keeping bad company, as I explain to Tommy.

Our tempers begin to go, especially as our female

fellow travellers begin to point out how sure they have always been that we were doing the wrong thing the wrong way with the wrong people. The Apache has now subsided into an alcoholic stupor on my cabin trunk.

At this point an unusually well-dressed official appears and demands with stern ferocity what we are doing here. We explain. He declines our explanation, and says we must go away at once. We agree joyfully, but are crushed by his ukase that our luggage must remain. Why? we ask timidly. With growing indignation he tells us loudly because it has not been examined by the customs officers. We implore him to inform us how we can get this done. He, speaking still louder, says we cannot get this done, as the time has passed for the examination of the baggage of passengers from this steamship, and in this he is confirmed by a small crowd of officials, porters and loafers, who have assembled round us, and who all talk at once.

We ask still mildly, by exercising miracles of self-control, what are we then to do? That, bellows the official, is not his affair. We must go and come back to-morrow.

But we urge, with a pressure of some thousands of pounds to the inch in our boilers, we wish to catch the six o'clock train to Paris. At this he almost screams with rage, and the remainder of the crowd bellow with excitement. We gather that he does not really care whether we go to Paris or elsewhere. As a last chance we point out that in the next shed the passengers of another liner are having their baggage examined. Could it not be done there? This nearly produces an apoplectic fit; apparently mixing passengers is against every principle he has. It is, to judge by his demeanour, a vile act, with which no honest sub-deputy assistant examiner of customs would stain his reputation and honour.

Every one now lets himself go, and we all shout and gesticulate.

Tommy now reveals the true greatness of his character. He strides up to the gibbering official, and demands in courteous but firm language to be immediately taken to the Director of Customs, to lodge a complaint of the outrageous way in which two senior officials of the Egyptian Government and two English ladies have been treated.

Every one pauses and then the discussion is resumed, but our adversary is shaken. One must not treat officials like the general public. His friends reason with him and make suggestions. Finally, with a dramatic gesture of despair, he rushes at our baggage, chalks it all over, and says we may go. We thank him profusely and we bow to each other. Every one congratulates us and him, and we feel like the heroes of a duel. Our luggage is whisked away and put on cabs. An outlet for any remains of animosity is found in the Apache, who is abused, arrested, fined and dismissed, or is going to be, which is doubtless the same thing.

CHAPTER X   MARSEILLES TO PARIS

NEXT to the barbarity of cooping one up on board ship in a cabin wet with fellow sufferers, the most disgraceful relic of the dark ages is the arrangement of a sleeping car. I reflect this sadly as I find myself in a four cabin, of which all the three other berths are occupied. Two of the occupants are standing outside in the passage, gloomily watching the conductor making up what are by a polite fiction called the beds. My co-voyagers are, I imagine from their countenances, at any time of severe and gloomy dispositions, and under the present circumstances they appear to be in their element. They would make excellent models for a historical picture—Puritans watching the preparations for their own execution.

By the few hoarse gutturals which they exchange, I conclude that they are of Scottish origin. I suspect them of being elders who have been to see with their own eyes the horrors of those sinks of iniquity, Nice and Monte Carlo.

They have certainly not been corrupted into any form of unfitting levity during their visit.

The fourth victim of overcrowding is not there, but a miscellaneous selection of articles scattered carelessly on his berth look foreign. I notice a huge music case

As it is impossible to sit in the compartment and the beds are down, we stand in the passage while the train moves slowly out of the station. Luckily we are to have dinner at once, so we totter towards the restaurant car in single file along the narrow passage, banging against the sides and holding on with difficulty, like very drunk Red Indians on the war-path. The march of the column, which Tommy joins in the next car, is checked from time to time by the elders, who are portly men, having to squeeze past other passengers. It is an embarrassing process, and some people never see that by reason of their stoutness this cannot be done, and they must step back into their cabins. In the case of one old French-man, the leading elder sticks, and for a moment it looks as if we should either have to give up our dinner or climb over them. The second elder, however, whose implacable purpose to reach the restaurant any one could read in his eye, solves the matter by pitching forward and driving his com-panion from his position, leaving the unhappy Frenchman breathless, and I believe permanently dented in front.

We arrive at last at our destination, to find a perspiring head waiter doing a sort of step dance up and down the car, trying to get people into their proper places. Some people have lost the numbers they were given, others never had them, and the whole car is a scene of rocking, bumping confusion. A small but energetic boy is struggling with a pile of plates, a bread basket and eight bottles through the mob at the risk of his life. The head waiter has as usual put every one at every one else's table, and this is bitterly resented by the public. One old Australian, finding that he and his wife were placed at opposite ends of the car, has broken out into open mutiny, and has annexed a table for two. " Dis lady," says the distracted waiter, " is not 18, ze is 24." " She is more than that, my lad," says the Australian genially but firmly, " but we have been together nigh on forty years and we don't separate now."

At this excellent sentiment the waiter swears to himself in French, and with a dramatic gesture of despair flings the remaining tickets into the air, and retires to the kitchen, presumably to commit suicide in the saucepan.

We sort ourselves, and I find myself at a four table with Mrs. X., Mrs. H. and Tommy, H. having been judiciously ridden off by the latter and placed at a table with the elders, where they can bore each other in peace.

Dinner on a restaurant car is invariably the same in whatever country you eat it. I always wonder if it has been standardised, and thus an economy effected. They, however, keep up the farce of giving you a menu which, in addition to the vermicelli soup, fish of a peculiar nature which I believe are bred in the engine tanks, small slices of wear-resisting beef, eight-legged winners of the chicken Marathon race, and caramel pudding, tells you all sorts of other things.

I suppose advertisements pay, but why one should decide to buy a steam pump or electric light installation while one is making shots to get something which one doesn't like into one's mouth is a puzzle. Perhaps people of modern ideas in the agony of the moment promise their patron saint a complete electric light plant, instead of the old-fashioned candles, if they ever get out of the car uninjured.

Mrs. H. under this shaking becomes very violent, and Tommy, who is next her, and I who am opposite, have an exciting time.

Early in the proceedings she flings a spoonful of soup at me, and empties the salt cellar over Tommy. She has, too, a huge drooping plume in her hat, which just touches the bald head of an irritable old Frenchman behind her, who keeps on slapping at the imaginary flies, until he nearly pulls her hat off, and discovers his mistake.

She reminds me of those men at fairs who play four or five instruments at once—she soups me, salts Tommy and feathers the old Frenchman all at the same time.

Soup, which is always a dangerous moment, has passed when the small boy enters with a huge plate of fish. At this moment we take a curve, and he is thrown violently against Mrs. H., whom he partially sits on, still with an expression of rigid despair, holding the dish up as the hot water trickles on to his devoted waistcoat.

On my return to my compartment, I find the two elders have already occupied their berths and I climb up into mine, where I proceed to go through the various acrobatic feats necessary to undress when lying down in a rocking and jolting train. I have hardly finished, when we hear coming down the passage unusually uncertain steps and the carolling of an Italian air, and our fourth companion arrives.

He proves to be a rather stoutish gentleman of about thirty, very dark and Italian looking, and having obviously dined very well.

He wishes all an affectionate good evening in Italian, French, and English, and as an unusually severe jolt occurs at this minute, sits down suddenly on the fatter elder, who gives vent to an exclamation of surprise and pain in no civil tones. Our operatic singer, for so I am sure he is, apologises profusely and insists on shaking hands with the elder, much to that gentleman's wrath. He then pats him affectionately on the shoulder, begs him to be cheerful, and turns to the other pillar of the Scottish Church, and insists on shaking hands with him. " I don't want," begins that individual, but seeing that the Italian may at any moment collapse on to him in his turn, he thinks better of it, and grudgingly gives him an enormous and unsympathetic paw. " I hope now," he says in his drawling caw, " we may all be allowed to go to sleep." The singer does not understand, but breaks into a merry laugh, claps him on the shoulder, informs him he is an original, and starts to climb into his berth. It is a ticklish job, even if one has not passed a convivial evening, and the Italian, though he goes at it with plenty of dash, is a trifle unsteady in his movements, with the result that he falls back on elder number one, who fairly bellows with rage. More apologies, and the tenor, full of the milk of human kindness, insists on again shaking hands all round. The elders by this time are in a most unclerical frame of mind, and though I cannot follow their remarks, I gather they are in the nature of a reproof.

The tenor, for so he is, undismayed and smiling brightly, winks at me, and climbs with præter-human luck this time successfully into his berth. He then begs to introduce himself. His name is Antonelli, he is an operatic tenor, but I may already know. No? He is surprised, but perhaps I come from far Egypt. Ah, that explains it, because frankly he has had some success, yes, some. Egypt, ah, Egypt, the land of Aïda—he then bursts into song.

" Will you ask that lunatic up there to let us go to sleep? " growls the fat elder querulously, whilst the other growls out his intention to complain. " He is in a disgraceful condition and should be ashamed of himself," he adds.

I translate the desire for sleep to the signor, who immediately offers to sing a lullaby, which he does. The fat elder presses the button of the electric bell furiously, but this as usual produces no effect at all. I never knew a sleeping-car bell that did. The tenor meanwhile has unpacked a small bag, the principal contents of which seem to be a sleeping cap of a weird shape, a large spirit flask and a cabinet portrait of a very good-looking lady in very scanty attire.

This he kisses passionately and then shows to me. I admire it duly. " What a woman! Ah, what a dream! She adores me, but that is the same with them all. A tenor they cannot resist. My faith, they weary me, poor things. But she—she is lovely. What eyes! What a skin! What a figure!" etc. etc. I am glad elders do not understand French.

The tenor now leans over his berth and insists on showing the photograph to the suffering followers of John Knox below, eliciting furious remonstrances from them, which most unfairly are addressed to me. " Ah ha, what say they? They are jealous, the two quaint ones." I remonstrate, pointing out that they are reverend gentlemen, and that he is offending them.

He declines to believe this. All really great men admire the beautiful, he says, and they are therefore not great but metaphorically little. The fatter elder now asks me with weary fury if I cannot stop that intoxicated idiot talking. The tenor, having put away his photograph, tells me of his early life and his leanings towards religion, which he found, however, too petty for him. He has nevertheless a great respect for it. Will I assure the two " clergimans " of this? It will comfort them.

I urge again the propriety of his going to sleep. Not, he says with solemn dignity, without cementing the friendship which has sprung up between us, and which he feels will last our lives. I am sympathetic, I love life, beauty, woman, wine, and all that makes life (hiccup) worth living.—I am glad my family cannot hear this character sketch.—Not like those black beetles below, for whom he has a deep respect, but they are undoubtedly black beetles.

He now unscrews the flask, produces a glass and

pours out some brandy, only a portion of which reaches its intended destination, the remainder descending in an alcoholic spray on the respected ones beneath.

"Drink," says the tenor, "there is no better brandy. If those black beetles below had been amiable they too should have shared, for generosity is my failing. I give away all I have, I cannot help it. I am like that, but they—what do they know of this beautiful nectar of the (hiccup) gods? They swill their rough whisky, gin and porter beer, which reduces their muddy brains to a degraded pulp. But you, you are different—therefore drink to the divine Massenet or to your love, whoever she is, doubtless superb (hiccup)!"

I accept the brandy with joy, because I see that a very little more liquor will reduce our king of song to a quiescent state. My hopes are quickly fulfilled as the tenor takes a long pull at the flask, and after an ineffectual attempt at song, falls into a heavy sleep. I compose myself to follow his example, wondering why the reek of the brandy is so unpleasantly powerful.

When I awake we are circling Paris and the tenor is gone; he left us apparently at the Gare de Lyon. The elders, worn out with their troubles, are still asleep, and I slip off to the washing place to go through all the miseries of a railway toilet. However, it is not the first time I have shaved with my head knocking against the sides of the cabin, or washed in half a pint of the peculiar mixture of coal dust, oil and water, which the sleeping cars provide for the purpose, and I just get back to my compartment as we enter the Nord.

The two elders, when dressed, look at me with sour dislike, but I notice an expression of anxious dismay on the one who slept in the berth under the tenor, and who by the way, like his companion, I notice sports the blue ribbon. " It is very awkward," he is saying to his companion, " and very difficult to explain. How will I make Janet and the rest believe I slept under a God-forsaken lunatic who went to sleep with a full bottle of brandy uncorked in his hand, and fairly drenched me with it all night? " The fatter elder, whose natural sourness has been accentuated by his recent sufferings, remarks that if people sleep so heavily they are liable to all sorts of inconveniences, and generally implies it is the fault of the sleeper.

.   .   .   .   .   .

As we stop they gather up their belongings, and get out to change on to some other route. I watch with interest their meeting with a group of gaunt females and solemn, blue-ribboned men on the platform. The bebrandied elder gingerly embraces the most forbidding of the women, who starts back with horror, and they drift from my sight up the platform, the unhappy man evidently explaining to an unsympathetic and incredulous audience the reason for his brandy-flavoured condition. It is a sad story and must have a moral which I cannot think of. I will ask Tommy.

CHAPTER XI   PARIS TO CALAIS

I FEEL a sinking of the heart as we leave the station. Mrs. H. has that restlessness which all women of a certain sort have. It is not the restlessness of the efficient housekeeper, but the restlessness of innate discontent. A woman has to think about herself, and many of her type get so naturally self-centred, that they really cease to care for anything else. The result is a natural discontent and desire for change.

It makes travelling rather a sad business, especially in cold weather when one is well wrapped up. I begin by enveloping her in her rug, and making her as comfortable as possible, and then proceed to do the same for myself. As for some reason the heating arrangements of the carriage have gone wrong, and as Mrs. H. is at present a believer in a fresh air doctor and insists on all windows being down, it is bitter; and even with a muffler, heavy greatcoat and wool gloves, I am pretty chilly.

I get out my book, a fairly interesting yellow-back novel which I picked up at Marseilles, at the price of a first edition, and am soon in the state of trying to follow the somewhat diffuse story of the author. I have just begun to follow the thread of the story, when Mrs. H. asks me if I would mind getting her her bag which is on the rack over my head. I unwind myself, put down my book and get down the bag. Mrs. H. wishes me, she says, to open it. I take off my gloves and find the catch ; as she frankly admits, it is hard to manage. I split a nail and sprain my thumb, but restrain any comment and get it open.

Now if she will only leave me quiet for a moment, I might get on with my book. It is interesting, though like most modern sensational novels it makes me a little dizzy, because no one acts in a way that one conceives it possible they would. They also seem to have all sorts of principles and laws, social and moral, which are all their own. Perhaps these writers belonged to a concealed and secret religion, with a different set of morals and ethics from ours. For instance, Jones's grandfather shoots Miss Smith's uncle dead, then Jones and Miss Smith cannot marry, though both families were glad when the shooting part of the occurrence terminated so satisfactorily.

Again you must, according to their laws, never call in the police, or if you do you must tell them transparent falsehoods, so as, I conclude, like the old riddle about the hen, to make it more difficult. If ever a friend, relation or even a stranger asks you a simple and straightforward question such as, When does the Scotch express start and from where? you must either tell him an incredible story about its going from the Marble Arch at four in the morning or, even better, you must get deathly pale, hold on to the lamp-post, and say in broken accents, " Would to God I could answer you, but the secret is not mine." You should then faint or disappear into the darkness—the latter, I should imagine, if your questioner is muscular and irritable. In cases where action instead of words is wanted, such as stopping a man braining your benefactor as he sits at his desk, you being the stronger and well-armed and having no expectations from the old gentleman; or preventing a woman from leaving your house by the window with all your wife's jewels under her arm—the first thing to do is to become numb and to allow everything to rush through your mind till it is too late to do anything.

This power of getting numb is very important and must need much practice, but must also be, when acquired, an accomplishment much admired in criminal circles. It makes professional matters so much easier for them. As I say, you should remain numb until it is too late to do anything and then compromise yourself as quickly as possible. In the case of murder, you should cover yourself with blood, transfer all portable property from the victim's to your own pockets, take the murderous weapon firmly in the right hand and wait for arrest. If a word or two of explanation would have got you out of the difficulty, get dazed or numb again and say nothing.

On the other hand, if by action you can do nothing useful, take it at once. Always when unarmed, feeble from illness or loss of blood, rush at fourteen professional murderers who are looking for you. Similarly, throw yourself in front of express trains, steam-rollers and such like, if the heroine is being carried off in them. Naturally, after these efforts you will wake up in hospital wondering where you are, and fight your way back to life.

Another difficult point is, when you should or should not suspect people. When you find your beloved uncle, a hale and powerful man of forty, on the high road of a winter's night, in a condition which looks as if he had been put through a pulping machine, you must suspect his ward—a frail, ethereal girl of eighteen—who is your *fiancée*, and must rush off and bury yourself in South America for a few years, because you noticed a flower like the one she wore the winter before last lying near the body. You may occasionally wonder how she did it, but take no steps to clear the matter up. On the other hand, if you enter a church and see your *fiancée* being married privately to a stranger who embraces her fondly as she gets into the motor car to drive away, you must not be surprised if your young woman, when asked for explanations, says, " Heavens! I cannot explain; you must trust me." It is, of course, difficult, but you will reproach yourself bitterly for ever suspecting her afterwards, and live a broken man if you do.

Again, never suspect a leading criminal or other Bohemian acquaintance who offers to lead you to this same *fiancée*, who has got temporarily mislaid, and who, stipulating that you shall be alone and unarmed, takes you to the worst quarter of the town and then down a dark passage. If the proceeding appears too childish, you can be impelled by an unseen power (from behind presumably), but go on unsuspectingly until you are quietly knocked on the head or thrown into the river, or whatever it is they want to do with you.

You should also give criminals a sporting chance. If some one gives you a paper with the name and address of the gentleman or lady who, after committing a series of atrocious crimes, is supposed, with the assistance of a thumbscrew, to be extracting cheques by torture from your respected aunt, in their lair, never open it or send it to the police. No, you should begin a series of futile inquiries, which will give them time to cash your aunt's cheques, and in the end, when by a colossal series of flukes you catch them, your aunt will thank you profusely. If the series of flukes are really too disgraceful, you can put them down to Providence.

I could go on for hours on this subject, which really fascinates me, as I have a theory about it. It is that these works are all written by gentlemen or ladies who are in establishments under medical charge, and sold for the benefit of the institution and by the management. This is really why there are so many.

At this moment I recognise Marley coming down the corridor, and we greet each other, and he seats himself next to me. He is a great authority on the Near East, and I have known him on and off for years. He travels about and gives rather cryptic advice gratis to any one he can catch. He began life as some great man's private secretary and was, I think, employed by the Foreign Office at one time. He writes on Egypt particularly, and sometimes

comes to us to check his information, figures, etc. I
could bear with him better if he were not deaf, as
when I talk to him I have to shout, and it drives me
crazy, besides making my head ache.

He begins at once in the monotonous, low-pitched
voice of the deaf man whom some fiend of a friend
has told he speaks too loud, asking me how things are
in Egypt. On my replying that they are much as
usual, he informs me that Lord Palmerston remarked
once to the late Duke of Essex, " The East is always
as usual, which is usually bad." I give a rudi-
mentary smile and nod to save my voice. He then
tells me that he has just come from Constantinople.
I ask him how things are there, at which he shakes
his head and says, " Not as good perhaps as they
might be." He adds that the late Lord Dufferin
once said to Sheriff Pachs, " Turkey is a knot which
no one but a Turk dare cut." I ask if there is any
danger of further fighting. He replies, " Yes, but
not enough," which surprises me. I ask if he thinks
much is wanted. " Oh," he says, " the same
amount as elsewhere," which fogs me completely.
He adds, however, that the late Lord Lytton once
observed that the mysterious darkness of the East
was the result of mental fog.

If that is the case, I am in the blackest Eastern
night. It now strikes me he thought I was talking
of lighting, not fighting, so I scream an almost
piteous prayer to be told how the present Grand
Vizier is getting on with the committee. He shakes
his head sadly, and says, " Well enough at present."
I yell, " Who are his particular friends?" He says,

" Much too much and without result." He continues that Lord Beaconsfield stated to Sir Arthur Doughnut, our ambassador at Vienna, that he believed that Turkish expenditure and a speech of Mr. Gladstone's were the only two things of which the wisest men could not predict the extent.

I shall die if this goes on. If I don't scream he does not hear, and if I do Mrs. H. looks daggers at me, as it makes her head worse. Well, she has been a pig to me, so I'll introduce them, which I do, and then, murmuring that I left my tickets in the other carriage, stagger miserably down the train to Mrs. Despard's compartment, where I find, to my delight, there is a vacant seat next her, and I sit down to a comfortable chat, which by good luck is what she wants, as she has been suffering under H., she tells me in a whisper, but he mercifully has dropped off to sleep. We talk on pleasantly and my temper returns, when an idiotic man with a punch comes round and punches our tickets. This, of course, wakes H. up.

H., of course, begins by having a row with the collector or puncher, because the official who previously dealt with the ticket has punched or torn out some portion of it which, according to H., he should not have done. In vain the unhappy collector explains that he is an employé of the Nord Railway, and the delinquent, if he was a delinquent, was belonging to the P.L.M. H. looks at him with a cold but distrustful eye and says, " Ça n'importe. Vous avez donné cette billette à moi et vous êtes responsable pour tout."

The man appeals to me, and I try to reason with H., but he is obdurate, and the employé gets very excited and H. coldly angry, whilst I begin to get confused and fussed between the two, when Mrs. Despard intervenes. She speaks beautiful French and looks trustingly at the employé, who becomes, as they all do, her devoted slave from that minute, and her firm adherent whatever she may say or do.

She explains the whole matter according to her view, and we all get so hopelessly fogged that we don't know what we are talking or even thinking about. " You see," she says triumphantly, " if you travelled from France through Russia and they punched your ticket in Italy, it would be just the same, only in this case they are both Frenchmen, and I don't myself believe the ticket was punched wrong at all, and certainly not by monsieur,"—indicating the ticket collector—" who I am sure would never do such a thing, but if you "—speaking to H.—" wish your ticket punched anywhere else, I am sure monsieur will do it at once."

The ticket collector then solemnly announces, with as magnificent a bow as can be made in a rocking, jolting train, that to please Madame he would punch anything anywhere. I wish she would ask him to punch H.'s ear. H. is silenced, and is obviously making heroic efforts to follow her reasoning. Mrs. D., taking advantage of the lull, as she afterwards says, to put an end to an unpleasant scene, asks the ticket collector to punch the ticket which she now holds in a place she indicates, which he does without even looking, and receives the sweetest thanks, and retires bowing and hopelessly enslaved. H. takes back the ticket mechanically, murmuring, " And the ticket was punched in Italy. But you would not go through Italy." " Don't be tiresome," says Mrs. D., " that was only an illustration. And, anyhow, now it is punched right through all the coupons." Which indeed is the case, and I hear from time to time during all the rest of the journey, H. explaining to various officials who ask why this has been done: " *Une dame qui était avec moi dans la voiture a fait faire ça pour s'amuser,*" which reduces his interlocutor to a condition of mystified astonishment. It gives H. quite a lot to do and keeps him busy.

No further untoward incident mars our further journey, except the untiring bag straying into the next compartment but one, and being brought back by a lady's maid who happens to know Mrs. D., and hence the bag.

" I think," says Mrs. D., as we arrive at Calais, " that it is going to be quite calm." H. and I look gloomily seawards and hold our peace. On these occasions I am always a pessimist.

·   ·   ·   ·   ·   ·   ·